W9-DBP-110

Advance Praise for

Why Foucault?

"Do we really need another book on Foucault? We certainly need this one. It is original and accessible and grounded. It is not about Foucault, it is about using Foucault in productive ways within educational research. It shows us what we can do with Foucault. I think he might have approved of this book!"

Stephen J. Ball, Karl Mannheim Professor of Sociology of Education,
Editor, Journal of Education Policy, *Institute of Education, University of London*

"Michael A. Peters and Tina (A.C.) Besley have brought together an impressive collection of essays on the cutting edge of educational philosophy, method and theory. Using Michel Foucault's work as a springboard, the authors engage in wide-ranging and evocative discussions across a broad spectrum of topics including, amongst others: method, pedagogy, ethics, self formation, governmentality, forms of government, management, and education policy.

It is a unique collection which also, very importantly, underscores the truly international and ongoingly productive impact of Foucault's work amongst educational scholars, with contributors from across the English-speaking world and from Belgium, Germany, and Malta. This work is an invaluable, indeed essential resource both for those already working with Foucault's ideas in education and also for those seeking an overview and entrée into current research in the area."

Clare O'Farrell, School of Cultural and Language Studies in Education,
Queensland University of Technology, Brisbane, Australia

"This book is an important contribution to studies of education. The book poignantly underscores the intellectual reach of Foucault's historical concerns with the systems of reason that govern conduct. The technologies in the construction of subjectivities are richly explored in multiple national sites and in the intersection of schooling and social work. Challenged are the orthodoxies of school policy and research that separate theory and practice and inscribed notions of the autonomous subject. The volume continually and cogently points to how contemporary policy, pedagogy, and research may undermine inclusive public interests."

Thomas S. Popkewitz, The University of Wisconsin-Madison

Why Foucault?

COUNTERPOINTS

Studies in the
Postmodern Theory of Education

Joe L. Kincheloe and Shirley R. Steinberg
General Editors

Vol. 292

PETER LANG
New York • Washington, D.C./Baltimore • Bern
Frankfurt am Main • Berlin • Brussels • Vienna • Oxford

Why Foucault?

New Directions *in* Educational Research

Edited by Michael A. Peters
& Tina (A.C) Besley

PETER LANG
New York • Washington, D.C./Baltimore • Bern
Frankfurt am Main • Berlin • Brussels • Vienna • Oxford

Library of Congress Cataloging-in-Publication Data

Why Foucault?: new directions in educational research / edited by
Michael A. Peters, Tina (A.C.) Besley.
p. cm. — (Counterpoints / studies in the postmodern
theory of education; v. 292)
Includes bibliographical references and index.
1. Foucault, Michel, 1926–1984. 2. Education—Philosophy.
3. Postmodernism and education. I. Peters, Michael.
II. Besley, Tina.
LB880.F682W49   370.7'2—dc22   2006023767
ISBN 978-0-8204-7890-6
ISSN 1058-1634

Bibliographic information published by **Die Deutsche Bibliothek**.
Die Deutsche Bibliothek lists this publication in the "Deutsche
Nationalbibliografie"; detailed bibliographic data is available
on the Internet at http://dnb.ddb.de/.

Cover design by Sophie Boorsch Appel

The paper in this book meets the guidelines for permanence and durability
of the Committee on Production Guidelines for Book Longevity
of the Council of Library Resources.

© 2007, 2008 Peter Lang Publishing, Inc., New York
29 Broadway, 18th floor, New York, NY 10006
www.peterlang.com

All rights reserved.
Reprint or reproduction, even partially, in all forms such as microfilm,
xerography, microfiche, microcard, and offset strictly prohibited.

Printed in the United States of America

ဆ Table of Contents ര

Received
JAN 2013
Acquisitions
C.U. Library

Campbell University Library
Buies Creek, NC 27506

🐬 Preface ᴄ꒓

All academic works require the effort of many people-researchers, academics and writers, publishers, editors, proofreaders, printers, programers and all those who give advice and support along the way. It is not often recognized the extent to which edited collections are collective works in the true sense that orchestrate the different activities of many people. This collective aspect often goes unnoticed as the focus settles on the *individual* author or editor at the expense of others. Foucault was clear about such matters when he addressed himself to the question of the 'author-function' and saw the present set of author practices as an aspect of modernity that in part sustained the public sphere. In another albeit different way the author-function has been regulated and produced through the law and in particular according to the proprietary model of academic production that began with the law of copyright with the Statue of Anne in 1710 that was the first copyright act in the world, although scholars also mention the Venetian Statute of 1474 as the first patent law and the Statute of Monopolies in 1623 enacted under King James I of England. This was the beginning of granting 'letters patent' (as opposed to 'sealed letters') that granted monopolies to favored persons or those who were prepared to pay. It was a system that was open to abuse and James I was forced to revoke all previous monopolies and declare that patents were to be used only for 'projects of new inventions'. The Statute of Anne was titled 'An Act for the Encouragement of Learning, by Vesting the Copies of Printed Books in the Authors or Purchasers of such Copies, during the Times therein mentioned.' The Statute, named after Queen Anne, was a response to the control over the written word by booksellers ('stationers' who later became publishers) who the Crown had empowered to destroy books considered to be seditious and heretical. The Statute refers to 'manner[s] of new manufacture…[by] inventors' and granted authors and inventors, rather than printers, a fourteen year term of exclusive ownership with the right to renew for one more term. This provision remains the foundation for patent law in New Zealand and Australia, and is also the basis for U.S. copyright law embodied in the Constitution. This has changed dramatically with the World Wide Web that has made it easy for virtually anyone to publish texts, images or music.

The production of academic works have also been marked by the bourgeois ideology that celebrates the individual author/writer that began with German Romanticism and has since developed around the cult of the individual, 'originality' and 'genius'. Roland Barth in his famous essay 'The Death of the Author' that strongly influenced Foucault, emphasized Marx's observation that it is history that makes man and *not* vice versa, as Hegel supposed. Barthes emphasized that author does not exist prior to or outside of language; it is writing that makes the author. On this basis Barthes criticized the tendency in criticism for the reader to understand the text by reference to the author's intentions or aspects of the author's identity, using biography as the touchstone for textual meaning. The notion of the author with academic works is different from literature as a whole and needs to be unraveled and deconstructed, as do the works of academics—including edited collections, sole authored books, academic papers and all the genres that make up the panoply of academic publishing world.

With these brief observations, we would like to acknowledge and thank the general editors, Joe Kincheloe and Shirley Steinberg for their support in bringing this collection to publication. We would also like to thank the publisher, Chris Myers at Peter Lang, New York, for his encouragement and support. We would like to acknowledge the goodwill and the collegiality of all contributors who wrote chapters for this international collection. We would like to thank Casey George who is pursuing her doctoral work in higher education at the University of Illinois at Urbana-Champaign for undertaking the arduous and demanding role of formating the manuscript. Finally, a word for all the students, especially at our Universities of Glasgow and Auckland (and elsewhere in Germany, Taiwan, Mexico, China) who have helped us to refine and think more deeply about Foucault, a thinker who is the most energetic and enigmatic talisman of our times.

℘ Chapter 1 ℘

Introduction: Why Foucault? New Directions in Educational Research

Michael A. Peters and Tina (A.C.) Besley

Why Read Foucault Today?[1]

Why read Foucault today? Why study him at all? Is the Foucault we read today institutionally castrated, old and toothless? And have we made him so? After twenty years have we domesticated and tamed his politics, institutionalised him, finally nailed his coffin home and categorised his work once and for all? In reader response criticism where the primary focus falls on the reader and the process of reading rather than on the author or the text, it is accepted that the reader—the audience—is not passive but constructs the text and the writer. The 'death' of Foucault, like the death of God, as Nietzsche's madman reminds us, is a feat performed by the believer, the reader: "Foucault is dead and we have killed him," we might paraphrase Nietzsche. Terry Eagleton (2003), perhaps the United Kingdom's most able Marxist literary critic, has written a book called *After Theory*. By 'after' he means that the explosion of interest in cultural studies that took place in the 1970s is *over*. Cultural studies fuelled by the work of contemporary French philosophers have moved beyond their poststructuralist phase: Foucault, Lyotard, Deleuze and Derrida are dead. Habermas, while often hostile to poststructuralist thought especially in the early 1980s, is one of the last remaining intellectuals of this era. These philosophers were marked by the tragic events and huge human wastage of WWII and the political events of the post-war settlement. These giants drew the big philosophical pictures and we were left with colouring them in. The question becomes even more pressing—why read Foucault '*after* theory'?[2]

But then the question is too melodramatic. It is also wrong-headed. Why 'we' read Foucault today is different from why 'we' read him twenty years ago (if at all).[3] Let us say that the question of *reception* is paramount here and that the reception of Foucault is a hermeneutical question in the philosophy of reading and the sociology of knowledge and culture. The reception of Foucault is very different in different national and cultural contexts, especially when he is read by different audiences and generations and often for different reasons. We can get some sense of the cultural dynamics and complexities by examining Foucault's reception in the English-speaking world.

The reception of Foucault in the English-speaking world has been both varied and uneven, as has the wider movement 'poststructuralism.' 'Poststructuralism,' as an Americanism that tends to obscure the often deep-seated differences and individual styles of thinkers grouped together under this term, was initially most readily received in departments of literature than in departments of philosophy. Indeed, where the latter were especially hostile, the former were more than hospitable. Much of the poststructuralist canon dealt with the act of literature and developed forms of criticism that were not easily contained within disciplinary boundaries spilling over into philosophy, literature, and cultural studies. Analytic philosophers, in particular, have found the question of style difficult to deal with; they were unhappy with the new methods—deconstruction, semanalysis (Kristeva), and genealogy—questioning whether they were sufficiently 'philosophical' and rigorous. Yet, as the philosophers quarrelled and engaged in demarcation disputes the work of first generation poststructuralist thinkers became more absorbed into the fabric of the humanities and social sciences. While poststructuralist thought was seized upon in the emerging fields of cultural studies and film studies, it was also opposed by traditional and neo-Marxists, and especially in the early days by self-styled critical theorists.

The question of the reception of Foucault needs to be written for specific countries, locations and disciplines for the American and British experience differ considerably, as it does for other countries. Colin Gordon (1996), for instance, remarks that "the British reception of Foucault's work has been difficult and uncertain" (p. 253) and yet he goes on to observe the way in which "Foucault drew attention to an element of critical thought in the Scots creators of political economy" (p. 255) and attached particular important to Fergusson's idea of civil society (a point that contemporary Scottish theorists themselves have not yet picked up on). Gordon also begins to flesh out an account of the differences between Foucault and the British historians, especially those who see Marxism as the science of history. As he says, the intellectual signature of the British Left is the way in which social history replaces historical sociology as the vehicle for Gramscian "organic" intellectuals to live their lives as part of the existential task of recreating democratic elements of a common culture.[4] Perhaps, today we are more sensitive to the valences of cultural context and less likely to parade our ideological commitments as 'truths.' The bitter antagonisms on the Left which characterized the 1980s seem to have given way to a greater theoretical sophistication and creativity; perhaps, even a preparedness to entertain what might have seemed like heresy only a mere decade ago. This antagonism was evident, for example, in the endless arguments over State Theory. On the one hand, Foucault, as Gordon (1996) acknowledges, "was inclined to make fun of what he called a tendency . . . toward 'State-phobia'" (p.

263) and, on the other, he offended the moralists by mistrusting the social bond, reading it, rather, as a field for the application of governmental techniques. State phobia, perhaps, a result of the experiment of National Socialism, as Foucault (2004) remarks in *Naissance de la Biopolitique*, is a characteristic of the particular post-war generation.

The question for the German reception of Foucault's work (and Foucault himself) is also very complex: the question of why it was largely postponed has much to do with the lack of interpenetration of philosophical traditions, intellectual antipathies and defensiveness on both sides (French and German), and Habermas' early polemical intervention when he accepted the Adorno prize from the City of Frankfurt in 1980. His acceptance speech drew up sides of the debate in terms of an exhaustive modernity versus postmodernity, indicating that he held that modernity was an "incomplete project" and calling the French poststructuralists "neo-conservatives" likening them to the conservatives of the Weimar Republic.

An alternative title for this chapter might be "Relativizing Foucault to the Contexts of His Uses." We suggest this because in the field of education scholars and theorists deform him: they use him or elements of his thought; they abuse him in countless ways; they unmake him and remake him; they twist and turn him and his words; sometimes they spread him very thinly; at other times they squeeze him into small spaces; often they appeal to Foucault, beginning with a quote only to do something very conventional and mundane, against his original intent.

Foucault is Mr. Elastic Man, the original portmanteau thinker. We can pick up on aspects of his thought or influences in his thinking to demonstrate a proposition, elucidate a point, examine an argument or window dress our own theoretical hunches. Foucault almost encourages this piecemeal, unsystematic, and poetical appropriation of his work. He spoke of his own "toolbox approach" to Nietzsche and Heidegger and of using them for his own ends. So it is not surprising that Foucault might inspire what we refer to as a constructivist theory of interpretation, which emphasizes political contexts of *use*. Yet, it is *not* the case that we can make of him and his work anything at all. There are bad, wrong, or misleading interpretations of Foucault, even if there is not one single true or correct reading. This is what is called the principle of *interpretive asymmetry* that opens up the work or the author (the text, context and the intertext) to multiple interpretations, while at the same time protecting the future against closure and providing for an open horizon of interpretations. Foucault is, as he says of Nietzsche, Freud, Marx, a *figure of discursivity* (Foucault, 1998a) That a text stimulates and allows novel interpretations is a sign of its richness, depth and complexity.

Who, What and Why Foucault?

The questions "who or what is Foucault?" have more often been asked than "why Foucault?" For instance, James Faubion begins his Introduction to the edited collection of Foucault's work (Faubion, 1998) with exactly this question to which he answers: "The possibilities seem endless: structuralist, idealist, neoconservative, post-structuralist, antihumanist, irrationalist, radical relativist, theorist of power, missionary of transgression, aestheticist, dying man, saint, or, if nothing else 'postmodern'" (p. xiii).

These labels designed to answer the "who" or "what" of Foucault, are, of course, not necessarily mutually contradictory but they are not categories or descriptions that Foucault would apply to himself. And Foucault was very testy and vitriolic against those who ascribed him positions he didn't hold or those who offered descriptions of him that didn't fit. Remember his Foreword to the English edition of *The Order of Things* (1973) where he wrote: "In France, certain half-witted 'commentators' persist in labelling me a 'structuralist.' I have been unable to get it into their tiny minds that I have used none of the methods, concepts, or key terms that characterise structural analysis" (p. xiv).

He went on to acknowledge "certain similarities" between his own work and that of the structuralists (identifiable only in retrospect) and went on to suggest—in terms consonant with the problematic of structuralism that emphasised the unconscious and a decentering of the author—that it would be strange for him to claim that his work was "independent of conditions and rules of which I am very largely unaware" (p. xiv). Elsewhere he denied he knew what the term "postmodernism" meant—or indeed, even the term 'modernity'—(Foucault, 1998b, p. 448), yet he granted that structuralism had a determinate meaning although only in retrospect. In the same interview he was to remark: "I have never been a Freudian, I have never been a Marxist, and I have never been a structuralist" (p. 437).

In another autobiographical comment Foucault (1984) proceeds negatively, by noting how others have classified him and by taking considerable enjoyment from casting aspersions on these descriptions:

> I think I have been situated in most squares on the political checkerboard, one after another and sometimes simultaneously: as anarchist, leftist, ostentatious or disguised Marxist, nihilist, explicit or secret anti-marxist, technocrat in the service of Gaullism, new liberal etc. An American professor complained that a crypto-marxist like me was invited to the US, and I was denounced by the press in Eastern Europe for being an accomplice of the dissidents. None of these descriptions is important by itself; taken together, on the other hand, they mean something. And I must admit that I rather like what they mean (pp. 383–384)

He once famously remarked "The coming into being of the 'author' constitutes the privileged moment of individualization in the history of ideas, knowledge, literature, philosophy and the sciences" (Foucault, 1998c: 205). Such a statement is doubly paradoxical when applied to Foucault himself for the so-called "disappearance or death of the author" significantly is not something that applies to Foucault, either as a scholar who during his productive life initiated new inquiries and approaches or as the name for a body or corpus of 'work' that connects with contemporary movements and goes beyond them. Nor is it apt for the consideration of Foucault and his role in contemporary 'theory' when the processes of reification and canonisation of both the man and his work began even before his death in 1984. Yet, Foucault was acutely aware of the Nietzschean trope of an 'aesthetics of existence' and the ways in which we can or should remake ourselves—principles of self-constitution that are at once ethical and political and readily apply to the public intellectual, to the writer, and to the theorist.

Foucault constantly remodels his position and his thinking changes and evolves. Indeed, he was forever reformulating what he saw as his own project. In their study of Foucault's work, Dreyfus and Rabinow (1982) propose four stages: a Heideggerian stage (typified by his study of madness and reason), an archaeological or quasi-structuralist stage (characterised by *The Archaeology of Knowledge* and *The Order of Things*), a genealogical stage and, finally an ethical stage. The shift from the archaeological to the genealogical stage in Foucault's writings is well represented in *Discipline and Punish*, a work that has direct relevance to educational theory. Like *The History of Sexuality*, *Discipline and Punish* exhibits a Nietzschean genealogical turn focused upon studies of the *will to knowledge* understood as reflecting both discursive and non-discursive (i.e., institutional) practices and, in particular, the complex relations among power, knowledge and the body. In *Discipline and Punish*, Foucault is concerned with the body as an object of certain disciplinary technologies of power and he examines the genealogy of forms of punishment and the development of the modern penal institution, discussing in turn torture (beginning with the gruesome account of Damien the regicide), punishment (with clear echoes of Nietzsche's famous list of meanings in the *Genealogy*, 1956, p. 213), discipline, and the prison.

In the early eighties, Denis Huisman asked François Ewald to reedit the entry on Foucault for a new edition of the *Dictionnaire des Philosophes*. As Robert Hurley, the translator, remarks in a footnote to the text entitled 'Foucault,' "The text submitted to Huisman was written almost entirely by Foucault himself, and signed anonymously 'Maurice Florence'" (p. 459, fn). Foucault (1998d) begins the dictionary entry on himself with the following words: "To the extent that

Foucault fits into the philosophical tradition, it is the *critical* tradition of Kant, and his project could be called *A Critical History of Thought* (p. 459). Later, he defines a critical history of thought as an analysis of the conditions under which certain relations of subject to object are formed or modified, insofar as those relations constitute a possible knowledge [*savoir*]…In short, it is a matter of determining its mode of 'subjectivation'…and objectivation…What are the processes of subjectivation and objectivation that make it possible for the subject qua subject to become an object of knowledge [*connaissance*] as a subject? (pp. 450–460).

He describes himself as undertaking the constitution of the subject both as an object of knowledge within certain scientific discourses or truth games we call the 'human sciences' (both empirical and normative) and as an object for himself, that is the history of subjectivity insofar as it involves "the way the subject experiences himself in a game of truth where it relates to himself" (p. 461), such as in the history of sexuality.

It is the kind of self-description that Foucault gives elsewhere. In an interview a year before his death, Foucault (1983) confessed to Paul Rabinow and Hubert Dreyfus that his real quarry was *not* an investigation of power but rather the history of the ways in which human beings are constituted as subjects, a process that involved power relations as an integral aspect of the production of discourses involving truths.

> My objective…has been to create a history of the different modes by which, in our culture, human beings are made subjects. My work has dealt with three modes of objectification which transform human beings into subjects…The first is the modes of inquiry which try to give themselves the status of the sciences…In the second part of my work, I have studied the objectivizating of the subject in what I shall call "dividing practices"… Finally, I have sought to study—it is my current work—the way a human being turns him- or herself into a subject. For example, I have chosen the domain of sexuality…Thus it is not power, but the subject, that is the general theme of my research (p. 209).

Paul Veyne (1997) commented after Foucault's death that in his very first lecture at the College de France,

> Foucault contrasted an 'analytic philosophy of truth in general' with his own preference 'for critical thought that would take the form of an ontology of ourselves, of an ontology of the present'; he went so far, that day, as to relate his own work to 'the form of reflection that extends from Hegel to the Frankfurt School via Nietzsche and Max Weber.' (p. 226)

Veyne warns us not to take that circumstantial analogy too far and he puts us on a course that connects Foucault strongly to Nietzsche and Heidegger, correctly in my view.

Foucault, undoubtedly, was strongly influenced by his readings of both Nietzsche and Heidegger and indebted to them for ideas that led him to emphasize and unpack the conceptual and historical relations between notions of truth, power and subjectivity in his genealogical investigations. He started reading these two philosophers in the early 1950s and while he wrote only one substantial paper on Nietzsche (Foucault, 1977) and nothing directly on Heidegger, it is clear that Foucault's works bear the unmistakable imprints of these two great thinkers.[5] Nietzsche's work, in particular, provided Foucault with novel ways to re-theorize and conceive anew the operation of *power* and *desire* in the constitution and self-overcoming of human subjects. It enabled him to analyse the modes by which human beings become subjects without according either power or desire conceptual priority over the other, as had been the case in the discourses of Marxism (with its accent on *power*) and of Freudianism (with its accent on *desire*).

This is our general account of "why Foucault?" and why Foucault has appealed to the present generation of Foucault scholars in educational research. Foucault has provided an understanding of the educational subject—the pupil, the student, the teacher etc.—in terms of a history of subjectivity and a genealogical investigation that allowed educational theorists to understand the effects of education and pedagogies both as disciplines and practices. It is a question that might also be profitably phrased as "where Foucault?" that is, a spatial analysis of Foucault, not the man but the corpus of work, its parameters, its thematizations and problematizations with earlier questions, its connections to thinkers—contemporary, modern and classical. It is an answer that we think Foucault would have preferred.[6]

The use and development of Foucault's work is not yet well enough established in educational research to begin to talk about clear differences or orientations in English-speaking countries in the way that we might distinguish the French Foucaultians (Donzelot, Ewald, etc.) from the Anglo-Australasians (Rose, Hindess, Hunt, Dean, Hunter, O'Malley, etc. based around the journal *Economy and Society*) or the US, French, or Australian feminists. Ian Hunter's (1994) book is worthy of mention in this regard as an early development of Foucault's work in relation to rethinking the school.

In Britain during the mid 1980s Walkerdine's (1984, 1988) critical psychology approach to child development exerted a strong influence in British educational circles. Thereafter, the use of Foucault has been dominated by the ethno-sociological orientation of Stephen Ball (1990, 1994), although David

Hoskin's (1979) work has exerted an important influence, as has Norman Fairclough's (1989, 1992), whose discourse analysis based on Foucault has been usefully applied to understandings of educational policy. In North America a more epistemological and feminist appropriation of his work can be seen in the writings of Tom Popkewitz (Popkewitz & Brennan, 1997), Bernadette Baker (2001), and Maureen Ford (1995), whereas, perhaps strangely for such a small country, in New Zealand, the philosophical appropriation of Foucault's work by James Marshall (1989, 1996) has exercised a strong critical and philosophical direction not only over his students in his own home country, but also internationally. New Zealanders have worked on Foucault in diverse ways: Mark Olssen's (1999, 2002) materialist interpretation of Foucault seeks to view him in close proximity to Gramsci; Tina (A.C.) Besley (2002) has put Foucault to work in understanding the significance of power relations in school counselling and, more broadly, in the construction of self and youth cultures; Sue Middleton (1998), as a feminist, has appropriated his work on sexuality, while Peters (1996) has sought to understand Foucault within the wider context of "poststructuralism," focusing on themes of governance, subjectivity and ethics in relation to education policy. A group of scholars established a Foucault SIG at the American Educational Research Association in the mid 1990s "dedicated to the historical and philosophical studies of education that engage the writings of Michel Foucault."[7]

The Organization of this Book

We are pleased to be able to present the work of some of the authors already discussed in this introduction: James Marshall and Mark Olssen. Marshall in Chapter 1 has developed a theme on education research as problematization and Olssen in Chapter 14 has contributed an original thesis on Foucault's conception of democracy. Both chapters offer strong new research directions in education. Alongside these authors and our own work as representative of Foucault scholarship in the English-speaking world, the collection uniquely brings together this corpus with work completed by scholars working in various German universities—Ludwig Pongratz, Thomas Coelen, Fabian Kessl, Susanne Weber and Susanne Maurer.

The collaboration with German scholars came about through an initial invitation from Hermann Forneck (Geissen University) and Ludwig Pongratz (Technical University of Darmstadt) to us to attend a small conference focused on Foucault held in a beautiful location in the hills above Verona, Italy in April 2003 which issued in the collection *Nach Foucault: Diskurs- und machtanalytische Perpsektiven der Pädagogik* (Pongratz et al., 2004). It was there also that we met

Susanne Weber, who with her colleague Susanne Maurer, invited us (and Robert Doherty, our Scottish colleague), to a workshop in January 2005 at Philips University in the historic city of Marburg. At these two sessions we met the German scholars who have contributed to this collection and laid the basis for ongoing research collaborations. (There were many more scholars attending these two events than those contributing to this collection). What started as collaboration between the editors of this collection (Michael A. Peters and Tina Besley, two New Zealanders working at the University of Glasgow) was extended first to Robert Doherty, a colleague from Glasgow University who is completing doctoral research on Foucault in relation to education policy, and, second, to our New Zealand colleagues and friends, James Marshall and Mark Olssen. Finally, we extended the invitation to our colleagues working in the field of Foucault studies, Jan Masschelein and Maarten Simons (Leuven, Belgium), James Wong (Canada) and Kenneth Wain (Malta). The result is an international collection that focuses on exploring aspects of Foucault's work for new directions in educational research.

The collection begins with some general themes explored in this introduction to focus on a general account of education as problematization by James Marshall (Chapter 1) and contributions designed to explore in new ways the significance of Foucault's work based on questions surrounding the notion of pedagogy. Ludwig Pongratz in Chapter 2 investigates the relation between the concepts of freedom and discipline in Foucault's work examining transformation in pedagogic punishment, while Thomas Coelen in Chapter 3 provides a study of pedagogical relationships between master and student in Antiquity presenting them as alternatives to modern confessional and disciplinary alternatives. Tina (A.C.) Besley in Chapter 4 investigates the centrality of the technology of the confessional self to schooling, investigating the significance of the practice of truth-telling and James Wong in Chapter 5 provides a critical ontology of the developmental model of childhood.

In Chapter 6 Fabian Kessl turns his attention to an analysis of power in social work suggesting that normalization studies of education and social work often tend to reproduce the assumption of repressive power, while in Chapter 7 Susanne Weber takes the figure of the 'entrepreneur'—so prevalent in neoliberal discussions of culture—to investigate it within the field organizational development in Germany as an example of both the normalization of subjects and the reconstruction of organization cultures. Her chapter is particularly nuanced and sensitive to contemporary discourses concerning affirmative action for women considered as support for 'human resources'. In Chapter 8 Susanne Maurer, exploring similar themes, uses the notion of governmentality to investigate in the context of radical social work connections to social movements and new mobile and shifting collective actors. These essays have a distinctive German flavour; they analyze the German tradition of social work, which institutionally, are strongly related to pedagogy and education, and often taught in same or related departments within the university.

In Chapter 9 Maarten Simons and Jan Masschelein use Foucault's analysis of truth-telling as a means of investigating the 'scientific truth-telling' of the institution of the university yet their interest is not epistemological so much as 'the way scientific truth-telling is being practised and being distinguished from non-scientific speech, an ethical concern.' Kenneth Wain in Chapter 10 is also interested in the late Foucault and his approach to ethics. He usefully maintains that for Foucault where ethics concerns freedom, morality has to do with truth. 'Games of truth,' connected to questions of governance and control, constitute a different language game from ethics. Wain then provides an account of self-creation in relation to care of the self and the future of education. In Chapter 11 Michael Peters focuses on Foucault's conception of 'games of truth,' using this as a means for elucidating aspects of subjectivity and ethics in educational research and in Chapter 12 Robert Doherty uses Foucault notion of governmentality as a link with discourse and as a basis for critically framing education policy. Finally, in Chapter 13 Mark Olssen explores Foucault's suggestion of a kind of democracy that takes us beyond current practices and institutions.

Foucault studies in education provide tools for analysis that have inspired historical, sociological and philosophical approaches that cover a bewildering array of topics: genealogies of pupils, students, teachers, and counsellors; the social constructions of children, adolescence, and youth; social epistemologies of the school in its changing institutional forms, and studies of the emergence of the disciplines and of their relation with regimes of discipline and punishment; philosophical studies of educational concepts that grew up with European humanism, especially in its Enlightenment and specifically Kantian formations—Man, freedom, autonomy, punishment, government and authority. In all cases, the Foucaultian archive provides an approach to problematize concepts and practices that seemed resistant to further analysis *before* Foucault, that seemed, in other words, institutionalised, ossified and destined to endless repetition in academic understandings and interpretations. After Foucault, it is as though we must revisit most of the important questions to do with power, knowledge, subjectivity and freedom in education.

Notes

1   The first part of this introduction is drawn from a paper entitled "Why Foucault: New Directions in Anglo-American Research" presented at the conference *After Foucault: Perspectives of the Analysis of Discourse and Power in Education*, 29–31 October, 2004 held in Verona and organized by the University of Dortmund. We would like to extend our thanks to Hermann Forneck and Ludwig Pongratz for the invitation to attend this conference. This first acquaintance became the basis for an ongoing collaboration of which this collection is part. A version of the original paper, which is much fuller and comments specifically on Foucault studies in education in the English-speaking world, appears in *Nach Foucault: Diskurs- und machtanalytische Perpsektiven der Pädagogik* (Pongratz et al., 2004).

2   We do not accept Eagleton's position, even though it is a handy trope in this context. What we desperately need 'after theory' is a theory of knowledge capitalism and this is something that cultural studies, at least in its present guise, is unable to provide partly because it has no grasp of economics and does not focus on the question of the economics of knowledge or information.

3   Why Foucault was read in Germany in the 1970s, Michael Wimmer (Hamburg University) assures us, is different from why Foucault is read today.

4   We were, nevertheless, disturbed to discover that in early July, 2002 the original department of Cultural Studies at Birmingham had been closed because it scored low in the 2001 Research Assessment Exercise which determines research funding for british universities, even though it had a high ranking for teaching and many students.

5   On Nietzsche's influence on Foucault see Shrift (1995). On Heidegger's influence on Foucault see Dreyfus (1989; 1996). Foucault's books are, of course, scattered with references to both thinkers. In regard to Heidegger, it is an interesting question, given his intellectual debts, why Foucault provided little direct acknowledgement of his work or influence upon him.

6   In the paper "Why Foucault? New Directions in Anglo-American Educational Research" Peters (2004) indicated the 'new directions' by reference to a series of possible descriptions of Foucault (Foucault as….) and developments out of Foucault that explore the use to which he has been put in educational theory by scholars in the Anglo-American community, focusing on work by James Marshall, Stephen Ball, Mark Olssen, Tina Besley, Bernadette Baker, Tom Popkewitz & Marie Brennan, Sue Middleton, and Michael Peters. Peters specifically excluded general accounts of Foucault's influence on educational research that advocate a poststructuralist orientation to education or recommend a synthesis or integration between poststructuralism and critical pedagogy in order to focus exclusively on Foucault studies. For such accounts see Marshall (1989) and Olssen (1999, Chapter 10).

7   See the website *http://facstaff.uww.edu/heyningk/foucault/sitemap.htm* (accessed 2nd August, 2005). See, for example, the roundtables "Foucault and Education: How do we know what we know?" (chaired by Katharina Heyning with participation by Andrea Allard, Colin Green, Ruth Gustafson, Michael Ferrari & Rosa Lynn Pinkius, Stephen Thorpe, Cathy Toll, Kevin Vinson, Huey-li Li) and "Tinkering with Foucault's Tool-kit Down Under" (chaired by Stephen Ball, with participation by Elizabeth McKinley, Mary Hill, Nesta Devine, Michael Peters, James Marshall, Sue Middleton).

Bibliography

Baker, B. (2001). *In perpetual motion: Theories of power, educational history, and the child*. New York: Peter Lang.

Ball, S. J. (1990). (Ed.). *Foucault and education*. London: Routledge.

————. (1994). *Education reform, a critical and post-structural approach*. Buckingham: Open University Press.

Besley, A.C. (2002). *Counselling youth: Foucault, power and the ethics of subjectivity*. Westport, CT: Praeger.

Dreyfus, H. (1989) On the ordering of things: Being and Power in Heidegger and Foucault, *Michel Foucault, Philosophy*. Paris: LeSeuil.

————. (1996) Being and power: Heidegger and Foucault. *International Journal of Philosophical Studies*, Volume 4, pp. 1–16.

Dreyfus, H. & Rabinow, P. (1983) *Michel Foucault. Beyond structuralism and hermeneutics*. Chicago: University of Chicago Press.

Eagleton, T. (2003) *After theory*. London: Allen Lane/Penguin.

Faubion, J.D. (1998) Introduction. In *Aesthetics, Method and Epistemology: Essential Works of Foucault 1954–1984*, Volume 2, James D. Faubion (Ed.), New York, The New Press, pp. xiii–xliii.

Fairclough, N. (1989). *Language and power*. London: Longman.

————. (1992). *Discourse and social change*. Cambridge: Polity Press.

Ford, M. (1995) "Willed" to Choose: Educational Reform and Busno-power. (Response to Marshall). *Philosophy of Education Yearbook*, [retrieved on July 6, 2006 from *http://www.ed.uiuc.edu/EPS/PES-Yearbook/95_docs/ford.html*.

Foucault, M. (1973*). The Order of Things: An archaeology of the human sciences*. New York: Random House.

————. (1977) Nietzsche, Genealogy, History. In *Language, Counter-Memory, Practice: Selected Interviews and Essays*. D.F. Bouchard (Ed.), Ithaca: Cornell University Press.

————. (1982) The subject and power. In H. Dreyfus and P. Rabinow (Eds.) *Michel Foucault: Beyond structuralism and hermeneutics*. Brighton: Harvester Press, pp. 208–226.

————. (1983) Afterword: The subject and power. In Michel Foucault. *structuralism and hermeneutics*. Chicago: University of Chicago Press, pp. 208-226.

————. (1984) Polemics, politics and problematisation. In P. Rabinow (Ed.), *The Foucault reader* (pp. 18–24). Harmondsworth: Penguin.

————. (1998a) Nietzsche, Freud, Marx. In *Aesthetics, Method and Epistemology: Essential Works of Foucault 1954–1984*, Volume 2, (pp. 269–278) James D. Faubion (Ed.), New York, The New Press.

————. (1998b) Structuralism and poststructuralism. In *Aesthetics, Method and Epistemology: Essential Works of Foucault 1954–1984*, Volume 2, (pp. 433–458) James D. Faubion (Ed.), New York, The New Press.

————. (1998c) What is an author? In *Aesthetics, Method and Epistemology: Essential Works of Foucault 1954–1984*, Volume 2, (pp. 205–222) James D. Faubion (Ed.), New York, The New Press.

————. (1998d) Foucault. In *Aesthetics, Method and Epistemology: Essential Works of Foucault 1954–1984*, Volume 2, (pp. 459–464) James D. Faubion (Ed.), New York, The New Press.

————. (2004) *Naissance de la biopolitique: Cours au Collège de France, 1978–1979.* Paris: Gallimard Seuil.

Gordon, C. (1996). Foucault in Britain. In A. Barry, T. Osborne & N. Rose (Eds.), *Foucault and political reason* (pp. 253–270). London: UCL Press.

Hoskin, K. (1979). The examination, disciplinary power and rational schooling. *History of Education 8 (2)*, 135–146.

Hunter, I. (1994). *Rethinking the school: Subjectivity, bureaucracy, criticism.* Sydney, AU: Allen & Unwin.

Marshall, J. D. (1989). Foucault and education, *Australian Journal of Education 2*, 97–111.

————. (1996). *Michel Foucault: Personal autonomy and education.* London: Kluwer Academic.

Middleton, S. (1998). *Disciplining sexuality: Foucault, life histories, and education.* New York: Teachers College, Columbia University.

Nietzsche, F. (1956). *The birth of tragedy and the genealogy of morals.* (F. Golffing, Trans.). New York: Anchor Books.

Olssen, M. (1999). *Michel Foucault: Materialism and education.* Westport, CT: Bergin & Garvey.

————. (2002). Invoking Democracy: Foucault's conception (with insights from Hobbes), *Policy Futures in Education*, 1(3) at *http://www.triangle.co.uk/PFIE*

Peters, M. (1996) *Poststructuralism, Politics and Education.* Westport, CT & London: Bergin & Garvey.

————. (2004) Why Foucault? New directions in Anglo-American educational research. In *Nach Foucault-Diskurs-und machtanalytische perspektiven der pädagogik.* W. Nieke, M. Wimmer, & J. Masschelein (Eds.). Wiesbaden: V.S.-Verlag für Sozialwissenschaften.

Pongratz, L., Wimmer, M., Nieke, W., & Massschelein, J. (2004). (Eds.), *Nach Foucault: Diskurs- und machtanalytische perpsektiven der pädagogik.* DGfE, VS Verlag.

Popkewitz, T., & Brennan, M. (1997). (Eds.). *Foucault's challenge: Discourse, knowledge and power in education.* New York: Teachers College Press.

Schrift, A. (1995) *Nietzsche's French legacy: A geneaology of French Poststructuralism.* New York & London: Routledge.

Veyne, P. (1997). The Final Foucault and His Ethics. (C. Porter & A. I. Davidson, Trans.) In A.I. Davidson (Ed.), *Foucault and his interlocutors*, (pp. xxx–xli). Chicago: University of Chicago Press.

Walkerdine, V. (1984). Developmental psychology and the child-centred pedagogy: the insertion of Piaget into early Education. In J. Henriques et al., *Changing the subject* (pp. 157–174). London: Methuen.

————. (1988). *The mastery of reason: Cognitive development and the production of rationality.* London: Routledge.

ᔓ Chapter 2 ᔕ

Michel Foucault: Educational Research as Problematisation

James D. Marshall

The title for this book suggests that we need new directions for educational research. Michel Foucault, however, would not have offered *new directions* for educational research, though he might have offered suggestions as to how research might be done. He often claimed that he did not advocate theories or methodologies which were to be adopted or followed. Nevertheless, the book title suggests that for some reason educational research needs to be re-thought. I will look at an approach to research by Foucault which can be considered as a possibility for doing educational research. This approach can be called *problematisation,* and it is exhibited in the second half of the paper by an example.

In educational research and in the theories underlying educational research there have been long standing debates about how to approach, and how to do research. There seems to have been nothing agreed upon as a *paradigm* of educational research.[1] For example, should educational research follow the models of science and/or philosophy of science? However, even if there was agreement on following scientific research there seems to have been nothing agreed upon as *the paradigm* for scientific research. Thus, should one be a Popperian, attempting to falsify hypotheses, or should one be a positivist like B.F. Skinner and Emile Durkheim? Another debate has been called the *quantitative* vs. the *qualitative.* Here the issue concerns the collection of scientific data (often mirroring the medical double blind crossover model) or should it be concerned with case studies which, far from trying to develop general principles concentrate through an extensive holistic study upon the particular institution, practice, or individual 'actors'? Or should educational research be abandoned altogether because it is believed by some people in education that theory and research have little to offer to the practices of education?[2] These debates have often been sharp and vitriolic, and have resulted in what can be called ideological standoffs in which proponents asserting the 'truth' of their differing theories and approaches cannot find any common ground which may be a way forward to establishing new 'truths.'

Underlying these ideological positions are two fundamentally opposed views about knowledge of human beings. Is knowledge of ourselves and our practices best understood by the establishment and the adoption of universal truths from the social or human sciences, or is it best understood, not in this universal sense, but in a singular, particular, and unique manner? Foucault sees the relationship between knowledge and the self as having undergone huge shifts post-Descartes, and that this can be exemplified by noting changes in the practices of the self in relation to truth. He claims that in Western culture "up to the sixteenth century, asceticism and access to truth are always more or less obscurely linked" (Foucault, 1983, p. 279). But this is not to continue. Foucault explains the changes which occurred, the break or rupture[3] between the Renaissance and the classical age, with this example:

> ...Pascal was still in a (Renaissance) tradition in which practices of the self, the practice of asceticism, were tied up with the knowledge of the world . . . we must not forget that Descartes wrote 'meditations'—and meditations are a practice of the self. But the extraordinary thing in Descartes' texts is that he succeeded in substituting a subject as founder of practices of knowledge for a subject constituted through practices of the self. (Foucault, 1983, p. 278f) (my enclosure)

This is important as it is to lead to the prioritizing of universal general knowledge from the human sciences over self-knowledge. It also leads to the subject being conceived as autonomous and the foundation of knowledge and signification—the meaning giving subject. Foucault continues:

> This is very important. Even if it is true that Greek philosophy founded rationality, it always held that a subject could not have access to the truth if he did not first operate upon himself a certain work that would make him susceptible to knowing the truth – a work of purification . . .(Foucault, 1983, p. 278f.)

According to Foucault:

> Descartes, I think, broke this when he said, "To accede to truth, it suffices that I be *any* subject that can see what is evident." Evidence is substituted for ascesis at the point where the relationship to the self no longer needs to be ascetic to get into relation to the truth. It suffices that the relationship to the self reveals to me the obvious truth of what I see for me to apprehend the truth definitively. Thus, I can be immoral, and know the truth. (1983, pp. 279)

This break between the self and knowledge is 'attacked' by several French philosophers before Foucault, though not necessarily in his terms (and he is not proposing a return to Greek culture). This break is taken up, by Henri Bergson in the late 19th century. Bergson (1895), an early critic of this new relationship between the self and knowledge, of positivism (Comte and Durkheim) and the human sciences, believes that they merely place us as one amongst groups, destroying, what is unique about ourselves as individuals. This knowledge is what "*any* subject...can see" (Foucault, 1983, p. 279). In the approach of the human sciences we are not seen as uniquely individual but as one of a group. But what Bergson argues is that we have *self-knowledge* which is not caught by the human sciences. Bergson prioritises this *self-knowledge* over the universal knowledge provided by the human sciences. But is Bergson's view of the subject a continuation of Descartes in French philosophy? The short answer is no, but we need to pursue the history of French philosophy further.

Foucault himself has remarked that since Descartes French philosophy has prioritised the philosophy of the subject:

> In the years that preceded the Second World War, and even more so after the war, philosophy in continental Europe and in France was dominated by the philosophy of the subject. I mean that philosophy took as its task par excellence the foundation of all knowledge and the principle of all signification as stemming from the meaningful subject. The importance given to this question was due to the impact of Husserl, but the centrality of the subject was also tied to an institutional context, for the French university, since philosophy began with Descartes, could only advance in a Cartesian manner. (Foucault, 1981, p. 176)

Whilst Foucault is confining himself to a certain time period, one philosopher who was initially very influential upon the philosophers of those times was Bergson. Though he attacked Cartesianism on a number of fronts he certainly argued for the notion of the embodied self and the possibility of multiple selves. He influenced both Maurice Merleau-Ponty and Simone de Beauvoir on the importance of immediate experience. However, it was Emmanuel Levinas, strongly influenced in his early thought by Bergson, who introduced phenomenology into French philosophy in both Heideggerian and Husserlean terms (Matthews, 1996, p. 158). In turn, Merleau-Ponty and both Sartre and Beauvoir are to be influenced by Husserl, and indeed Beauvoir developed a (later) Husserlean philosophy of lived experience (see Holveck, 2002).

Foucault sought a resolution of the theoretical problems in the philosophy of the subject as he believed that this philosophy had paradoxically failed:

> With the leisure and the distance which came after the war, this emphasis on the philosophy of the subject no longer seemed self-evident. Hitherto, hidden theoretical paradoxes could no longer be avoided. This philosophy of consciousness had paradoxically failed to found a philosophy of knowledge, and especially of scientific knowledge. Also, this philosophy of meaning had failed to take into account the formative mechanisms of signification and the structure of systems of meaning. (Foucault, 1981, p. 176)

Foucault continues, saying that the directions which followed this 'breakdown,' were first

> ...the theory of objective knowledge as an analysis of systems of meaning, as semiology [e.g., logical positivism]...and second...a certain school of linguistics, psychoanalysis, and anthropology—all grouped under the rubric of structuralism. These were not the directions I took. (Foucault, 1981, p.176) (my enclosure)[4]

Foucault then talks of the direction which he was to take. This way was, he says, through a "genealogy of the modern subject as a historical and cultural reality—which means as something that can eventually change" (1981, p. 177). This direction will be followed below and linked to a version of ascesis (not the Greek version[s]).

Even so, whilst we have a direction which he intended to follow, if we are to talk of Foucault and doing educational research we may think that we need to have some idea of where he 'comes' from, from what 'discipline'—was he an idealist, marxist, nihilist . . . and so on? In the interview with Paul Rabinow just before his death, Foucault said in an answer to such a question:

> I think I have in fact been situated in most of the squares of the checkerboard, one after another and sometimes simultaneously: as anarchist, leftist, ostentatious or disguised marxist, nihilist, explicit or secret marxist, technocrat in the service of Gaullism, new liberal, and so on. An American Professor claimed that a crypto-Marxist like me was invited to the US, and I was denounced by the Press in Easter European Countries for being an accomplice of the dissidents. None of these descriptions is important by itself; taken together, on the other hand, they mean something. And I must admit that I rather like what they mean. (Foucault, 1984, p. 113)

But Foucault did understand the label 'researcher,' that it applied to him, and that he approached his 'teaching' as a researcher. According to Ewald & Fontana:

> Michel Foucault approached his teaching as a researcher. He explored possibilities for books in preparation, outlined fields of problematisation, as though he were handing out invitations to potential researchers . . . the lectures given at Le Collège de France . . . are not outlines for books, even though the books and lectures do sometimes have themes in common. They have a status of their own. They belong to a specific discursive regime within the sum total of the 'philosophical acts' performed by Michel Foucault. (2003, p. xi)

At the start of his 1975–1976 course at Le Collège de France Foucault said this on research:

> After all, the fact that the work that I described to you looked both fragmented, repetitive and discontinuous was quite in keeping with what might be called a 'feverish laziness.' It's a character trait of people who love libraries, documents, references, dusty manuscript, texts

that have never been read, books which, no sooner printed, were closed and then slept on the shelves and were only taken down centuries later. All this quite suits the busy inertia of those who profess useless knowledge, a sort of sumptuary knowledge, the wealth of a parvenu and, as you well know, its external signs are found at the foot of the page. (2003 p. 4)

I wish to characterize this account of doing research as an indication of a modern form of ascesis, because, as quoted above, for Foucault the self has to "first operate upon himself a certain work that would make him susceptible to knowing the truth" (See further below when we look at an example of problematisation).

In this chapter I look at Foucault's notion of problematisation and suggest, if not argue, that this notion provides a way forward, a way through endless ideological disputes and polemical argument, though it does not claim to offer solutions (see below). I provide an illustration of Foucault's notion of problematising—the abolition of corporal punishment in New Zealand's (public) schools. Foucault's *Discipline and Punish* (1979) is an example of what he means by problematising an object of *Thought* (see below) but *how* that is done is in the text, but not explicitly. My example provides a schematic account of what *might* be done. My conclusion will be that Foucault's notion of problematisation provides a way forward, an approach which is different from, and steps aside from, the ideological and the polemical.

Problematisation

In his interview with Michel Foucault (1984), Paul Rabinow's opening question on problematics and problematising was: "You have been talking about a 'history of problematics.' What is a history of problematics?" (1984, p. 117).

Foucault's answer begins with an exposition on the history of *thought*. (He had, of course, named his chair at the Collège de France in 1969–1970 as 'The History of Systems of Thought'). His aim for some time had been to describe a history of *thought* that was not a history of ideas and was not a history of attitudes and types of action:

It seemed to me that there was one element that was capable of describing the history of *thought*—this was what one could call the element of problems or, more exactly, problematisations . (Foucault, 1984, p. 117)

He distinguished the history of *thought* from the history of ideas and from the domain of attitudes that might underline and determine behaviour. The history of ideas may take one of at least two forms. First, we may compare and/or contrast the concept of justice in Plato's *Republic* with that found in John Rawl's modern works. Second, we might look at the King's concept of punishment to be found in the opening pages of *Discipline and Punish* with contemporary views, so as to criticise the earlier views and/or to show how more humane and civilised we have become. These are *not* the history of *thought*. Nor is the examination and elucidation of underlying attitudes, beliefs, and customs which, while not articulated may govern, if not determine, practices and policies. Thus *thought*, Foucault argues, is

> something quite different from the set of representations that underlies a certain behaviour;
> it is also quite different from the domain of attitudes that can determine this behaviour.
> Thought is not what inhabits a certain conduct and gives it its meaning; rather, it is what
> allows one to step back from this way of acting or reacting, to present it to oneself as an
> object of thought and question it as to its meaning, its conditions and its goals. (1984, p.
> 117)

The notion of stepping back is very important. Stepping back is different from the notion of unearthing an underlying knowledge or set of practices, an episteme, which permit utterances to be considered true or false. Hacking (1981) talked of a depth knowledge or savoir. Depth knowledge is used in *Discipline and Punish* and discussed formally in *The Archaeology of Knowledge*. But to step back is not merely to seek depth knowledge or an episteme.

Stepping back is at the same time a freedom for Foucault. It is a freedom to detach oneself from what one does, it is the motion by which one detaches oneself from what one does, so as to establish it as an *object of thought* and to reflect upon it as a problem. An object of *thought* as a problem carries no "baggage," (i.e., prior theory, presuppositions and possibilities or hints of solutions). To question meaning, conditions and goals is at the same time freedom in relation to what one does. It is to treat the object of *thought* as a *problem*. A system of *thought* would be a history of problems or a problematisation. It would involve developing a set of conditions within which possible responses can be proposed. But it would not present itself as a solution or response. How does something become a problem and enter the domain of *thought*? For a domain of action, a behaviour, or practice to enter the field of *thought*: " . . . it is necessary for a certain number of factors to have made it uncertain, to have made it lose its familiarity, or to have provoked a certain number of difficulties around it. These elements result from social, economic or political processes (Foucault, 1984, p. 117). The elements—social, economic and political processes—can be described as "the politics." It is the elements of practices, the politics as he calls them, to which Foucault directs his questions.

Finally, to problematise is not to pose questions to the politics from any particular position. One must not approach problematising as either an adversary or as a committed theorist or ideologue.

Problematising

In this section I will look at how a certain practice entered a field of *thought* and how it might be problematised. The example is the abolition of corporal punishment in New Zealand's State Schools (i.e, public) in 1992 (for a fuller background discussion on punishment in New Zealand, see Marshall & Marshall, 1997). First, we will look at how the practice of corporal punishment entered the domain of *thought*, how it became uncertain as a practice in public schools, and how it had become 'unfamiliar' to a number of teachers and parents. Second, how it might be problematised from a Foucauldean position.

How Corporal Punishment Became Uncertain?

The Social. Since WWII there has been a rising disquiet in New Zealand society over discipline of the young, accompanied by an increasing and substantial knowledge of the effects of certain child rearing practices upon the young, including corporal punishment and spanking. There was a rising problem of teenage delinquency from the 1950s and, more recently, justified concern over deaths of young children and early suicides. New Zealand does not fare at all well amongst international statistics on these matters.

In education the (old) State Department of Education had tried to 'tackle' these issues, first by learning from overseas experts. From the 1930s a string of experts visited the country to offer advice on the effects of corporal punishment (e.g., psychologists Sir Cyril Burt and Dr. Joseph Mercurio). But their advice in the late 1930s and 1950s was virtually ignored by the populace, or those who claimed to be able to divine what the populace believed on these issues. Comics, rock and roll and films (e.g., James Dean's *East of Eden*) came under attack as 'causes' of these problems. But no political solution was attained. Schools attempted to ameliorate these problems through the introduction of counseling services and the beginnings of other forms of disciplining.

These issues bubbled over in education in the 1970s but, again, corporal punishment was not abolished. By the 1980s however, new forms of disciplining the young were being used, and for those teachers wavering on the fence, the tide began to turn against corporal punishment in schools. Yet, there was still a number of teachers—the 'old school'—who opposed abolition, resorting to such soothsayings as "What could theorists tell *us*?; *we* teach" and "Statistics can be used any way one wishes."

The Economic. Corporal punishment was certainly more economic than the alternatives that were being proposed, some of which have been installed since abolition. In some state schools the head prefect was permitted to cane. The author attended a state boarding school where the disciplining was done by prefects and punishment given by the head prefect. This was certainly economic for it saved extra appointments of teachers to the boarding establishment. But it was also economic in another sense for it removed the object of resentment by recipients from the teachers to the prefects.

The Political. The problem was that the nation was divided on this issue of corporal punishment. On the one hand, the National Party (conservative) was scared of losing the rural vote which had held it in power for so long. On the other hand, the Labour Party had promised to abolish it and did so on the eve of losing power in 1992. But now in power again, the Labour Party has not addressed the thorny question of the Crimes Act, article 529 and the meaning of 'reasonable force.' This notion, unclear as it remains, was used to oppose abolition.

Problematising Corporal Punishment

New Zealand was one of the last nations in the Western world to abolish corporal punishment in public (i.e., state) schools. Great Britain was forced to abolish corporal punishment in state schools in 1986 because of a ruling of the European Committee of Human Rights in 1982. At that time, corporal punishment was legal only in Great Britain, Australia and New Zealand. New Zealand suspended it in 1987 and legislated against it in 1992, but there is still a section of the Crimes Act which permits parents and teachers to use reasonable force and which is in conflict with Article 7 of the United Nations Convention on Civil and Political Rights, ratified by New Zealand in 1992. Article 7 of the UN Convention states that: "No one shall be subjected to torture or to cruel, inhuman, or degrading treatment or punishment."

At present, a debate is simmering in New Zealand to stop parents from smacking their children. Some people fear that discipline is (again) declining in New Zealand society and, of course, in schools. There are demands for the return of corporal punishment regardless of the fact that by signing the UN convention we are held to the contrary by international law. In other words, the notion of reasonable force in New Zealand's Crimes Act is being challenged (once again) as it is not defined in Section 52 of the Crimes Act   Does the notion of reasonable force cover corporal punishment and spanking, as it seems to in relation to corporal punishment in private schools and spanking by parents and/or care givers in homes? If it does and section 59 of the Crimes Act is not repealed or altered then New Zealand remains in contravention of the UN Convention, both legally and morally. Thus, the debate, and 'political' uncertainty between legalists, politicians, teachers and parents continues. How could New Zealand have retained corporal punishment in public schools when legally it was about to ratify (and did ratify in 1992 as planned) the United Nations Convention on Civil and Political Rights?[5]

In order now to problematise the object of thought we need to direct questions at the 'politics.' By 'politics' in Foucault I understand the social, economic and political processes found in an amalgamation of laws (Legal Acts of Education), public institutions (Education Boards, schools, universities, etc.), Boards of Trustees (Governors), teachers, parents and students/children. I will refer to this amalgamation as the "Forum." The Forum needs to be questioned along the parameters of meaning, conditions and goals by questions probing the areas of the social, the economic and the political, and along those parameters we need to look at historical factors.

Questions

Across all three parameters there is no meaning assigned to 'reasonable force' in section 59 of the Crimes Act. This must be pursued through questions of both the meaning of 'punishment' and how it is to be justified. Questions must also be asked to the Forum as to their understanding of the section on reasonable force in the Crimes Act. (In what follows, I have written the three sections differently to indicate differing possibilities for questioning the Forum).

Questions of *Meaning* (to the Forum)

Q.1. The term 'reasonable force' is used in Section 59 of The Crimes Act. It is not defined in the Act, but it is clearly either restraint or punishment. In terms of corporal punishment in education how do you understand 'reasonable force'?

A.1. Reasonable force has not been defined in the acts though it has, to a certain extent, been defined in the Courts by case law. What is reasonable is in part defined by practices of child rearing in homes and institutions. The history of those practices shows a change towards more 'humane' practices. For example, young criminal offenders are no longer whipped, in part because of inconsistencies in its administration, and this too has been tightened in education.

Q.2 . But do you see punishment, for example, as retributive, as a sort of 'paying back' to someone who deserves it for their behaviour?

A.2. Well! In education there are some teachers and administrators who think in that way or believe that corporal punishment is deserved, but there are others who see it as a deterrent, in that it acts against the offender, in that it deters that person and deters others from offending because of the consequences. It is interesting that some people see corporal punishment as educative or as reformative, but the former is more like training than education, and the latter needs other activities, processes and programmes—reform is reform. So we are left then with retribution and deterrence, and teachers who support corporal punishment are pretty much divided on this issue.

Q.3. Okay! Given that retribution and deterrence are the competing meanings for punishment I suppose that the justifications follow in part from those meanings. Thus, retribution is justified as a deserved paying back for wrong doing and deterrence is justified because it stops or tends to stop future offending. But isn't that a little odd, if not morally questionable, in the case of young children? Retribution is a payback but for what? An offence, or a part-offence, or for being innocent but in a group situation punished, or for not knowing rules or rules under a number of different formulations or descriptions? Deterrence has the same problems about guiding the young, but it has the added problem of threatening the young, offenders and non-offenders alike. Do these justifications really work with the young? Furthermore, is paying back or threatening young people about their future behaviour the kind of thing which we should be doing with children, as well as inflicting unpleasantness?

A.4 We might not see it that way. As has been said the wisdom of the age supports corporal punishment as a kind of necessary evil, and the beliefs are that it works better than other proposals.

Q.5 If I hear you correctly you do not see agreement on punishment being defined and justified as either retributive or deterrent which are, after all, the two main and competing philosophical contenders. By appealing to 'the wisdom of the age' as an explanation of why corporal punishment is permitted to continue, you seem to mean something like inducting or initiating young people into society's practices and norms—perhaps a sort of training to take one's place in society.

A.5 Well! We don't know much about philosophy but seeing it as kind of initiation or training seems to be quite useful.

Q.6 Have you read a book by Michel Foucault entitled *Discipline and Punish: the Birth of the Prison?*

Questioning the *Conditions*

In this section on conditions I will talk of the *types* of questions which might be asked.

Questions must be asked as to whether the Crimes Act Section 59 which permits 'reasonable force' should be abolished or reworded to cover issues of the meaning of 'reasonable force.' Or the section might be totally abolished. There are other conditions, (e.g., issues) of self-protection from minors. Under the parameter of the social would fall questions about the long-term psychological effects of punishment, including corporal punishment, and of child abuse (what research has been done in New Zealand, for example), the disruption of order in schools and the effects upon society (e.g., of the need for counseling and psychiatric services), the breaking up of families and the provision of a whole coterie of child services. It must be noted that New Zealand is very high amongst the developed Western countries for early childhood deaths.

Questions must be asked about the economic effects of corporal punishment, smacking and child abuse. I am not just talking about the economic effects of providing children's courts and welfare services and the economic effects of losing potentially well adjusted citizens to anti-social behaviour and the courts. Rather, I am talking about the actual 'loss of life' of young people who may have contributed to the well being of society, who might have led useful and practical lives as good parents and citizens, and who may have contributed to society.

Further questions could be raised about alternative measures to corporal punishment, and the education of principals, staff and administrators. Schools are required to keep records of cases of corporal punishment and these need to be studied: there are questions concerning the numbers of instances, the socioeconomic status and ethnic status of recipients (are certain individuals and groups receiving more punishment than others?) and the details of the offence for which the punishment is given. These are examples only of the questions which might be posed of the *object* 'corporal punishments' under this heading of conditions; it is far from being an exhaustive list.

Questions of *Goals*

Goals and aims are notoriously difficult things to specify—they are left in general terms only—nor is this an exhaustive list.

1. To care for all children.
2. To provide order in the school grounds and classroom.
   a.   to provide general order
   b.   to ensure that there is no bullying.
   c.   to ensure that pupils can learn.
   d.   to assure parents on such matters.
   e.   to develop socially responsible citizens
   f.   to ensure that all in the school are treated with respect
          and dignity.
3. To pursue equity goals.
4. To pursue excellence in teaching and learning.
5. To maintain good communication, relationships and involvement
    with parents and the community.

Summary

Let us assume that we have our problematisation. This has been arrived at from a series of questions addressed at the 'Politics' (or Forum as it was named here). Let us assume further that no more questions will be asked, or need to be asked.

But how is this research, it might be asked? (e.g. by a funding authority). Research is meant to be *research*, i.e., to find out things and to get positive answers to questions asked, or to provide recommendations for solving problems and/or guiding policy. We don't even have a solution or positive answers to the actual questions asked, or failing that, as to what further research should be done. Is that *doing* research, is that what 'you' call research? What was the hypothesis that was being tested? And what conclusion was arrived at from all of those questions?

At which point the researcher might reply by asking another set of questions.

Q.1. (Researcher) Your list of questions implies a problem. Do you have a problem?
A.1. Of course! Look at all of those interminable questions! Why can't they be reduced to something more manageable so that we have clear principles and clear hypotheses to be tested? How could we present this research, as a solution to questions concerning the corporal punishment of children—as a practice it has become very uncertain, and this research needs to be simplified and made logically watertight. Also, we will need a one pager for the Minister of Education. You don't appear to have done anything—you are lazy and we are frenzied! (See Foucault above on his research at Le Collège de France).
Q.2. Oh dear! Have you read Henri Bergson? If you want wise judgments to be made in education then perhaps this might interest you—from Bergson (1895, p. 352)

> The education of good sense (i.e., wise judgment) will thus not only consist in rescuing intelligence from ready-made ideas, but also in turning it away from excessively simple ideas, stopping it on the slippery slope of deductions and generalizations, and finally preserving it from excessive self-confidence. Let us go further: the greatest risk that education could represent to good sense would be to encourage our tendency to judge men (sic.) and things from a purely intellectual view (i.e., scientific) to measure our value and that of others according to mental merit alone, to extend this principle to societies themselves, to only approve institutions, laws and customs which bear the outward mark of logical clarity and simple organization (my enclosures).

Conclusion

What Foucault's notions of problematisation and research reveal, or at least indicate, is that he is striving for a modern form of *ascesis,* of getting oneself into a position that "would make him susceptible to knowing the truth" (Foucault, 1983, p. 279). Problematising involves the production of an Object of Thought devoid of *a priori* views, and the 'wisdom' of recognized practices and beliefs. Instead of establishing sound research designs based upon established knowledge of the problem/practice to be researched in advance as the Forum's last question proposes (Q.2 in the summary), what is required is research that is "frenzied laziness," as Foucault calls it. It is these general questions that make it susceptible (possible?) to know the truth.

In my view, the problematisation of objects of thought is Foucault's approach to restoring the right relationship between a subject and truth. It is a rejection of both Descartes' view, and the directions taken by semiology and structuralism to challenge that view (see Foucault, 1981, pp. 176–177). But nor is it a return for Foucault to the Greek notion of ascesis.

Notes

1   In Kuhn's (1962) sense of paradigm.
2   I was once interviewed for a position at a northern English university where the Professor of Education, a distinguished WWII veteran, abhorred educational theory. Needless to say I did not receive an offer for that position and the professor later returned to school mastering.
3   A term ascribed to Foucault's works.
4   At this point in the text, Foucault takes yet another ironic swipe at being labelled a structuralist. "Let me announce for once and for all that I am not a structuralist, and I confess, with the appropriate chagrin, that I am not an analytic philosopher. Nobody is perfect."
5   In May 2006 a Bill is before the House of Parliament to abolish 'reasonable force' in the Crimes Act, as a *defence*.

Bibliography

Bergson, H. (1895). Good sense and classical studies. In K. Ansell Pearson & J. Mullarkey (2002) (Eds.), *Henri Bergson: Key Writings* (pp.345–352). New York & London: Continuum.

Bertani, M., & Fontano, A. (Eds.). (2003). *Michel Foucault: Society must be defended* (D. Macey, Trans.). New York: Picador

Eribon, D. (1991) *Michel Foucault*, (Betsy Wing, Trans.). Cambridge, Mass.: Harvard University Press.

Ewald, F., & Fontano, A. (2003). Foreword. In M. Bertani & A. Fontano (2003) (Eds.). *Michel Foucault: Society must be defended* (pp. ix–xiv). New York: Picador.

Foucault, M. (1979). *Discipline and punish: The birth of the prison*, New York: Vintage.

——————. (1981). Sexuality and solitude. In P. Rabinow (1997) (Ed.), *Michel Foucault: Ethics, subjectivity, and truth* (pp. 175–184). New York: New Press.

——————. (1983). On the genealogy of ethics: An overview of work in progress. In P. Rabinow (1997) (Ed.), *Michel Foucault: Ethics, subjectivity, and truth* (pp. 254–280). New York: New Press.

——————. (1984). Polemics, politics, and problematisations: An Interview with Michel Foucault. In P. Rabinow (1997) (Ed.), *Michel Foucault: Ethics, subjectivity, truth*. (pp.113–119). New York: The New Press.

——————. (2003). *Michel Foucault: Society must Be Defended*, M. Bertani & A. Fontano (Eds.). New York: Picador.

Hacking, I. (1981). The archaeology of knowledge. *The New York Review of Books.*
Holveck, E. (2002) *Simone de Beauvoir's philosophy of lived excperience,* New York: Rowman & Littlefield.
Kuhn, T. (1962) *The structure of scientific revolutions.* Chicago: The University of Chicago Press.
Marshall, J. D. & D. J. Marshall (1997). *Discipline and punishment in NewZealand education.* Palmerston
    North: Dunmore Press.
Matthews, E. (1996). *Twentieth century French philosophy.* Oxford: Oxford University Press
Rabinow, P. (1984) Polemics, politics, and problematisations: An Interview with Michel Foucault. In
    (Ed.) Paul Rabinow (1997).
Rabinow, P. (Ed.). (1997) *Michel Foucault: Ethics, subjectivity, truth.* New York: The
    New Press.

℅ Chapter 3 ℆

Freedom and Discipline: Transformations in Pedagogic Punishment

Ludwig Pongratz

Modern Contradictions—Contradictions of Modernity

"Why Foucault?" Well, the most obvious answer is, because he invites us to abandon established modes of thinking and to turn accepted perspectives on their head. Whoever gets involved with Foucault has to reckon with irritation. Foucault calls to account everyone, in the past as well as today, who hopes to play the guardian of democracy and freedom: instead of presenting the history of the modern world as a history of achievement and emancipation (a perspective which mostly serves the supposed 'victors of history'), Foucault draws our attention to the network of subtle tactics and constraints which have long been at work beneath the surface of proclaimed bourgeois freedoms. "Discipline is the other side of democracy" (Foucault, 1977, p. 126), this is one of the disillusioning insights that Foucault provides his readers along the way.

It is this 'dark view' (as Foucault's critics have referred to it) which generates responses which go beyond sympathy—including among educationalists. This is clearly illustrated by the question of punishment, a theme which educationalists would gladly like to be rid of. To speak of punishment produces unease: to all appearances, punishments demonstrate the failure of well-meaning pedagogic intentions. This is why today educationalists would rather speak of classroom management, self-steering or prevention, instead of discipline and constraint. Not without reason are they proud of the fact that tough physical punishments, which in the premodern world were considered 'normal' educational tools, were rejected and abolished by enlightened bourgeois society. But it remains debatable whether contemporary pedagogy, instead of excessive, painful punishments, has not replaced them with quite different modes of punishment, which may be more silent and unconscious than their predecessors, but certainly no less effective.

We should remember that *the basic framework of medieval-feudal forms of punishment* was modelled on the figure of *'repressive exclusion.'* Anything that opposed the expressions of hierarchically organised social power was excised. The thief lost his hand, the murderer his life, the recalcitrant school pupil was heavily disciplined. Not without reason did the switch become the symbol of schoolmasterly discipline. However, this direct violence rapidly came to be called into question as the medieval social world began to disintegrate. The critique of domination bound up in Enlightenment philosophy eventually deprived it of legitimation. For, how can individual domination exist alongside the rationally-founded claim to 'universal freedom'? How can the irrationality of pedagogic power be combined with the right to the rational conduct of life? Modern pedagogy has laboured at this dilemma since the beginning of the Enlightenment. And this contradiction is not simply internal to pedagogy itself. It constitutes *the contradiction of modernity itself, which manifests itself in the pedagogic problem of punishment* in an accentuated form.

At least since the emergence of Enlightenment pedagogy, then, penalty has had to legitimate itself: pedagogic punishment now had to appear rational. It is precisely this contradiction that makes Kant's lecture 'On Pegagogy,' in the winter semester of 1776–1777, a far-sighted engagement with the issues:

> One of the greatest problems in education is how to combine the subjection to the required discipline with the capacity to make use of one's freedom. For discipline is necessary! How do I cultivate freedom alongside discipline? (Kant 1899, p. 711).

Kant's answer to this question runs as follows: one must

> show the child that one imposes discipline on him in order to lead him to the use of his own freedom, that one cultivates the child so that he eventually becomes free, i.e., so that he does not need to be dependent on the assistance of others. (Kant, 1899, p. 711)

In other words, the child should be subject to pedagogic discipline in the interests of his later independence. *The freedom of the bourgeois subject* remains systematically *coupled to forms of internalised domination.* And this manifests itself particularly in pedagogic penalty. It is clear: pure rationality, which is what Kant is concerned with, gets its hands dirty on its entry into bourgeois society. Rationality must—alongside all it claims regarding freedom —at the same time legitimate the societally-required degree of domination and discipline. Irrationality lies at the heart of social processes of rationalisation. The rationality of modernity reveals, in the course of its progression through history, more than ever before how its essence is characterized by domination. "Torture," observes Foucault (1977) in relation to this disillusioning aspect of the processes of Enlightenment, "that is what reason is" (p. 65).

'Enlightened Punishment': Ethical Consciousness and Morality

We can concede that in the first place this insight captures only half the truth.

Yet, it does give expression to a scepticism which modern optimism about progress (including among educationalists) is much too anxious to sweep under the carpet. Foucault's *Instrumentarium* makes it possible to show not just how the Enlightenment deprived feudalism's repressive forms of punishment of their legitimacy, but also how *new procedures of power appear in enlightened punishments*, which advance the contradiction between freedom and discipline in a new form. The rest of this paper examines this historical process of transformation, with particular reference to the German-speaking regions of Europe.

Pedagogic arrangements underwent a decisive change: setting out from the fundamental conviction of Enlightenment pedagogy, that the social integration of the individual is to be anchored in the formation of consciousness, the new practices of punishment *no longer aimed primarily at the body* and its habitus, but at an internal space, whether it is called the soul, imagination, consciousness or reason. In particular, this shift can already be seen in the early Enlightenment, in the sublimated strict pedagogic discipline in the ensemble of diverse pedagogic institutions established in Halle by the theologian and pedagogue, August Hermann Francke (1663–1727).

Certainly Francke's maxim, that the child's will was to be broken, has come to be understood as the epitome of repressive education. However, it was more a matter of the beginning of a theologically-based *technique of the psyche or the soul*. The rescue of the ruined soul is Francke's ultimate aim, and this is why the physical discipline in Francke's homes lost the form of mindless repression. Discipline was consciously exercised not as vengeful violence, but as paternal care. It was to operate without anger, retribution, indeed without any kind of passion. Self-control was imposed on the teacher. The punishment was recorded in a 'morals register.' In the final ritual element of the punishment one can see how this form of punishment only made sense in terms of the shared virtue of both tutor and pupil: "…and when the punishment is completed, the child shall offer his hands to the tutor…and solemnly promise improvement" (Francke, 1957, 116).

It is obviously difficult to say how much rationalised sadism remained bound up with this controlled form of punishment; nonetheless, completely raw pedagogic aggression was not intended and this would destroy what Francke was aiming for: the child's capacity for personal insight, on which this moral improvement depends. The offering of hands at the conclusion of the punishment symbolises—in contrast to the situation as a whole—the requirement that the bond between tutor and pupil should not be broken. And this bond was established in *ever more subtle ways in the Enlightenment pedagogy of the 18th century*. Correspondingly, the situational conditions and arrangements of punishment became increasingly precise. But physical discipline did not disappear completely. For example, in Salzmann's (1744–181) Schnepfenthaler educational institute (like the 'Dessauer Philanthropin' of Johann Bernhard Basedow (1724–1790), a model Enlightenment institution), punishment was approached as follows: corporal punishment was to take place "in complete secrecy, following prior solemn warnings" (Salzmann, 1884, p. 30). The intimidatory effects of public repression are no longer mentioned. Punishment takes place precisely with the exclusion of the public, perhaps also with the pedagogues secret shame about its still uneven impact. When punishment is brought into the public arena, it is not that of the bloodthirsty mob at the gallows, but the *controlled public arena of a civilized community:* in the 'merit tables' in the Dessauer homes, everyone could scrutinize the virtuousness of everyone else, like a sort of public accounting system. Punishment was noted as a loss of points, (i.e., as a loss of public esteem). (This anticipates considerably modern forms of managements and behaviour modification).

Public disparagement can also, however, serve other ends, such as the establishment of (moral) maturity:

> The usual punishment of mistakes and nuisances is a reduction of the merit points; turning a study hour into an hour of manual labour; a long period in an empty room, where one cannot see out the window and where one can hear the nearby sounds of other pupils studying or enjoying themselves. (Basedow, 1965, p. 216)

The obvious point of attack for these forms of punishment and discipline is no longer the body; what is coerced instead is the soul, which is shamed, exposed or disappointed. Very generally, one can distinguish *three forms of control* with which Enlightenment pedagogy occupied the subject's inner space: (1) structuring the field of internal observation, to focus their attention and repress undesirable ideas; (2) guidelines consisting of positively sanctioned projected models, which were to operate as ideals of civility continually in view of 'the inner eye'; and finally—accepted only as a last resort by the 'philanthropists' (as the progressive German Enlightenment pedagogies referred to themselves)—(3) breaking the will by means of corporal discipline (Pongratz, 1989).

'Disciplinary Punishment': Body Drill and the Machine

Enlightenment punishment certainly became more refined. The 18th century laid the groundwork for more subtle forms of pedagogic control, which are still propagated and used today. None the less, with the turn of the century one can see a clear *shift in punishment techniques* and their pedagogic rationale: *instead of moral exhortation* and humiliation, there appear *forms of disciplinary formation and bodily drill.* The distinction which is decisive for the question of punishment lies in the discernible displacement of punitive violence exercised by an authorised person. The 18th century Enlightenment pedagogues punished in the name of a general and rational civility, which was clearly represented by the school community and its inner ordering. The disciplinary institutions of the 19th century, in contrast, increasingly made use of drill, silent training, continual correction, behind which a *personal relationship*—in the act of punishment itself also—plays less and less of a role. Punishment becomes an administrative act within a thoroughly rationalised system of learning.

It should be added that this made it necessary that school and teaching were reconstructed as a 'system.' One could possibly interpret this as a far-reaching consequence of the 'elementary method' with which Pestalozzi (1746–1827) put his particular stamp on the public schools at the beginning of the 19th century. However, one could easily reverse the relationship. The development of the modern disciplinary society in the 19th century demanded a learning system for which Pestalozzi's teaching style provided a decisive stimulus. His 'elementary method' introduced a new teaching method in which punishment also took on a transformed meaning.

Pestalozzi's new method of teaching not only made it possible, but precisely necessary, to subdivide the teaching programme both in content and in its temporal arrangement. It introduced a requirement for the formulation of binding, structured teaching plans and for an improved, more regular sequencing of the learning process. The new temporal regulation of teaching, however, brings to life a new picture of the school-age child, characterized by Kost (1985) as the "normalised school pupil" (p. 39). The new teaching method and its associated techniques of practice and examination created the possibility of characterizing the school pupil with reference to an objective, their fellow pupils and a particular method. The fictional 'normal pupil' also goes hand-in-hand with the division of classes according to age and learning and performance capabilities. All of this *makes the 'elementary method' an integral part of a new technique of power,* geared to a differentiated treatment of receptive bodies in order to increase their useful capacities as well as their compliance.

Using the example of the Zurich pedagogue Ignaz Thomas Scherr's practical writings on teaching from the 1830s, Kost has shown how the school reform inspired by Pestalozzi was seamlessly integrated and bound up with architectural and organisational disciplinary forms: with a particular ordering of school space, which established in schools what Foucault referred to as the "disciplinary gaze" (Pongratz, 1988, p. 155); with the introduction of a gender-specific code; with a 'microjustice' which regulated correct behaviour in the schoolroom; with a minute control of the body, beginning with the identification of the pupil's seat, establishing a language code—ranging from the teacher's commands to the pupils' ordered 'reporting'—and even military-style exercises with chalk and blackboard.

This drill, with which corporeal power (bio-power) was, so to speak, inscribed into the fabric of the school's everyday life, in order sublimely to target the school pupil, is part of the inner core of 19th century pedagogy. This is true not only of Pestalozzi's reform of the primary school (which was intended for the poorer population groups), but also of the reform of the Gymnasium (which was normally reserved for the wealthy children of the bourgeoisie). In the most 'progressive' pedagogic institutions, new procedures were implemented which boiled down to transforming people into 'learning machines' and schools into 'pedagogic machines' (Dreßen, 1982).

> Disciplinary power installs particular forms of acting on individuals, by arranging them spatially (through confinement, subdivision, assignment to functions and hierarchical classification), by controlling their activities temporally (by breaking down operations and establishing time units), by harnessing them to ultimate time frames (with a definitive sequence of guidelines concerning means and ends, with exercises and examinations) and by frequently linking these 'techniques' to each other. (Pongratz, 1989, p. 203)

What is disciplined is thus the process of learning itself—that is, the absorption and digestion of didactically processed knowledge. What also takes place is *the methodical discipline of the senses, of bodily posture, of correct behaviour in the classroom*. For example, Ziller (1817–1882, a leading German 19th century pedagogue), in his *Authorised Punishments for Teacher and Pupil* (1886), pays painfully close attention to the pupil's every movement. From the numbering of exercise book pages, through the cleanliness of benches and slates and pointing to lines and words during reading with a pencil or stick, to the clock striking the time beginning and ending the class, everything was controlled.

"Every activity, every movement," it was said dogmatically, "which diverts the children from the instruction, is to be treated as disturbance" (Ziller as cited in Rutschky 1977, p. 212). And such disturbance was subject to sanction. Nonetheless, the forms taken by such sanctions were fundamentally distinct from the punishment practices of repressive or integrative power. *Disciplinary punishment* aims at reducing deviation from the norm. This is why it is essentially *corrective* and works in terms of practice, learning which is intensive, duplicated and repeated. Disciplinary punishment *does not exact revenge* (like the repressive corporal punishment of the feudal era), it generates *no spectacle of punishment* (like Enlightenment pedagogy), but establishes itself through *a mechanics of training* which aims at repetition and firm inoculation. This is precisely why Ziller insisted that until an established habit has been formed, all of the teacher's instructions "should be executed, at the moment of the teacher's particular command, and that once the habit has been established, it must be constantly supervised, like any other custom" (ibid., p. 213).

Finally, disciplinary punishment is only one integrative element in a comprehensive system of rewards and sanctions, of conditioning and denial, which encompass the individual. It operates as a micropower acting on the learning body and seeks to link minimal expenditure with maximum effect. This is why Ziller generally rejects corporal punishment; it is not a means of education and can be 'left to the police.' The permissible forms of punishment, in contrast, work within a subtle differentiation of sanctions:

> Punishments during class in ascending order:
> a.   pause, disapproving look
> b.   a wave of the hand, tapping or striking the desk;
> c.   a warning call;
> d.   reprimand with earnest, generally restrained threat;
> e.   call out from the bench, place to one side or in the background, generally isolation, especially separate seating;
> f.   personal reporting of pupil to the head teacher;
> g.   to the Director (ibid., p. 213).

This punishment practice shows how much the effect of sanctions is coupled with a *structured distribution of sanctions* in the school institution (and beyond that in the whole social body). In this apparatus of punishment, the teacher's punitive gaze has only a casual place, but none the less with a more intensive effect than in earlier techniques of punishment, because it contains, in a mute form, the sanctioning force of the whole system. In the act of punishment the educator is only an *agent of an impersonal power*, for which he provides his voice for a precisely outlined period of time.

'Panoptic Punishment': Soft Control and Integration

With the transformation of the school into a disciplinary institution, the character of techniques of punishment becomes increasingly abstract and anonymous. Certainly, corporal punishment is increasingly subject to criticism and comes to be ostracized, but the process of disciplining still has a contradictory character: the humanisation of forms of punishment rests on a generalised and increasingly comprehensive control over individuals. Punishment becomes, in a sense, preventive. It does not need to be actually exercised, because it has already had an unconscious effect. Disciplinary procedures demonstrate their complete effectiveness only at the point where they no longer even need to be visible. In this sense, the 19th century school operating with its open, rigid discipline is by no means the apex of disciplinary power. On the contrary, it provided an ample basis for contradiction, bringing to life, towards the end of the 19th century, the opposition to school life organised around drill and rote-learning. "For a free school!" was the call of the reform pedagogues announcing their attack on traditional institutions during the first third of the 20th century.

However, even the model of reform pedagogy was unable to resolve the contradiction between freedom and discipline. It was simply disguised with *the establishment of new, softer forms of control*, but not eliminated. Reform pedagogy's focus of attention turned decisively away from the school's system of discipline towards 'the child.' What was now thematised was less the external arrangements for the regulation of learning bodies (school bench, school hygiene, the management of time and space in the school building, etc), but *much more the internal arrangements* (motivational structures, psychic dispositions, 'school life,' social forms) in order to established attention and independence in the process of learning. Corresponding to this there emerged new, flexible organisational structures, often referred to as 'free,' not only at the level of individual classes (free seating, free conversation among pupils, open learning plans) but equally at the level of the school as an institution (free school community, innovative 'school plans,' free school enrolment). As an aside, today's dominant neo-liberal discourse favours linking up with reform pedagogy's rhetoric of freedom, in order to effect current, governmental strategies of control.

Reform pedagogy's programme emphasises proximity to the 'real' world of life beyond the school: teaching becomes 'community teaching,' the school class turns into a 'living and working community,' educating becomes 'self education.' Certainly, the school pupil is taken more seriously as an autonomous subject than he had been previously, but not least in order to integrate him more smoothly into the institutionally established framework of the school. Kost (1985) has illustrated this *shift from "drill pedagogy" to "reform pedagogy"* (p. 190) with the example of the pedagogue's relationship to the school pupil's trouser pockets: the 'old' pedagogy examined trouser pockets only to ensure they contained clean handkerchiefs, the 'new pedagogy' did precisely the reverse, emptying all the contents onto the table in order to gain an insight into school life and to make the youthful collector's passions pedagogically useful. The subjective interest in the school pupil is thus imperceptible coupled with the objective interest of the school system in the development of individual capacities and the reintegration of these capacities into a unified whole, the functional principles of which remain concealed from the individual—precisely because everything appears to be out in the open. In this way, the learning situation is reorganized according to the principle of 'panopticism,' the primary effect of which is the creation of a conscious and permanent state of visibility for the school pupils: "He who is subjected to a field of visibility, and who knows it, assumes responsibility for the constraints of power; he makes them play spontaneously upon himself" (Foucault 1977, p. 202).

In this way the *disciplinary network* is *no longer organised in terms of administrative decrees*, but more in terms of the *ultra-flexible steering mechanisms of 'school life.'* One speaks now of the 'free dynamics' of capacities, to be released from the 'soil' of the community. The school advances to being a 'stage of life' which—in the terminology of the leading reform pedagogue Hugo Gaudig (1860–1923)—is understood more as a 'sphere of capacities.' The reformists' conceptual toolbox leads towards new, more subtle social techniques which are introduced, according to their own self-understanding, as models of liberation. Superficially, at least, this rhetoric of liberation is based on reality: for there is no longer an external instance which makes demands of the individual, the demands are now of a general nature. Everyone is subject to the same social arrangements, but at the same time they participate in their reproduction. In this way, individuals find themselves in a dual position: they can experience themselves as the subject of processes to which they remain completely subjected. The pegagogic code for this soft discipline is education for the 'community' through 'school life.' It is a programmatic feature of almost all the statements of pedagogic reform and puts a particular stamp on their practices of punishment. For example, Landahl (a teacher in the Hamburg Lichtwark school, an exemplary reform pedagogy model early in the 20th century), wrote about his decision "to place the whole responsibility for order and school discipline" in his class, "in the hands of the pupils themselves":

> In the one year in which we had already come together, the class established a whole range of self-governance arrangements through which, and this is naturally of particular importance for the question before us, an extraordinarily lively community feeling had developed. The feeling of belonging was for the individual no longer merely an external feeling, reserved for the work time, it had become purely human, extending beyond the class time, beyond school time and creating for all of us a strong feeling of unity. With such a class, naturally all doubts about the introduction of self-governance could recede into the background. For us school discipline has now become a matter for our class community. Punishment or teacher-led education has been replaced by community education. (Landahl, as cited in Reble 1980, p. 44f.)

Clearly, the most severe punishment in this arrangement is exclusion from the school or class community itself. This could be preceded by graded sanctions, such as the loss of a position or the right to hold a position, the right to vote in the class meetings or exclusion from communal activities, such as excursion, parties, and so on. The teacher's or the school system's sanctioning authority disappears behind the veil of a general regulation, which thus has a more lasting effect. "Since the class community decides on all transgressions against order discipline in its tribunal," reported Landahl, "all these transgressions have more or less completely ceased, despite the fact that they had become, as I said earlier, very frequent, not least because of the difficult space conditions in our school" (ibid., p. 46). The involvement of adults can, with a clear conscience, be restricted to "moderating punishments proposed by the school community" (Ilgner, as cited in Reble, 1980, p. 49). The actually sanctioning coercion arises from an ultimately irrational instance: 'school life' and this 'life' cannot—following a dictum of the philosophical doyen of German reform pedagogy, Wilhelm Dilthey (1833–1911)—be brought before the court of reason.

This anti-Enlightenment shift is to a certain extent characteristic of reform pedagogy. The overextension of the rational moment of teaching resulted only in "shallowness and platitudes" (Petersen, 1970, p. 203), wrote one of the leading thinkers of reform pedagogy, Peter Petersen (1884–1952). The actual "irrationality of the self-developing human soul" (ibid., p. 196) obstructs all methodological schemas, and offers in their place a teaching arrangement in which all the school pupils' irrational 'motivational forces' were "made to serve the learning and educational processes," so that "the laws of life could unfold to the full extent and power" (ibid., p. 131). This was precisely what Petersen's "pedagogic group" achieved, which wanted to become much more than a social group: It is the omnipresent control organ, indirectly steering habits, conduct and the acquisition of knowledge, without having to resort to "prescriptions and laws in a juridical sense" (ibid., p. 74).

Petersen could hardly formulate his distance from the rigid school system of the 19th century more clearly. The effects of the pedagogic groups as communities, however, were by no means inferior to the old disciplinary institutions. In the group, every member is always "completely extended and occupied" (ibid., p. 74). "We are not concerned with order," proclaimed Petersen with a nonchalant gesture,

> as teachers then only have to do the little that is left over, dealing with unsuitable or fragmented or genuinely damaging group formations or especially to keep an eye on them, but they have become visible and so clearly brought out into the open, that they cannot cause any serious damage. (p. 103).

Soft control has an easy job of it, because it brings every underground countermovement to light: "Visibility is a trap" (Foucault, 1977, p. 200). A general form of control emerges based on irrational premises, but pursuing rational instrumental ends. "Ultimately," comments Heinz-Joachim Heydorn (1916–1974) one of the most striking figures in German critical pedagogy,

> a pseudo-totality comes into being, including everything, but excluding all contradiction. Everything is spontaneity, nothing is spontaneous; everything is experienced as nature, nothing is nature; everything conforms to the system, to ideology, to production. The experience of freedom presumes the absence of all freedom. (1979, p. 242f.)

This insight does turn on their heads the well-intentioned premises of the reform pedagogues, but it brings into view *some fundamental tendencies* which probably remained hidden to the reform pedagogy actors themselves (although current management conceptions gladly take up their inheritance):

- There is a *functional-integrative aspect* of reform, in which the individual becomes an involuntary coproducer of the control effects of social arrangements.
- There is furthermore a *manipulative aspect*, which tends to undermine individual resistance; for the functional processes of 'community life' are, in their flexibility, difficult to attack.
- There is also an *anonymizing aspect*, resulting from the invisibility and collective nature of the circulating structures of power and influence; individual persons are for the functionality of 'community life' not the last instance—so-called 'life' trumps them every time. (It is thus not surprising that Foucault in his later work paid particular attention to 'bio-power').
- And finally, there is an *ideological aspect*, because the real dependencies in the experience of participation are made to disappear. Consciousness persists in the fine appearance of integrative participation, without even perceiving the actual constraints and fractures.

Reform pedagogy, conceived and proclaimed as a pedagogy of freedom, promotes the moment of external control in accordance with a mobilised, flexible society. *The old contradiction between freedom and discipline has been transformed into a new form of socialization*, in which intuitive experience and creativity is interwoven with planned management, irrationality with technical rationality, to such an extent that soft control takes the form of a generalised "political technology" (Foucault, 1977, p. 205).

Subjection as Humanisation?

The act of punishment itself, which had been celebrated as a ritual in face-to-face situations, is dissolved in a network of circulating controls. When life as a whole becomes an institution of improvement, the detention centre becomes unnecessary. The reform pedagogue's delight at this, however, implies a misunderstanding: that discipline, external control and domination lie behind us in a past pedagogic era. In fact, however, *external control only sheds its antiquated form, in order to dominate with new, softer methods.*

- This raises the question of the extent to which pedagogic reforms can be understood as advances in freedom. Given the transformation of forms of pedagogic punishment, one could insist, with good reason, that *a progressive improvement* has taken place—and this would be correct. There is no reason to hark back to the pedagogy of drills and beatings.
- Others would say, in contrast, that the anonymous hood of all-pervasive regulation simply disguises the real *continuing control*—and this is also correct: The new sanctioning mechanisms function, in their abstraction, in a more silent, sustained and profound way.
- The 'advantage' of traditional rites of punishment, in which the pedagogic authority relation appeared as a personal relationship, so that everyone was able to know 'what was what,' encompassed at the same time an ideological moment: for general control appeared stripped of its societal form, that is, personalised.
- The ideological moment of soft control systems, on the other hand, lies in their generality: no one knows 'what's what,' since no one can be pinned down as the source of social un-freedom. Control appears with its concrete form removed—that is, rendered anonymous.

The transformation of pedagogic forms of punishment remains bound up with the more deeply rooted change in the social contradictions of modernity, from which no abstract leap into the realm of freedom can save us. Even the simplest pedagogic scene labours under these contradictions, which bring into play both subjection and freedom as determining counter-movements. They often turn pedagogic praxis into a tightrope walk—and, at the same time, demonstrate the impossibility of adjusting to the societal status quo.

Pedagogic punishment is modern society's 'writing on the wall': an expression of its internal fragmentation, which no pedagogy has the power to heal, but which is even more difficult to accept. In its negativity, it makes it necessary to strive constantly towards that which transcends the dumb coercion of circumstance and, despite everything, puts pedagogy in its rightful place: towards the demand, arising from modern society itself, for a life "without sacrifice and without vengeance" (Adorno, 1973, p. 141).

Bibliography

Adorno, T. (1973). *Negative dialectics.* London: Routledge & Kegan Paul.

Basedow, J. B. (1965). *Ausgewählte pädagogische Schriften.* Paderborn, Germany: Schöningh.

Dreßen, W. (1982). *Die pädogogische maschine. Zur Geschichte des industrialiserten bewusstseins in Preußen/Deutschland* Frankfurt a.M.: Ullstein.

Foucault, M. (1977). Die Folter, das ist die Vernunft. *Literaturmagazin, 8*

————. (1977). *Discipline and punish.* London: Allen & Unwin

Francke, A. H. (1957). *Pädagogische Schriften.* Paderborn, Germany: Schöningh.

Heydorn, H-J. (1979). *Über den Widerspruch von Bildung und Herrschaft.* Frankfurt a.M.: Syndikat

Kant, I. (1899). *Kant on education.* Trans. Annette Churton. London: Routledge and Kegan Paul, 1899.

Kost, F. (1985). *Volksschule und Disziplin.* Zürich: Limmat

Landahl, H. (1980). Die Schulstrafen in der Hamburger Lichtwarkschule. In Reble, A. (Ed.) *Das Strafproblem in Beispielen.* Bad Heilbrunn, Germany: Klinkhardt.

Petersen, P. (1970). *Führungslehre des Unterrichts* (9th ed.). Weinheim, Germany: Beltz

Pongratz, L.A. (1989). *Pädagogik im Prozeß der Moderne. Studien zur Sozial- und Theoriegeschichte der Schule.* Weinheim, Germany: DSV

————. (1988). Michel Foucault. Seine Bedeutung für die historische Bildungsforschung. *Informationen zur Erziehungs- und bildungshistorischen Forschung, 32*

Reble, A. (Ed.). (1980). *Das Strafproblem in Beispielen.* Bad Heilbrunn, Germany: Klinkhardt.

Rutschky, K. (Ed.). (1977). *Schwarze Pädagogik.* Frankfurt a.M.: Ullstein.

Salzmann, G. (1884). Ankündigung einer Erziehungsanstalt. *Festschrift zur hundertjährigen Jubelfeier der Erziehungsanstalt Schnepfenthal.* Schnepfenthal: Erziehungsanstalt.

Ziller, T. (1977). Regierungsmaßregeln für Lehrer und Schüler. In K. Rutschky (Ed.), *Schwarze Pädagogik.* Frankfurt a.M.: Ullstein

Pedagogy and Self-Concern in Master-Student Relationships in Antiquity

Thomas Coelen

An Alternative to Disciplinary Methods and Coercion to Confess?

Michel Foucault wrote specifically in the last four years of his life on the topic which never ceased to interest him, the historical connections between power and knowledge which continue up to this day. In those four years he used the forms of constituting the subject in Greco-Roman antiquity as the basis for his writings. He developed this focus from a general concern with 'governmentality,' a way of thinking combined with the ability to lead and control oneself and other people, and hence addressed topics of prime importance for pedagogy. However, his works on pedagogy and self-concern in Antiquity have been ignored in the field of educational science, particularly in Germany.[1] This is particularly regrettable as, in the work on antiquity, a great deal of importance is placed on pedagogic questions. As a result of the missing debate, the following is simply a list with comments the aspects relevant to pedagogic questions, not a comprehensive, critical discussion.

It is however the case that educational science and *pedagogy* simply cannot ignore the studies on governmentality, because for both terms the verb 'to lead' is constitutive: It has been traditionally understood that an adolescent learns to attain maturity via the educational process: *educare* (to educate) or *educere* (to show the way—away from immaturity). In particular in his works on medicine and psychiatry ('*Naissance de la clinique*' and '*Histoire de la folie à l'âge classique*') Foucault reveals the monologue of the superiority of reason to non-reason. For educational science the challenge of these early works consists of having to ask oneself how much, in the tradition of enlightenment, educational science itself perpetuates a monologue of the reasonable adults regarding children, who are 'not yet reasonable.' Moreover, the challenge of '*Les mots et les choses*' consists of deciphering the idea of the 'human being' which, according to Foucault, has achieved a normative character and become self-evident and is now considered to be universally applicable. This would mean that, as a human science par excellence, educational science too is covered by Foucault's verdict of being "unscientific" (1989, p. 420).

Furthermore the constitutive *paidagogos* was the youth leader of antiquity, who accompanied a boy from the parental *oikos* via the public area of the *polis* to the *gymnasion* of the city state. And, throughout the ages up till today the pedagogue is the mediator between family and state in the public sphere (which also includes the market). 'Leading,' we can see, is at least semantically constitutive for our discipline in two different ways. Moreover, on the basis of a detailed study, I will show in the following the extent to which—according to Foucault—this is also substantially true.

To start off with, let's refer briefly to three types of pedagogic topic in Foucault's work ('Why Foucault?' in the sense of *pedagogy* according to the interpretation used by Foucault). Educational practice according to Foucault can be defined on the one hand using the term 'discipline': In '*Surveiller et punir*,' it is first of all clear to what extent disciplinary methods, for example those used at school, have the exact control of bodily activities as their aim, with the result that the disciplinary manifestation of power is integrated in the personality. On the other hand, educational activities and reflections upon them from Foucault's perspective can be perceived via the term 'confession': Particularly in the first volume of '*Histoire de la sexualité*,' it is clear to what extent those being educated must yield to 'a will for knowledge' in order to reveal the hidden truth supposedly present in them. Thirdly, 'education of the self' (*culture de soi*) is emphasised in Foucault's work on philosophy in antiquity: In these later works, it is clear that the *pedagogy* of that time is interlaced with a *psychagogy*, which in the first instance requires the teacher to take pains to achieve access to truth and to his own self.

Foucault's shift of perspective from discipline via confession to education can be clearly inferred from his opinion on pedagogic institutions (in late interview):

> I really can't see what is so objectionable in the practice of those who know more in a given truth game than another participant and tell the latter what he must do, teach him, and pass on knowledge and explain techniques to him. The problem arises much more in knowing how, when using these practices (in which power is neither avoidable nor intrinsically unacceptable), to avoid effects of dominance. Such effects would make a small boy subservient to the pointless and arbitrary authority of a primary school teacher, or make a student dependent upon the professor who abuses his position etc. I believe this problem must be understood in terms of the relevant laws, rational methods of control, and also ethics, practice of the self and freedom'. (1985a, p. 26)

No mention any more of the 'pedagogic machine' and 'methods of administering discipline,' for example as used at school, or of 'coercion to confess.' Everything is now left to the ethics of the teacher. The *mutual* influence of educational circumstances and those of upbringing is, according to Foucault, however, only of importance with respect to intrinsic differences in discipline and/or the coercion to confess. This fact—and it must be seen as a criticism—corresponds to a significant emphasis on the role and personality of the teacher in Foucault's reconstruction of the philosophy of antiquity.

With his journey back to antiquity Foucault attempts inter alias to research into the genealogy of the modern coercion to confess and of "verbalisation techniques" (1993a, p. 62). In the course of this he makes use of alternative practices and methods of thought—all described in the analytical-normative and apparently random manner unique to his style of writing. His basic hypothesis with respect to the confession topic is that the "method of self-disclosure" (*exagoreusis*) (ibid., pp. 56–61)—based on verbalisation—has attained right from the first centuries A.D. a greater importance than the contrasting "method of penance" (*exolologesis*) (ibid., pp. 52–56). Moreover,

> since the 18th-century and right up to the present, verbalisation methods of the so-called social sciences have been transformed in to another context, where they have been instrumental in creating a new self. (ibid., p. 62)

As far back as the heyday of the monasteries, a teacher/pupil duality would be developed by a monk or a novice, in which the pedagogic voice was turned inwards and in this way became so much aware of the own ignorance and incompetence that these became completely dominant. Moreover, modern educational-scientific research has become suspected of wishing to reveal hidden truths of the subjects investigated, to accumulate knowledge of them and to define this knowledge (implicitly) as the norm.

What other connection between subject and truths does Foucault see in Greek antiquity? Or, more precisely, how does Foucault reconstruct the unbroken line in the course of a generation, from 'governing one's self' to 'governing others'? Furthermore, does it methodologically make sense to observe this unbroken line in reverse: How can an adolescent be governed by other people in order later to be able to govern himself and others too in a sensible way?

I do that in four steps. First of all, in each of the pairs of terms, *pedagogy/psychagogy* and self-concern/self-knowledge, the terms are differentiated. Next, the core task and attitude of the master (i.e., truth telling, cf. 1988), is explained. Finally, using examples from antiquity, a pedagogic *paradoxon* is described.[2]

Pedagogy und Psychagogy

In the last years of his life Foucault occupied himself specifically with *pedagogy*. He described *pedagogy* as

> passing on a truth to others, the function of which consists of providing one individual or another with an outlook, ability, knowledge etc. which the individual did not possess before receiving pedagogic support but which he should possess afterwards. (2004, 496–497)

Foucault differentiates *pedagogy* from passing on a truth, of which the function consists of changing "the essential being of the subject" (ibid., p. 497). His name for the latter is *'psychagogy.'*

These latter, psychagogical processes met, according to Foucault, with considerable changes between Greco-Roman philosophy and Christianity. At first, the pedagogical processes were connected very closely to the psychagogical processes characterised by the knowledge of the master/teacher/adviser/friend and his transfer of this knowledge, but later they became disconnected. As Foucault continues, the subject being instructed now has an obligation to truth. Whereas it was exclusively the master in the Greco-Roman era who was always required to tell the truth, to accept all rules, and to change his essential being, in the Christian *psychagogy* it is the instructed and led subject who has to pay the price. It is his 'soul' which is required to bear witness to truth, "which only those who are in possession of the truth can do" (ibid., p. 498). It is now required of the pupil to admit that his essential being has changed, possibly prompted by a psychological pedagogic approach. The pupil is not asked about his knowledge, his abilities, his attitude but about his soul. He must undergo tests, bear witness to his knowledge and produce truths about himself.

In these illustrations of *psychagogy*, analogies can be seen to *pedagogy* or educational science operating as a practice and science of confession.

Self-Concern and Self-Knowledge

The difference between *pedagogy* and *psychagogy* was established by Foucault in the years 1982–1984 within the wide framework of his lectures and writings: Foucault occupied himself at that time with the question of the form of thinking in antiquity in which subject and truth were connected. The *epimeleia heautou* (self-concern, *souci de soi, cura sui*) was for him a concept of prime importance. Foucault differentiated the *epimeleia* from self-knowledge as this is only one particular part of self-concern.

Self-concern, according to Foucault, is a pedagogic, ethical and ontological condition for being a 'good (responsible) governor,' and prevents the person concerned from abusing his power. It is constituted as conscious dealing rather than just a general disposition (i.e., it is an active political and erotic status).

Analogously to the thesis of Christian dissociation and to changing the relative order of *psychagogy* and *pedagogy*, Foucault asked himself, why does "Western philosophy assigns self-knowledge such a privileged position *vis-à-vis* self-concern" (1985b, p. 33). In other words, why has it become more important to be aware of one's inner being than to take care of oneself in everyday life?

Foucault developed a possible answer to this question by formulating that self-concern no longer seems to be a positive example of morals for society as a whole. The current generally accepted 'ethics of non-egoism' equates a concern with oneself with withdrawal and lack of consideration for others. Christian self-denial and/or the modern form of an obligation towards others (the collective, the class, etc.) look upon this concern with oneself with suspicion. After all, Cartesianism has indeed declared self-knowledge to be the general way to truth: In modernity age insight alone is sufficient to achieve the truth. Foucault continues: "The spiritual dimension is missing, (i.e., modifications and transformations are lacking which the subject carries out upon himself in order to have access to truth) (1985b, p. 34). Erotic and ascetic experiences no longer have a place today in the uncertain progress of cognition and the accumulation of knowledge. Self-knowledge became, as the first step of epistemology, the fundamental principle of modernism.

So we see that, according to Foucault's source analysis, a reversal of the order applicable in antiquity of the maxims 'take care of yourself' and 'know yourself' has taken place. The role of *pedagogy* in self-concern can now be shown on the basis of the relationship between master and pupil.

The Master's Truth Telling

Let's start with the role and the function of the master:

> In the absence of a master there can be no self-concern, but the position of a master is defined by the fact that he occupies himself with the self-concern of the person he leads, who can achieve this for himself. (2004, p. 86)

That sounds rather paradoxical and is in fact so: The master does not only take care of himself but also occupies himself with something else which first does not even exist. That means: In order to be a master, self-concern is not enough. 'Truth telling' (*parrhesia*) must also be practised.

But first of all let's look at the general case. The master assumes the position of mediator with respect to the subject constitution of the individual. The individual would have to strive for the status of subject—a status previously unknown to him—and not (only) for new knowledge.[3]

The individual himself cannot however lose the *stultitia* (simple status without self-practice) as this is characterised by a lack of reference to the self and by a lack of will. The immature person is unaware of his immaturity and that he needs the help and intervention of somebody else (cf. 2004, pp. 86–88). For this he needs someone who tells him the truth (cf. 1985a, p. 15). But this other person is neither an educator nor a master in memory training: *educere* instead of *educare* (i.e., show the way-out of maturity instead of educate, cf. 2004, p. 175).

Whoever tells the truth is neither an educator of young children, nor a pedagogue, nor a teacher but a philosopher! Without considering profession or institution, however, he is an instrument of social control. The master must waken the slumbering ability to achieve self-concern but can't quite manage this.[4] But Foucault does not explain the initial interaction which the immature person voluntarily undergoes. So how does the pupil recognise the master? And how does he extricate himself from the situation? This is also not explained.

It is the master's task "to tell everything" (2004, p. 447). In contrast to flattery and to rhetoric (cf. ibid., pp. 454–463) he must not only express the content of the truth but also apply this skilfully and live according to it. According to Foucault, this attitude and this process were described in antiquity as *"parrhesia"* (2004, p. 447).

Furthermore, Foucault continues, the term *parrhesia* was indeed used and mentioned in the philosophical writings of antiquity, but nobody really reflected upon it or accorded it much importance (cf. 1988, p. 19). Its exact structure is difficult to determine, it is distributed throughout many texts from that time right up to Christian religiosity. But, according to Foucault, the latter brings with it the danger that the concept is simplified and changed to confession: Christianity changed "revealing the truth of the own soul" (1985b, p. 58), which characterises the attitude of the master, into a pressure to reveal oneself. Furthermore, there is also a remarkable diminution in importance of the term compared with truth telling on the part of the pupil.

Regardless of all the interpretations, *parrhesia* is generally defined as 'telling everything,' the ability to speak freely. This makes it simultaneously a virtue, a talent, an ability and an obligation (cf. 2004, p. 454). It is therefore pedagogically extremely relevant, because above all it has to characterise the ones having "the task of leading others, in particular someone with the task of guiding others in their attempts to constitute themselves in their self-reference" (1988, p. 17).

In this context, Foucault reconstructs Plutarch's story of Plato and Dionysos, the tyrant of Syracuse.[5] In Plato's criticism of tyrants Foucault sees an excellent example of *parrhesia*. "A man stands up in the presence of a tyrant and tells him (possibly in danger of his life) the truth" (ibid, p. 24). In a discursive analysis of this and other examples Foucault establishes that *parrhesia* is neither a type of proof, nor persuasion (rhetoric), nor a form of dialogue (heuristics). According to Foucault's criterion, it is not a discursive strategy at all (cf. 2004, pp. 454–463), because it is not *pedagogy* either![6] *Parrhesia* is, in contrast, a genuine 'anti-pedagogic effect' (1988, p. 29).

Parrhesia, Foucault continues, is not pedagogic because there is "without doubt an unpleasant side to *parrhesia*—brutality and violence—which is completely different from a pedagogic process" (ibid., p. 32). *Parrhesia* is lacking in didactic techniques (from the known to the unknown, from the simple to the complex, from the part to the whole). *Parrhesia* is consequently not *pedagogy* because, on the one hand, it allows—regardless of practical considerations—the whole power of truth to be experienced and, on the other hand, the brutal features it possesses.

In a first approximation, Foucault's understanding of *pedagogy* in relation to antiquity can perhaps summed up indirectly as follows: *Pedagogy* must not be an example of telling somebody how to do something. It must not force a pupil to confess (even to his lack of knowledge). Furthermore, in contrast to *parrhesia*, *pedagogy* must not be inconsiderate of other people's feelings etc., or be violent. However, the master must 'tell the truth' to his pupils and live and act accordingly.

Foucault integrates his explanations of *parrhesia* in the larger context of self-concern and *psychagogy* when he establishes, "that the event of the statement influences the subject's essential being" (2004, p. 495). According to this, the truth teller is the true *psychagogue*—indeed of himself. A person who lives by truth changes the practice of his life by stating the truth and the type of connection which he establishes to this statement. The total weight of truth is born on the shoulders of the person speaking.

The Pedagogic Dilemma

Being occupied with oneself was seen in the whole Greco-Roman era as a task of the adult. When, however, does the self-concern start and, above all, how? What sets it in motion? In connection with this point in particular, Foucault is faced with a basic pedagogic problem. It's the central question of upbringing and education: How can immaturity lead to maturity?

First of all, Foucault establishes clearly that certain forms of the relation to truth are not given to the subject automatically—they have to be achieved:

> It is a general feature and a fundamental principle that the subject as such, in his current state of development, is not capable of truth unless he undergoes certain operations, transformations and modifications empowering him to truth. (1985b, p. 47)

Foucault locates the relation to truth in his further reflections in a spiritual dimension. In the antique pedagogic relationships this spirituality existed as a rule in the form of an erotic relationship between master and pupil. But, if we follow the thoughts of Foucault, the comprehensive literature of Greece at that time on pederasty reveals that a sexual relationship of this type raised problems:

> The problem was that they could not admit that a boy who would one day be a free citizen was being dominated and used as another person's object of lust . . . All the philosophical reflections on pederasty prove clearly that the Greeks could not integrate this practice in the framework of their social self. (1984, p. 73)

Hence, the role of a boy was determined by the status he would have in the future, namely that of a free citizen who should assume political office.[7] According to Foucault, a boy's lack of ability reflected only the degree of his incomplete development (cf. 1986, p. 275). The boy could therefore be an object of lust, but "it must not be forgotten that one day he will become a man, who will have to exercise powers and responsibilities and then, of course, can no longer be an object of lust. *To what degree could he have been such an object earlier?*" (ibid., p. 280, author's emphasis).

In the final analysis, this dilemma means that the boy cannot accept his role, for

> the relationship which he must form with himself in order to be a free man, master of himself, and to be capable of surpassing the others, cannot be consistent with a form of behaviour in which he would be an object of lust for others (ibid., pp. 280–281)

If an abstraction is made of the sexual implications and the problem is generalised, the perpetual challenge of these considerations for *pedagogy* consists of the question to what degree a child can have been an object of educational acts if it should be possible for him to become one day an independent and democratic citizen.

Apart from that, the Greeks obviously found it difficult to accept a physical interdependence or, in other words, justice within pederasty. They also couldn't imagine a commonality of feeling within homosexual romantic relationships. In addition, they believed it was "dishonourable" (ibid., p. 74) on the part of the boy if he felt desire of any kind in his relations to the master. Pederasty was always seen in the form of a dominant relationship (cf. ibid., p. 280). The behaviour of the boy was hence seen as a response to desire instead of requiting that desire. A number of conditions and expected benefits for the boy were connected to this granting of favours. Examples of these were "learning what it means to be a man, social protection for the future, a lasting friendship" (ibid., p. 284). It is even seen as the task of the older man to instruct the boy in how he can triumph over his lust (cf. ibid., p. 304).

Foucault now summarises the problem which can (also) be deciphered as an indisputably pedagogic problem: Are we capable of a system of ethics of behaviour and the corresponding feelings which could consider the needs of the other person involved? Are the needs of this other person something which can be integrated in our own feelings without having to refer to the law, to being an adult, or to some other (institutional) obligation (cf. ibid., p. 309).

Pedagogy following Foucault

The degree of importance Foucault accords *pedagogy* in his last work is really surprising. It is possible that he sees the *pedagogy* of antiquity in its connection with *psychagogy* and self-concern on the part of the master as the genuine *pedagogy*, which in modernity has been abandoned as a result of the separation of both aspects as well as the dominance of self-knowledge in 'methods of discipline' and in 'the practice or science of confession.' Foucault's analysis of the master-pupil relationship of antiquity indicates therefore a pedagogic relationship based on power rather than on dominance. However, in order to ensure the status of subject for both the master and the immature pupil, the link to an interactionistic approach is essential. The *pedagogy* of the master-student relationship of antiquity as instructions for achieving self-concern can hence be seen as a way of avoiding disciplinary methods and coercion to confess; however this does lead to further pedagogic and educational-scientific relevant questions (e.g., the entry and exit interaction), which can possibly be dealt with using a 'pedagogic discourse' (Richter, 1991) or 'social research as an educational process' (Richter, et al., 2003).

Notes

1   For the debate on Foucault in German Educational Science until the mid 1990s see Coelen (1996, pp. 21–27), for the current debate see Balzer (2004).

2   Every following quotation refers to Michel Foucault. The main source is the lecture *L'herméneutique du sujet* given in 1981 and 1982, published in German at first by H. Becker und L. Wolfstetter in 1985 (*Freiheit und Selbstsorge*) and again by Suhrkamp publishers (*Hermeneutik des Subjekts*), translated by U. Bokelman. I refer also to the lectures given in 1983 and 1984, translated in German by U. Reuter und L. Wolfstetter with the title *Das Wahrsprechen des Anderen* (1988).

3   Parallels can be drawn here to the difference between 'learning' and 'education' (cf. 2004, p. 69).

4   This phenomenon was described by Wilhelm Flitner (1962) as the "pedagogic paradox" (p. 53).

5   As further examples Foucault traces the episode of Oedipus and Kreon. In *Technologies of the Self,* he analyses the 'Alkibiades' by Platon. See also 2004, pp. 447–448.

6   Somewhat confusingly Foucault understands pedagogy here, in contrast to the above-mentioned text passage, as Socratic irony—which he characterises polemically as a "lecturing game" (1988, p. 29).

7   Dominant, educational relationships did not present problems as long as a woman or slave was concerned, for they would never have achieved the status of free citizens.

Bibliography

Balzer, N. (2004). Von den Schwierigkeiten, nicht oppositional zu denken. Linien der Foucault-Rezeption in der deutschsprachigen Erziehungswissenschaft. In N. Ricken & M. Rieger-Ladich (Ed.), *Michel Foucault: Pädagogische Lektüren* (pp. 15–35). Wiesbaden: VS.

Coelen, T. (1996). *Pädagogik als Geständniswissenschaft? Zum Ort der Erziehung bei Foucault.* Frankfurt a. M.: Lang.

Flitner, W. (1962). *Allgemeine Pädagogik.* Stuttgart: Klett

Foucault, M. (1984). Sex als Moral. Gespräch mit Hubert Dreyfus und Paul Rabinow. In M. Foucault (Ed.), *Von der Freundschaft als Lebensweise* (pp. 69–84). Berlin: Merve.

————. (1985a). Freiheit und Selbstsorge. In H. Becker & L. Wolfstetter (Eds.), *Freiheit und Selbstsorge. Interview 1984 und Vorlesung 1982* (pp. 7–28). Frankfurt a. M.

————. (1985b). Hermeneutik des Subjekts. In H. Becker & L. Wolfstetter (Eds.), *Freiheit und Selbstsorge. Interview 1984 und Vorlesung 1982* (pp. 32–60). Frankfurt a. M.

————. (1986). *Der Gebrauch der Lüste. Sexualität und Wahrheit Bd. 2* [Histoire de la sexualité. L'usage des plaisirs. Vol. 2.]. Frankfurt a. M.: Suhrkamp. (Original work published in 1984).

————. (1988). Das Wahrsprechen des Anderen. In U. Reuter & L. Wolfstetter (Eds.), *Das Wahrsprechen des Anderen. Zwei Vorlesungen 1983/84.* Frankfurt a. M.

————. (1989). *Die Ordnung der Dinge. Eine Archäologie der Humanwissenschaften* [Les mots et les choses. Une archéologie des sciences humaines]. Frankfurt a. M.: Suhrkamp. (Original work published in 1966).

————. (1993). Technologien des Selbst. In L. H. Marting, H. Gutman & P. H. Hutton (Eds.), *Technologien des Selbst* (pp. 24–62). Frankfurt a. M.: Suhrkamp.

————. (2004). *Hermeneutik des Subjekts. Vorlesung am Collège de France (1981/82)* [L'herméneutique du sujet. Cours au Collège de France. 1981–1982]. Frankfurt a. M.: Suhrkamp. (Original work published in 2001)

Richter, H. (1991). Der pädagogische Diskurs. Versuch über den pädagogischen Grundgedanken-gang. In H. Peukert & H. Scheuerl (Eds.), *Wilhelm Flitner und die Frage nach einer allgemeinen Erziehungswissenschaft im 20. Jahrhundert.* Zeitschrift für Pädagogik, 26. Beiheft (pp. 141–153). Weinheim und Basel: Beltz.

Richter, H., Coelen, T., Peters, L., & Mohr, E. (2003). Handlungspausenforschung - Sozialforschung als Bildungsprozess. Aus der Not der Reflexivität eine Tugend machen. In G. Oelerich, H.-U. Otto & H.-G. Micheel (Eds.), *Empirische Forschung und Soziale Arbeit. Ein Lehr- und Arbeitsbuch* (pp. 45–62). Weinheim: Luchterhand.

ဆ Chapter 5 ର

Foucault, Truth-Telling and Technologies of the Self: Confessional Practices of the Self and Schools[1]

Tina (A. C.) Besley

Introduction

The following scenario highlights a relatively common ethical dilemma in secondary schools. Rather than offering solutions for this dilemma, the paper presents it to highlight how Foucauldian philosophical notions of care of the self are relevant to the moral education of young people in secondary schools. However, any consideration of care of the self remains largely unwritten in school policies and moreover it is seldom an explicit goal of education, except when occasionally appearing in curricula such as health or personal and social education. Hence, it forms part of the hidden curriculum and something with which most teachers have no specific training or understanding. This paper is divided into the following sections that pursue Foucault's changing understandings about the self; truth-telling and technologies of the self; and his genealogy of confession. It ends with a brief conclusion.

Scenario

Imagine the following scenario: Jo is a top academic student and about to take the crucial exams that will provide a scholarship to attend university. The scholarship is vital because Jo's family is on welfare. Jo has just been discovered by a teacher who has always been very supportive, in the middle of a group of students who all seem to be sharing a joint of cannabis. Should the teacher 'confess' this knowledge to the school Principal? Should Jo confess?

Schools often hold very different policies and positions on how to deal with such incidents, so the consequences of truth-telling and confessing may be very different depending on which school Jo attends. In the process, this will have an effect on the ethical constitution of the self of the parties involved—that is, on

Jo and on the teacher. School A maintains a policy of expulsion for drug use so if either the teacher or Jo 'confessed,' Jo would be automatically excluded and being prevented from sitting the scholarship exams would make it an enormous struggle to attend university. The school has a team of support staff including a counsellor but the perceived seriousness of drug taking and the consequent expulsion would prevent involving him/her in Jo's situation. School B maintains a policy of intervening to help students caught with drugs to change their behaviour. School B has school counsellors, educational psychologists, social workers, youth workers and a mentoring system in place. Jo would be subject to the intervention of some of these professionals whose job might be to ascertain if this was a one off experiment and to help if serious drug abuse were revealed—an application of various 'psy' sciences (Rose, 1989; 1998). How the psy sciences of the 20th century have conceived of and positioned youth displays complex notions of self, the Other and is "intrinsically linked to the history of government" (not politics) which Nikolas Rose (1998) argues

> is part of the history of the ways in which human beings have regulated others and have regulated themselves in the light of certain games of truth. . . [The] regulatory role of psy is linked to questions of the organization and reorganization of political power that have been quite central to shaping our contemporary experience. (p. 11)

Schools are institutions that clearly involve such regulation and governance of the experience of their students. In turn, this constitutes the self.

For the teacher there are important personal, professional and ethical issues for his/her constitution of the self. Nevertheless, apart from the pragmatic implications and possible effects on Jo's educational and life chances, there are also implications for how both the student and the teacher each constitute their selves through their different practices of the self—care of the self, knowledge of self, confession and truth-telling —that are likely to be involved in the process. Questions that arise involve the effect of truth-telling or lying including saying nothing (i.e., lying by omission) and the effect of these practices will further shape the individual's understandings of their own self.

Foucault's Notion of the Self

Late in his life when discussing his work, Foucault (1988b) says that his project has been to historicise and analyse how in Western culture the specific 'truth games' in the social sciences such as economics, biology, psychiatry, medicine, and penology have developed knowledge and techniques for people to understand themselves. Foucault not only provides quite a shift from earlier discourses on the self, but also brings in notions of disciplinarity, governmentality, freedom and ethics as well as notions of corporeality, politics and power and its historic-social context into understandings of the self. His own understandings about the self shifted over the years. Late in his life he notes that he may have concentrated "too much on the technology of domination and power" (Foucault, 1988b, p. 19). Nevertheless, for Foucault both technologies of domination and technologies of the self produce effects that constitute the self. They define the individual and control their conduct as they make the individual a significant element for the state through the exercise of a form of power, which Foucault coined as "governmentality" in becoming useful, docile, practical citizens (Foucault, 1988c). Nietzsche inspired Foucault to analyse the modes by which human beings become subjects without privileging either power (as in Marxism) or desire (as in Freud). Foucault develops Nietzschean 'genealogy' and Heideggerian concepts into technologies of the self in a reconsideration of Greco-Roman antiquity and early Christianity (Foucault, 1988b; Nietzsche, 1956).

Foucault took up Heidegger's critiques of subjectivity and Cartesian-Kantian rationality in terms of power, knowledge and discourse—a stance against humanism that is a rejection of phenomenology, for Foucault sees the subject as being within a particular historic-cultural context or genealogical narrative. Foucault historicizes questions of ontology, substituting genealogical investigations of the subject for the philosophical attempt to define the essence of human nature, aiming to reveal the contingent and historical conditions of existence. For Foucault, the self or subject "is not a substance. It is a form, and this form is not primarily or always identical to itself" (Foucault, 1997a). Self means both *'auto'* or 'the same,' so understanding the self implies understanding one's identity.

Foucault also harnessed Heideggerian notions of *techne* and technology. Heidegger questions our relationship to the essence of modern technology which treats everything, including people, "as a resource that aims at efficiency—toward driving on to the maximum yield at the minimum expense" (Heidegger, 1977, p. 15). Unlike Heidegger, though, who focuses on understanding the 'essence' or coming into presence of being or *dasein*, Foucault historicises questions of ontology and in the process is therefore not concerned about notions of *aletheia* or uncovering any inner, hidden truth or essence of self (Heidegger, 1977). Dreyfus points out that for both Foucault and Heidegger, it is the practices of the modern world and modern technology that produce a different kind of subject—a subject who does not simply objectify and dominate the world through technology, but who is constituted by this technology (Dreyfus, 2002).

Foucault sets out a typology of four interrelated "technologies"—namely, technologies of production, technologies of sign systems, technologies of power (or domination) and technologies of the self. Each is a set of practical reason that is permeated by a form of domination that implies some type of training and changing or shaping of individuals. Instead of an instrumental understanding of 'technology,' Foucault uses technology in the Heideggerian sense as a way of revealing truth and focuses on technologies of power and technologies of the self.

Technologies of power "determine the conduct of individuals and submit them to certain ends or domination, an objectivizing of the subject" (Foucault, 1988b, p. 18). Technologies of the self are ways the various

> operations on their own bodies and souls, thoughts, conduct, and way of being, that people make either by themselves or with the help of others, in order to transform themselves to reach a state of happiness, purity, wisdom, perfection, or immortality. (ibid.)

These practices, activities, routines or disciplines will operate on a person's privately held, or inner self, on how they behave, act and think, such that currently existing self will be involved (sometimes with outside help) in choosing just what those practices might be and what the personal transformation goal might be. Subsequently, the self may then change and be re-constituted differently.

Thus, the self that Foucault espouses is not the Enlightenment version that aims to be a coherent, consistent, rational, harmonious, autonomous, unitary self. Instead, he favours de-centred, multiple, shifting and even contradictory forms of self and identity and ways of being.

His earlier work emphasised the application of technologies of domination through the political subjugation of 'docile bodies' in the grip of disciplinary powers and the way the self is produced by processes of objectification, classification and normalization in the human sciences (Foucault, 1977). Such work acknowledges the politico-anatomy of the body and the bio-politics of society as being inseparable parts of the general exercise of power, but does not allow sufficiently for agency or the self. Late in his life he considered that he may have concentrated "too much on the technology of domination and power" (Foucault, 1988b, p. 19). Criticism of the 'determinist' emphasis in *Discipline and Punish*, led to a re-definition of power to include agency as self-regulation thereby overcoming some of the problematic political implications in his earlier work (see Afterword in Rabinow, 1997; Foucault, 1985, 1988a, 1990; McNay, 1992).

He shifted his understanding of the self to emphasise that individuals are continually in the process of constituting themselves as ethical subjects through both technologies of the self and ethical self-constitution, and a notion of power that is not simply based upon repression, coercion, or domination. By this point Foucault sees individuals "as self-determining agents capable of challenging and resisting the structures of domination in modern society" (McNay, 1992, p. 4).

In *The Ethics of the Concern for Self as a Practice of Freedom* (Foucault, 1997a), an interview in 1984, the year of his death, Foucault explains the change in his thinking about the relations of subjectivity and truth. In his earlier thinking he had conceived of the relationship between the subject and 'games of truth' in terms of either coercive practices (psychiatry or prison) or theoretical-scientific discourses (the analysis of wealth, of language, of living beings, especially in *The Order of Things*). In his later writings he breaks with this relationship to emphasize games of truth not as a coercive practice, but rather as *an ascetic practice of self-formation*. 'Ascetic' in this context means an "exercise of self upon the self by which one attempts to develop and transform oneself, and to attain a certain mode of being" (Foucault, 1997a, p. 282). 'Work' completed by the self upon itself is an *ascetic* practice that is to be understood not in terms of more traditional left wing *models of liberation,* but rather as (Kantian) *practices of freedom.* This is an essential distinction for Foucault because the notion of liberation suggests that there is a hidden self or inner nature or essence that has been "concealed, alienated, or imprisoned in and by mechanisms of repression" (Foucault, 1997a, p. 282). The process of liberation, on this model, liberates the 'true' self from its bondage or repression. By contrast, Foucault historicizes questions of ontology: there are no essences only 'becomings,' only a phenomenology or hermeneutics of the self—the forging of an identity through processes of self-formation. To him, liberation is not enough and the practices of freedom do not preclude liberation, but they enable individuals and society to define "admissible and acceptable forms of existence or political society" (Foucault, 1997a, p. 283). He rejects Sartre's idea that power is evil, stating instead that "power is games of strategy" (Foucault, 1997a, p. 298) and that the ways of avoiding the application of arbitrary, unnecessary or abusive authority "must be framed in terms of rules of law, rational techniques of government and ethos, practices of the self and of freedom" (Foucault, 1997a, p. 299).

Truth-Telling and Technologies of the Self

Why truth? . . .and why must the care of the self occur only through the concern for truth? [This is] *the* question for the West. How did it come about that all of Western culture began to revolve around this obligation of truth. . .? (Foucault, 1997a, p. 281)

As Foucault indicates, the compulsion to tell the truth is highly valued in our society. It is enshrined in how our laws operate, for instance, in court witnesses are required to swear an oath to tell the truth or they may be charged with perjury if they lie and insurance will be cancelled if we do not tell the truth or disclose relevant information. Societal values are certainly operative in the disciplinary regimes of schools and how they pursue regimes of 'truth.' In doing so, schools shape the student's self and their identities. Yet, schools seldom formally perform this task or even consciously attempt it, despite government educational goals often referring to the type of person they are trying to form— variations on the theme of a 'good' citizen.

In *Technologies of the Self* (1988b), a seminar series held at University of Vermont in 1982, Foucault's emphasis shifts to the hermeneutics of the self in his study of the first two centuries A.D. of Greco-Roman philosophy and the fourth and fifth centuries of the Roman Empire when Christian spirituality and monastic principles were prevalent. What Foucault argues is that the Delphic moral principle, know yourself (*gnothi sauton*) became dominant, and took precedence over another ancient principle and set of practices that were to take care of yourself, or to be concerned with oneself (*epimelēsthai sautou*) (Foucault, 1988b). According to Foucault, care of the self formed one of the main rules for personal and social conduct and for the art of life in ancient Greek cities. The two principles were interconnected and it was from the principle of care of the self that the Delphic principle was brought into operation as a form of technical advice or rules to be followed when the oracle was consulted.

In modern day Western culture the moral principles have been transformed, maybe partly as a result of know thyself being the principle that Plato privileged which subsequently became hugely influential in philosophy. Foucault argues that know yourself is the fundamental austere principle nowadays because we tend to view care of the self as immoral, as something narcissistic, selfish and an escape from rules. Although there is no direct continuity from ancient to present times, Foucault's genealogy of sexuality does indicate some continuities and some of the Ancient Greek roots of our sexual ethics. First, Christianity adopted and modified themes from ancient philosophy and made renouncing the self the condition for salvation, but paradoxically, to know oneself required self-renunciation. Second, the basis of morality in our secular tradition involves concern for the self. Echoing Nietzsche (in *Genealogy of Morals,* 1956), Foucault argues that a respect for external law is in opposition to more internalized notions of morality associated with care of the self. Because our morality is an ascetic one the self can be rejected, so the principle know thyself has obscured take care of yourself. Furthermore, theoretical philosophy since Descartes has positioned the *cogito* or thinking subject and knowledge of the self as the starting point for Western epistemology. Foucault argued for the return of the ancient maxim of care of the self because since the Enlightenment, the Delphic maxim became overriding and inextricably linked with constituting subjects who were able to be governed.

Foucault elaborated on both the Greek (Platonic and Stoic) and Christian techniques of self. The Stoic techniques include first, "letters to friends and disclosure of self" second, the "examination of self and conscience, including a review of what was to be done, of what should have been done and a comparison of the two" and third, "*askēsis*, not a disclosure of the secret self but a remembering" and fourth, "the interpretation of dreams" (Foucault, 1988b, pp. 34–38). He points out that rather than renunciation, this is "the progressive consideration of self, or mastery over oneself, obtained not through the renunciation of reality but through the acquisition and assimilation of truth...that is characterised by *paraskeuazō* ('to get prepared')" (Foucault, 1988b, p. 35).

In fact, it transforms truth into a principle of action or *ethos,* or ethics of subjectivity that involved two sets of exercise—the *meletē* (or *epimelesthai*) or meditation and the *gymnasia* or training of oneself. The *meletē* was a philosophical meditation that trained one's *thoughts* about how one would respond to hypothetical situations. The *gymnasia* is a *physical* training experience that may involve physical privation, hardship, purification rituals and sexual abstinence. Foucault (1988b) remarks that despite being a popular practice, the Stoics where mostly critical and sceptical about the interpretation of dreams. It is interesting to note the re-emergence of many of these practices of the self in the different psy therapies of the 19th and 20th centuries and Foucault does a real service in pointing us to the philosophical and historical roots of some of these. Perhaps Foucault's emphasis on the centrality of truth in relation to the self is to be developed only through the notion of 'others' as an audience—intimate or public—a form of performance that allows for the politics of confession and (auto)biography.

In his discussion of ancient Greek (Plato, Socrates, Xenophon) philosophical notions of care of the self, Foucault (1997a) does not discuss the idea that care of the self involves 'care for others,' or that care for others is an explicit ethic in itself. He accepts that the ancient Greek notion embodied in care of the self is an inclusive one that precludes the possibility of tyranny because a tyrant does not, by definition, take care of the self since he[2] does not take care of others. Foucault seems to display a remarkable *naïveté* about the goodness of human beings in accepting this inclusive definition whereby care of the self involved a considerable generosity of spirit and benevolent relations for a ruler of others, be they one's slave, wife and children. He states that care for others became an explicit ethic later on and should not be put before care of the self (see Foucault, 1984).

Peters (2003) discusses truth-games that Foucault elaborated in a series of six lectures given at Berkeley in 1983, entitled *Discourse and Truth: The Problematization of Parrhesia* (Foucault, 2001).[3] Foucault's genealogy problematises the practices of *parrhesia* in classical Greek culture—a set of practices, that are deepseated culturally for the West and take various forms. He demonstrates that these practices link truth-telling and education in ways that are still operative in shaping our contemporary subjectivities, thus they are relevant in understanding the exercise of power and control in contemporary life.

In the classical Greek, the use of *parrhesia* and its cognates exemplify the changing practices of truth-telling. Foucault investigates the use of *parrhesia* in education to show that education was central to the 'care of the self,' public life and the crisis of democratic institutions, intending "not to deal with the problem of truth, but with the problem of truth-teller or truth-telling as an activity" (Foucault, 2001, p. 169). He claims that truth-telling as a speech activity emerged with Socrates as a distinct set of philosophical problems that revolves around four questions: "Who is able to tell the truth, about what, with what consequences, and with what relation to power" (Foucault, 2001, p. 170). Socrates pursued these in his "confrontations with the Sophists in dialogues concerning politics, rhetoric and ethics" (ibid). These lectures reveal how Foucault thought that the end of the PreSocratic philosophy allowed two traditions of Western philosophy that problematise 'truth' to begin. The 'critical' tradition in Western culture that is concerned "with the importance of telling the truth, knowing who is able to tell the truth, and knowing why we should tell the truth" (ibid.) begins at precisely the same time as an "analytics of truth" that characterises contemporary analytic philosophy. Foucault says that he aligns himself with the former 'critical' philosophical tradition, rather than the latter (Foucault, 2001).

A shift occurred in the classical Greek conception of *parrhesia* from a situation where someone demonstrated the courage to tell other people the truth, to a different truth game that focussed on the self and the courage that people displayed in disclosing the truth about themselves. This new kind of truth game of the self requires *askēsis* which is a form of practical training or exercise directed at the art of living (*techne tou biou*). The Greek practices of moral *askēsis* were concerned with "endowing the individual with the preparation and the moral equipment that will permit him to fully confront the world in an ethical and rational manner" (Foucault, 2001, p. 144) aiming at establishing a specific relationship to oneself —of self-possession, self-sovereignty, self-mastery. In marked contrast, Christian ascetic practices hold a different relationship to the self, since the theme of detachment from the world has its ultimate "aim or target the renunciation of the self" (Foucault, 2001, p. 143). Thus, Foucault elaborates on his earlier argument in "Technologies of the Self" (1988b) whereby the crucial difference in the ethical principle of self consists of ancient Greek *self-mastery* versus Christian *self-renunciation*.

Foucault's Genealogy of Confession as Practices of the Self

Contemporary notions of confession are derived not simply from the influence of the Catholic Church and its strategies for confessing one's sins where sin is mostly equated with sexual morality so that confession became the principal technology for managing the sexual lives of believers, but from ancient, pre-Christian philosophical notions (Foucault, 1980a, 1988b). They have also been profoundly influenced by confessional techniques embodied in Puritan notions of the self and its relation to God and by Romantic, Rousseauian notions of the self (Gutman, 1988; Paden, 1988). While confession means acknowledging, it also involves a declaration and disclosure, acknowledgement or admission of a crime, fault, or weakness. The acknowledgement is partly about making oneself known by disclosing one's private feelings or opinions that form part of one's identity. In its religious form, confession involves the verbal acknowledgement of one's sins to another. One is duty-bound to perform this confession as repentance in the hope of absolution.

Foucault points out the shift of confessional practices from the religious world to medical then to therapeutic and pedagogical models in secular contemporary societies. In confession, the agency of domination does not reside in the person that speaks, but in the one who questions and listens. Sexual confession became constituted in scientific terms through "a clinical codification of the inducement to speak; the postulate of a general and diffuse causality; the principle of a latency intrinsic to sexuality; the method of interpretation; and the medicalization of the effects of confession" (see Foucault, 1980a, pp. 59–70). However, he moves beyond simply focusing on confession of sexuality, to the more general importance of confession in the contemporary world. He concludes *Technologies of the Self* with the highly significant point that the verbalization techniques of confession have been important in the development of the human sciences into which they have been transposed and inserted and where they are used "without renunciation of the self but to constitute, positively, a new self. To use these techniques without renouncing oneself constitutes a decisive break" (Foucault, 1988b, p. 49).

In early Christianity two main forms of disclosing the self emerged—first, *exomologēsis,* then *exagoreusis.* Despite being very different, with the former a dramatic form, the latter a verbalized one, what they have in common is that disclosing the self involves renouncing one's self or will. Early on disclosure of self involved *exomologēsis* or "recognition of fact" with public avowal of the truth of their faith as Christians and "a ritual of recognizing oneself as a sinner and penitent" (Foucault, 1988b, p. 41). Foucault points out the paradox that "exposé is the heart of *exomologēsis*…it rubs out the sin and yet reveals the sinner" (Foucault, 1988b, p. 42). Penance became elaborated around notions of torture, martyrdom and death, of renouncing self, identity and life in preferring to die rather than compromising or abandoning one's faith. Foucault points out that Christian penance involves the refusal or renunciation of self, so that "self-revelation is at the same time self-destruction" (Foucault, 1988b, p. 43). Whereas for the Stoics the

> examination of self, judgement, and discipline [lead to] self-knowledge by superimposing truth about self through memory, that is memorizing rules, for Christians, "the penitent superimposes truth about self by violent rupture and dissociation. [Furthermore] *exomologēsis* is not verbal. It is symbolic, ritual and theatrical. (ibid.)

Foucault asserts that later, in the 4th century a different set of technologies for disclosing the self—*exagoreusis* —emerged in the form of verbalizing exercises or prayers that involve taking account of one's daily actions in relation to rules (as in Senecan self-examination). With monastic life, different confessional practices developed based on the principles of obedience and contemplation and confession developed a hermeneutic role in examining the self in relation to one's hidden inner thoughts and purity. The procedures of confession have altered considerably over time. But until the Council of Trent in the mid 16th century, when a new series of procedures for the training and purifying of church personnel emerged, confession in the church was an annual event, so the confession of and surveillance of sexuality was quite limited (Foucault, 1980b). After the Reformation, confession changed profoundly to involve not just one's acts but also one's thoughts. Then in the 18th century Foucault (1980b) suggested that there was

> a very sharp falling away, not in pressure and injunctions to confess, but in the refinement of techniques of confession. [This point in time saw] brutal medical techniques emerging, which consist in simply demanding that the subject tells his or her story, or narrate it in writing. (p. 215)

The History of Sexuality (Foucault, 1980a) points to the techniques of the examination and the confessional or therapeutic situation, where the person is required to speak about their psyche or emotions to a priest or therapist, who as an expert in both observation and interpretation, determines whether or not the truth, or an underlying truth that the person was unaware of, had been spoken. Accessing this inner self or 'truth' is facilitated by professionals in the psy sciences or helping professions (e.g., priests, doctors, psychiatrists, psychologists, psychoanalysts, counsellors, etc.) who may administer certain 'technologies' for speaking, listening, recording, transcribing, and redistributing what is said, such as examining the conscious, the unconscious, and confessing one's innermost thoughts, feelings, attitudes, desires and motives about the self and one's relationships with others. They may exert their expert knowledge to re-interpret and re-construct what a person says. However, in gaining this form of self-knowledge, one also becomes known to others involved in the therapeutic process. This can, in turn, constitute the self.

A further shift occurs from the medical model of healing where a patient 'confesses' the problem and inadvertently reveals the 'truth' as part of the diagnostic clinical examination to a therapeutic model where both the confession and examination are deliberately used for uncovering the truth about one's sexuality and one's self (Foucault, 1980a). In the process the therapy can create a new kind of pleasure: pleasure in telling the truth of pleasure. But speaking the truth is not only descriptive. In confession one is expected to tell the truth about oneself—a basic assumption that most counsellors continue to make about their clients. Because language has a performative function, speaking the truth about oneself also makes, constitutes, or constructs forms of one's self. By these discursive means and through these technologies a human being turns him or herself into a subject.

As confession became secularised, a range of techniques emerged in pedagogy, medicine, psychiatry, and literature, with a highpoint being psychoanalysis or Freud's 'talking cure.' Since Freud, the secular form of confession could be argued as having been 'scientised' through new techniques of normalization and individualization that included clinical codifications, personal examinations, case-study techniques, the general documentation and collection of personal data, the proliferation of interpretive schemas and the development of a whole host of therapeutic techniques for 'normalization.' In turn, these 'oblige' us to be free as self-inspection and new forms of self-regulation replace the confessional. This new form of confession is an affirmation of our self and our identity that involves "contemporary procedures of individualization" that "binds us to others at the very moment we affirm our identity" (Rose, 1989, p. 240). In truthfully confessing who one is to others (e.g., to parents, teachers, friends, lovers, etc. and oneself) "...one is subjectified by another"..."who prescribes the form of the confession, the words and rituals through which it should be made, who appreciates, judges, consoles, or understands" (ibid., p. 240). Through speech acts of confession a person constitutes their self.

Foucault (1985) in *The Use of Pleasure* talks of technologies of the self as "models proposed for setting up and developing relationships with the self, for self-reflection, self-knowledge, self-examination, for deciphering the self by oneself, for the transformation one seeks to accomplish with oneself as object" (p. 29). Foucault also examines the "arts of the self" which are designed to explore the "aesthetics of existence" and to inquire into the government of self and others. He discusses "self-writing" as a means of counteracting the dangers of solitude and of exposing our deeds to the gaze and at the same time because it works on thoughts as well as actions, it becomes a form of confession (Foucault, 1985, 1997b). It permits a retrospective analysis of "the role of writing in the philosophical culture of the self just prior to Christianity: its close tie with apprenticeship; its applicability to movements of thought; its role as a test of truth" (Foucault, 1997b, p. 235). In the literary sense then, confession contains elements of identifying the self in a deliberate, self-conscious attempt to explain and express oneself to an audience within which the individual exists and seeks confirmation (i.e., writing the self—see Peters, 2000).

Confession then is both a communicative and an expressive act, a narrative in which we (re)create ourselves by creating our own narrative, reworking the past, in public, or at least in dialogue with another. When the subject is confessing and creating its 'self,' it seems to feel compelled to tell the truth about itself. Therefore, confession involves a type of 'discipline' that

> entails training in the minute arts of self-scrutiny, self-evaluation, and self-regulation, ranging from the control of the body, speech, and movement in school, through the mental drill inculcated in school and university, to the Puritan practices of self-inspection and obedience to divine reason. (Rose, 1989, p. 222)

Whilst confession is autobiographical, compelling us to narratively recreate ourselves, it is also about assigning truth-seeking meaning to our lives. One can be assisted in this through therapies such as counselling or psychotherapy—the 'priesthood' of our secular society—who have replaced the theological form of confession. Although the use of listening techniques and the uncovering of self are similar, the elements of advice, admonition and punishment that are involved in the religious forms of confession are certainly no part of contemporary counselling either within or outside schools.

Conclusion

Foucault's discussion has strong and obvious relationships for schools in general and for school counselling as well as general counselling theories, in particular. Furthermore, his model of the care of the self in relation to practices of freedom provides a philosophical approach that offers schools and counsellors an ethically suitable way of dealing with the moral education of students. Foucault's account offers a very useful theory of power and also a Kantian-like basis for ethics based upon the way in which choices we make under certain conditions create who we become. Foucault's main aspects of the self's relationship to itself or 'ethical self-constitution' point to various ways that education of young people can help them to ethically constitute themselves: by ethical work that a person performs on their self with the aim of becoming an ethical subject; the way in which individuals relate to moral obligations and rules; and the type of person one aims to become in behaving ethically. One element that might be derived from Foucault is the importance of 'writing' and 'reading' the self alongside conversational or dialogical forms, and 'talking' or confessing the self. Whilst acknowledging their current existence as counselling techniques, the emphasis in school counselling might be widened to re-emphasize the forms of bibliotherapy, diaries, journal writing, personal narratives, autobiographies, biographies, together with the educative impulse of all forms of fiction, poetry and drama or role-play— both in film and television—that focus on the self.

In ancient schools of thought philosophy was considered to be a way of life, a quest for wisdom, a way of been and, ultimately a way of transforming the self. Spiritual exercises were form of pedagogy designed to teach its practitioners the philosophical life that had both a moral and existential value. These exercises were aimed at nothing less than a transformation of one's worldview and personality by involving all aspects of one's being, including intellect, imagination, sensibility and will. In the contemporary world, schools have frequently being seen as an appropriate location for the moral education of young people. Socrates provided a set of dialogical spiritual exercises that epitomised the injunction 'Know thyself!' and provided a model for a relationship of the self to itself that constituted the basis of all spiritual exercise that is at the very centre of a total transformation of one's being (see Davidson, 1997). In this model, the process of dealing with a problem takes primacy over the solution (Hadon, 1995). Foucault suggests re-instating care of the self, the maxim that know thyself supplanted. This provides schools with an ancient philosophical basis or model, at once transformative, ethical, dialogic and pedagogical that could both complement and correct certain emphases in Foucault's later thinking about truth and subjectivity and care of the self.

Current projects and even formal curricula with names such as values education, moral education, philosophy, civics, citizenship, personal and social education, and so on, have emerged alongside increasing concern about the moral state of young people and to deal with current social issues and as ways of dealing with 'social exclusion' in the UK. Regardless of whether or not learning about the self could or should be a formal curriculum item, schools do need to have some awareness of the part they play in constituting the self of their students. Schools need to be aware of the technologies of power (domination) and of the self that they bring to bear on their students and the effect these have in constituting the self. Furthermore, they need to more consciously provide the means to address care of the self, of which truth-telling and confession form only a part.

Notes

1   An earlier version of this paper was presented at the University of Warsaw, 2003 and appears in *Kwartalnik Pedagogiczny*, 2005, 1 (195), pp. 109–126 as Confessional Practices of the Self In Schools. A further version of this chapter appears as: Besley, T. (2005) Foucault, truth-telling and technologies of the self in schools, Journal of Educational Enquiry, 6, (1): 76–89. *http://www.literacy.unisa.edu.au/JEE/Papers/ JEEVol6No1/Paper%206.pdf*

2   The pronoun 'he' is used because these discussions about ancient Greek society only referred to free males as citizens, not to women.

3   These lectures were edited by Joseph Pearson and first appeared on the Internet and were published in 2001. Foucault did not write, correct, or edit any part of the text which is primarily a verbatim transcription of the lectures from the notes of one of the attendees. They have subsequently been published as *Fearless Speech* (see Foucault, 2001).

Bibliography

Davidson, A. I. (1997). Introductory remarks to Pierre Hadot. In A. I. Davidson (Ed.), *Foucault and his interlocutors* (pp. 195–202). Chicago: University of Chicago Press.

Dreyfus, H. (2002). *Heidegger and Foucault on the subject, agency and practices*. Retrieved on October 2002 from *http://socrates.berkeley.edu/~hdreyfus/html/paper_heidandfoucault.html*

Foucault, M. (1977). *Discipline and punish: The birth of the prison*. London: Penguin.

————. (1980a). *The History of sexuality*, Vol. I. New York: Vintage.

————. (1980b). The confession of the flesh. In C. Gordon (Ed.), *Power/knowledge: Selected interviews and other Writings 1972–1977 by Michel Foucault* (pp. 194–228). Hemel Hempstead, UK: Harvester Wheatsheaf.

————. (1984). Space, knowledge and power. In P. Rabinow (Ed.), *The Foucault reader* (pp. 239–256). New York: Pantheon Books.

————. (1985). *The use of pleasure: The history of sexuality,* Vol. II. New York: Vintage.

————. (1988a). Truth, power, self: an interview with Michel Foucault. In L. H. Martin, H. Gutman & P. H. Hutton (Eds.), *Technologies of the self* (pp. 9–15). Amherst: University of Massachusetts Press.

————. (1988b). Technologies of the self. In L. H. Martin, H. Gutman & P. H. Hutton (Eds.), *Technologies of the self* (pp. 16–49). Amherst: University of Massachusetts Press.

————. (1988c). The political technology of individuals. In L. H. Martin, H. Gutman & P. H. Hutton (Eds.), *Technologies of the self* (pp. 145–162). Amherst: University of Massachusetts Press.

————. (1990). *The care of the self: The history of sexuality,* Vol. III. London: Penguin.

————. (1997a). The ethics of the concern for self as a practice of freedom (R. Hurley et al., Trans.). In P. Rabinow (Ed.), *Michel Foucault: Ethics, subjectivity and truth, the essential works of Michel Foucault 1954–1984,* Vol 1 . (pp. 281–301). London: The Penguin Press.

————. (1997b). Writing the self. In A. Davidson (Ed.), *Foucault and his interlocutors* (pp. 234–247). Chicago: University of Chicago Press.

————. (2001). *Fearless speech*, J. PEARSON (ed.) (Los Angeles, CA, Semiotext(e))

Gutman, H. (1988). Rousseau's *confessions*: a technology of the self. In L. H. Martin, H. Gutman & P. H. Hutton (Eds.), *Technologies of the self* (pp. 99–120). Amherst: University of Massachusetts Press.

Hadot, P. (1995). Spiritual exercises and reflections on the idea of the cultivation of the self. In A. I. Davidson (Ed.), *Philosophy as a way of life* (pp. 83–125 & 206–213). Oxford: Blackwell.

Heidegger, M. (1977). *The question concerning and other essays.* Trans. William Lovitt. New York: Harper and Row.

McNay, L. (1992). *Foucault and feminism: Power, gender and self.* Boston: Northeastern University Press.

Nietzche, F. (1956). *The genealogy of morals* (F. Golffing, Trans.). New York: Doubleday. (Original work published in 1887)

Paden, W. E. (1988). Theaters of humility and suspicion: Desert saints and New England puritans. In L. H. Martin, H. Gutman & P. H. Hutton (Eds.), *Technologies of the self* (pp. 64–79). Amherst: University of Massachusetts Press.

Peters, M. A. (2000). Writing the self: Wittgenstein, confession and pedagogy. *Journal of Philosophy of Education,* 34(2), 353–368.

————. (2003). Truth-telling as an educational practice of the self: Foucault, parhessia and the ethics of subjectivity. *Oxford Review of Education,* 29(2), 207–223.

Rabinow, P. (1997). Preface and afterword. In P. Rabinow (Ed.), *Michel Foucault: Ethics, subjectivity and truth, The Essential Works of Michel Foucault 1954–1984,* Vol 1. London: The Penguin Press.

Rose, N. S. (1989). *Governing the soul: The shaping of the private self.* London: Routledge.

————. (1998). *Inventing our selves: Psychology, power, and personhood.* Cambridge: Cambridge University Press.

Paradox of Capacity and Power: Critical Ontology and the Developmental Model of Childhood[1]

James Wong

Introduction

Quite a lot of work has been done in philosophy of education relating to Foucault, to childhood and to development. What I wish to do in this paper is to draw these three areas of work together in a fresh way by focusing on Foucault's positive program of practical critique, what he calls 'critical ontology,' as it relates to the impact of the model of childhood development on children and their care providers. The development model of childhood is now central to the practices and policies of educators and other professionals who deal with children and their care providers such as healthcare providers and social workers. It should be emphasized at the outset that the focus of this paper is not intended to be a discussion specifically on the impact of Foucault's project of critical ontology on how we ought to think about children's education, including specific policy initiatives. The discussion is situated at the intersection between philosophy and philosophy of education, with particular emphasis on the effects of the developmental model, or 'developmental thinking,' on how children are perceived and dealt with today especially in the West. The contribution is, thus, more philosophical or conceptual than policy oriented.

The paper will proceed in four parts. I shall first present Foucault's project of critical ontology. I will then defend Foucault's approach against various criticisms. An account of the emergence and entrenchment of developmental thinking will then follow. The paper concludes with a discussion of the implications of Foucault's method of practical critique for practices grounded in the model of childhood development.

Critical Ontology

Given his scathing critiques of various features of modern societies, Foucault has been taken to be a standard bearer for anti-Enlightenment thought. But contrary to his critics, Foucault sees himself as following in the Enlightenment tradition, at least as outlined in Kant's 1784 essay "What is Enlightenment?" In his essay, Kant tells us that enlightenment consist in "the escape of men from their self-incurred tutelage" (1963, p. 9). To wake themselves from dogmatic slumbers, individuals, both singularly and collectively, must make use of their reason to challenge taken-for-granted assumptions guiding their beliefs. In short, they must analyse the state of affairs in which they find themselves. Hence, Kant proclaims *Sapere Aude* ('dare to know' taken from Horace) to be the motto for the Enlightenment.[2]

Foucault takes from Kant's essay that the hallmark of enlightenment is the attitude of challenging assumptions about what we know and how we act.[3] For him, the project of enlightenment commits us to a "permanent critique" (1984, p. 43). Lewis White Beck points out that, in the Preface to the first edition of *Critique of Pure Reason*, Kant had already written that "our age is, in especial degree, the age of criticism, and to criticism everything must submit" (1963, p. 8, note 4). Foucault is, of course, aware that much of Kant's philosophy is dedicated to 'critique' as a systematic philosophy. In *The Critique of Pure Reason*, Kant writes, "all the interests of my reason, speculative as well as practical, combine in the three following questions: What can I know? What ought I to do? What may I hope?" (1965, p. 635) Critical philosophy, then, yields theories about, as Foucault (1984) puts it, "what can be known, what must be done or what may be hoped" (p. 38). However, the project of a permanent critique will not attempt to "identify the universal structures of all knowledge or of all possible moral action", but rather, it will be "a practical critique that takes the form of a possible transgression" (pp. 46–45). [4] The project, Foucault (1984) tells us,

> implies a series of historical inquiries that are as precise as possible; and these inquiries will not be oriented retrospectively toward the 'essential kernel of rationality' that can be found in the Enlightenment and that would have to be preserved in any event; they will be oriented toward the 'contemporary limits of the necessary,' that is, toward what is not or is no longer indispensable for the constitution of ourselves as autonomous subjects (p. 43)

By 'limits,' Foucault means those taken-for-granted ways of thinking and acting which form the background framing our behaviour.[5] A critique of limits would then be an analysis of how we have constituted ourselves as subjects who think and act in particular ways in order to open up new spaces for thought and action (Norris 1994).

Because of its connection with self-constitution, different ways to be a person, Foucault also describes the permanent critique as a "critical ontology" of ourselves.[6] Foucault suggests that inquiries in critical ontology could be organized under three interrelated headings: "How are we constituted as subjects of our own knowledge? How are we constituted as subjects who exercise or submit to power relations? How are we constituted as moral subjects of our own actions" (Foucault 1984, p. 49)? Foucault describes these areas as "the axes of knowledge, power and ethics" (ibid.), representing different domains in which we constitute ourselves as subjects. For instance, under knowledge, what can be known about us as objects of knowledge at a particular moment will inform our thinking of ourselves as persons and the possibilities available to us. As an illustration, consider the idea of therapy in contemporary life. Therapy appears to be a prominent feature of Western culture today. Think of the volumes of self-help literature available in bookstores, and the talk of various addictions along with the establishment of the appropriate recovery programs. In the West, individuals have constituted several possible ways to be a person through what they say, think and do in terms of therapy, from victim or addict to survivor or recovering addict to confessor and much more. Of course, therapy is but one organizing principle informing possible ways to be a person in contemporary life. The point of critical ontology is to examine ideas and principles that organize our habitual ways of thinking and acting in order to think and act differently.

Foucault (1984) does not intend the project of critical ontology as a "gesture of rejection," rejecting everything, but rather as a practical critique for possible transformations (p. 45). He suggests that the project take on an "experimental" attitude towards "contemporary reality, both to grasp the points where change is possible and desirable, and to determine the precise form this change should take" (ibid. p. 46). One of the key issues addressed by critical ontology is what Foucault calls the "paradox of the relations of capacity and [disciplinary] power" (ibid. p. 47). The ability of individuals to be autonomous agents is linked with the development of capacity for thought and action (Tully, 1999, p. 93). So, encouraging, fostering, developing such capabilities would enable individuals to approach practices critically. But such capabilities are developed within disciplinary matrices of pedagogical and medical institutions, in which individuals are also normalized and hierarchized. Here, think of Foucault's remarks in *Discipline and Punish* (1979) where the routinization of tasks and the very spatial arrangements of individuals are geared towards the normalization and hierarchization of individuals. The question Foucault (1984) raises is, "how can the growth of capabilities be disconnected from the intensification of power relations" (p. 47)?[7] Notice that in raising the question, Foucault is *not* claiming that all that is given to us now as universal and necessary are problematic. His project is more modest, but no less audacious. It seeks to examine "in what is given to us as universal, necessary, obligatory, what place is occupied by whatever is singular, contingent and the product of arbitrary constraints" (ibid., p. 45). As suggested by the idea of an "experimental attitude," the practical critique is intended to challenge the taken-for-granted necessity of practices and the concepts and values informing such practices, and "where change is possible and desirable . . . to determine the precise form this change should take" (ibid., p. 45). In what follows, I will explore how such an experimental attitude might work in practice in the case study of child development. However, before that discussion can get off the ground, I will first consider some criticisms of Foucault's project.

Enlightenment Blackmail—Answering Critics

Jürgen Habermas (1986) asks "how can Foucault's self-understanding as a thinker in the tradition of the Enlightenment be compatible with his unmistakable criticisms of this very form of knowledge of modernity?" (p. 106). Rather than working within the Enlightenment tradition, he argues that Foucault's work actually undermines "modernity and its language games" (Habermas, 1987, p. 283). Against such criticism, Foucault warns against what he calls the "blackmail of the Enlightenment" (1984, p. 42). One is either for or against the Enlightenment *tout court*. Take, for example, the idea of 'reason,' one "recognizes reason or casts it into irrationalism—as if it were not possible to write a rational criticism of rationality" (Foucault, 1989, p. 242). But the dichotomy between either for reason or for irrationalism is a false one, and Foucault is right to reject it. As a set of political, economic, social, institutional and cultural transformations, the accomplishments of the Enlightenment are still felt today. Yet, *some* of the changes resulting from the enlightenment period may prove to be in conflict with the autonomy of individuals today. And it is the task of critical ontology to unmask such arbitrary constraints. Foucault's project, then, does not repudiate the values or institutions under the broad notion of 'modernity' or 'Enlightenment.' It is quite possible that *some* values and practices should turn out to be indispensable for our autonomy today. But, "where change is possible and desirable," Foucault (1984) adds, the project will attempt "to determine the precise form this change should take" (p. 46). Critical ontology, then, is not a global anarchist-deconstructionist project but a local and experimental, hence tentative, one.

Foucault (1984) acknowledges that the project of critical ontology abandons "hope of ever acceding to a point of view that could give us access to any complete and definitive knowledge of what may constitute our historical limits" (p. 47). From this admission, however, it does not follow that no critical judgements are possible. One must still provide reasons and evidence for why certain practices must be changed and how, except these reasons will not be cast as universal claims (Rouse, 1994). We can give partial justification for any particular suggestion by using other non-problematic practices or discourses. The transformed practices will then be put back in play. If in time those practices were to prove problematic, then the critical process would begin anew. Changes, on this view, are always provisional. The process of permanent critique is not dissimilar to the work of sailors on Neurath's boat rebuilding their ship while still at sea.[8]

But what do these changes accomplish? Would the end result be just substitution of one regime of power for another, as his critics suggest?[9] First, Foucault does not conceive of power just in terms of domination. His concerns are with relations of power in various settings, such as the family and other institutions rather than a theory of power *per se*. "When I speak of power relations," Foucault (1988b) tells us,

> I am not referring to Power—with a capital P—dominating and imposing its rationality upon the totality of the social body. In fact, there are power relations. They are multiple; they have different forms, they can be in play in family relations, or within an institution, or an administration – or between a dominating and a dominated class. ... It is a field of analysis and not at all a reference to any unique instance. [Furthermore] in studying these power relations, I in no way construct a theory of Power. But I wish to know how the reflexivity of the subject and the discourse of truth are linked – "How can the subject tell the truth about itself?" – and I think that relations of power exerting themselves upon one another constitute one of the determining elements in this relation I am trying to analyze. (p. 38)

For him, the idea of 'relations of power' is a general notion, describing the ways in which individuals direct the behaviour of one another and themselves (Foucault, 1983). These relationships range from one-sided domination over others to consensual and reciprocal relations between individuals. Foucault does not deny that there are cases of domination. For Foucault (1988a), a relationship of power is not necessarily identical with a relation of domination.

> When an individual or a social group manages to block a field of relations of power," [he writes] "to render them impassive and invariable and to prevent all reversibility of movement . . . we are facing what can be called a state of domination. It is certain that in such a state the practice of liberty does not exists or exists only unilaterally or is extremely confined and limited. (p. 3)

Individuals in relations of power other than domination, however, have the liberty to coordinate their actions in particular ways. In this kind of coordination problem, individuals align themselves according to certain goals that each want to achieve. The relationship may or may not be hierarchical, depending on the context in which it is situated. Nonetheless, even if it were hierarchical, individuals in various subject positions are constrained. When a manager, or a department chair, plans to implement new initiatives, she or he can do so only if others 'accept' the plans and work within them. Individuals in such circumstance can choose to act in accordance or resist. They can even attempt to modify the way in which they are connected to each other *to the degree they can*, by changing the rules governing the relation itself. In this sense, the relation of power is reciprocal between individuals, and requires that individuals have the freedom to make choices (Rouse, 1994; Tully, 1999). Change is, therefore, possible.[10] Indeed, the problem, Foucault (1988a) writes, "is to find out where resistance is going to be organized" (p. 12).

Second, Foucault is suspicious of overarching claims about liberation or emancipation.[11] Aside from the potential of merely uttering empty platitudes, the danger in such speculative universalist claims is that in their name, many heinous acts have been committed. Foucault (1984) reminds us that "we know from experience that the claim to escape from the system of contemporary reality so as to produce the overall programs of another society . . . has led only to the return of the most dangerous traditions" (p. 46). But he does not deny that, in concrete instances, liberation exists. "When a colonial people tries to free itself of its colonizer," he (1988a) tells us,

> that is truly an act of liberation, in the strict sense of the word. ... [But] this act of liberation is not sufficient to establish the practices of liberty that later on will be necessary for this people, this society and these individuals to decide upon receivable and acceptable forms of their existence or political society. (pp. 2–3)

Foucault here echoes Kant's view in his essay *What is Enlightenment?* Kant (1963) tells us that, "an age cannot bind itself and ordain to put the succeeding one into such a condition that it cannot extend its (at best very occasional) knowledge, purify itself of errors, and progress in general enlightenment" (p. 7). Rather than schemes of transformation that seek to establish 'freedom' once and for all, Foucault (1984) argues that we should focus on *specific* kinds of transformations concerning our ways of being and thinking instead. He tells us that he prefers "even these partial transformations that have been made . . . to the programs for a new man that the worst political systems have repeated throughout the twentieth century" (pp. 46–47).

Genetic Fallacy

There is another objection. Foucault (1988c) tells us one of the aims of his historical studies is

> to show people that a lot of things that are a part of their landscape—that people think are universal—are the result of some very precise historical changes. All my analyses are against the idea of universal necessities in human existence. They show the arbitrariness of institutions and show which space of freedom we can still enjoy and how many changes can still be made. (p. 11)

Showing that certain ways of thinking and acting are historically contingent, however, does not show that they are false or even problematic. If one were to hold that the unmasking of power relations behind concepts and practices by itself demonstrates that propositions informed by those concepts are false, then one would be committing the genetic fallacy.

Foucault (1988a), however, is well aware of this possible objection. He tells us that

> we can show, for example, that the medicalisation of madness . . . has been linked, at some time or other, to a whole series of social or economic processes, but also to institutions and practices of power. This fact in no way impairs the scientific validity of the therapeutic efficacy of psychiatry. It does not guarantee it but it does not cancel it out either. (p. 16)

Consider another example. Suppose, Foucault says, mathematics is linked to structures of power. What follows from that? Foucault tells us that this does not "mean that mathematics is *only* a game of power but that mathematics is linked, in a certain way and *without impairing its validity* [italics added] to games and institutions of power" (ibid.). In these passages, Foucault acknowledges that there is an epistemological or evidential side to knowledge claims. Whether or not a particular claim is true will depend on the evidence. Nevertheless, knowledge claims may be linked to and affected by relations of power. Feminist epistemologists have argued that not everyone is allowed to participate. Lorraine Code (1995) points out that the social order establishes structures of credulity and incredulity, which may exclude potentially good informants. Under such circumstances, it is likely that "there are truths which could have been and should have been transmitted, but were not" (Fricker, 1998, p. 173).[12]

For Foucault (1979), however, knowledge is not reducible to power, even though they directly imply one another. In an interview, Foucault (1988a) complains that, "when you point out to [others] that there can be a relation between truth and power, they say: 'Ah good! Then it is not the truth'" (p. 17).

The general perception of his idea of power/knowledge is that knowledge is reducible to power. Foucault chafes at such an interpretation. He (1988d) remarks acidly,

> I know that, as far as the general public is concerned, I am the guy who said that knowledge merged with power, that it was no more than a thin mask thrown over the structures of domination and that those structures were always ones of oppression, confinement, and so on. [This] point is so absurd as to be laughable. If I had said, or meant, that knowledge was power, I would have said so, and having said so, I would have had nothing more to say, since, having made them identical, I don't see why I would have taken the trouble to show the different relations between them. . . . Those who say that for me knowledge is the mask of power seem to me to be quite incapable of understanding. (pp. 264–265)

A full treatment of Foucault's idea of power/knowledge is beyond the scope of this paper, but perhaps it is enough for our purposes to point out that his studies reveal the connections between various knowledge claims and the practices by which they are justified and become intelligible. In *The Discourse on Language* (1972), Foucault tells us that, "a proposition must fulfil some onerous and complex conditions before it can be admitted within a discipline; before it can be pronounced true or false it must be, as Monsieur Canguilhem might say, 'within the true'" (p. 224). Yet, as Linda Alcoff (1996) points out, the "rules of discursive formations do not mandate specific truth-values for specific sentences, but open up a delimited space in which some statements can be meaningfully expressed" (p. 123). Since discursive formations, which are moulded by both intellectual and social events, only delineate what can be stated and what is capable of having truth values, it would be wrong to attribute to Foucault the view that knowledge is reducible to power relations.[13] The historical inquiries in critical ontology reveal the connections between knowledge and power in various taken-for-granted practices. That changes that are necessary in these customary ways of thinking and acting will be shown by problematic practices themselves because they pose arbitrary or unnecessary constraints on individuals.

The Developmental Model of Childhood

As an illustration of the workings of critical ontology, consider the case of child development. If we peruse literature from pediatricians' offices or off-the-shelf self-help books for parents, one idea that leaps out immediately is that children must develop according to physical, cognitive and psychological norms. It is difficult for us today to reason about what to do for children without thinking of them as having to develop according to such norms. Yet, the very idea that children must develop according to norms is recent, barely 200 years old.

Of course, people have always been aware that children grew up, or 'developed,' at different rates. How could they not? But their notion of development is not "theoretically well-formed" (Archard, 1993, p. 30). In contrast today, most people, especially in the West, are guided by a *scientific* idea of development, as a consequence of systematic explorations of childhood from the perspectives of biology, psychology, psychiatry and much else over the past century and a half. For example, consider Shakespeare's sketch of growing up in *As You Like It*:

> All the worlds' a stage
> and all the men and women merely players
> they have their exits and their entrances
> And one man in his time plays many parts
> His act being seven stages
> At first, the infant, mewling and puking in the nurse's arms
> Then the whining schoolboy, with his satchel, and shining morning face
> creeping like snail unwillingly to school
> And then the lover, sighing like furnace, with a woeful ballad
> made to his mistress' eyebrow. Then a soldier ... (II, vii, 1994, p. 151)

Of course, the bard is not an 'expert' on child development. But no one was then because the model of child development as we know it today has yet to be discovered. To be sure, philosophers writing roughly in the same period as Shakespeare, Hobbes and Locke for example, and even earlier, Plato in *The Republic*, discussed children in their works. However, their concerns are different from those in contemporary research on children's development. For instance, Hobbes's concern with children was primarily in the context of an account of the justification of political authority. Locke's case is more complicated. There were two contexts for his writings on children. On the one hand, he was interested in providing an alternative account of authority to Filmer's and Hobbes's in his *Two Treatises on Government*. On the other, in *Some Thoughts concerning Education* (1996), he was interested in providing an account of how best to raise future citizens. David Archard (1998) tells us that in *Some Thoughts* "Locke writes of children as the recipients of an ideal upbringing, citizens in the making, fledgling but imperfect reasoners, and blank sheets filled by experience" (p. 85). Locke presents children as beings with their own needs, and his counsel is wide ranging, including a program of study, possible punishment for misbehavior as well as dietary needs. Nonetheless, Locke did not write about children in today's framework of children's development. It is a far cry from the kind of general observation that Locke makes about children's abilities in *Some Thoughts*, such as when a child can talk, "it is time he should begin to *learn to read* …[But] a great care is to be taken that it be made a business to him, nor he look on it as a task" (1996, p. 113) to contemporary experiment-based claims about young children that, for example, from a few weeks of age on, they can distinguish people from inanimate objects (Bradley, 1989).[14]

It should also be noted that Jean-Jacques Rousseau's general remarks about children's abilities in his famous work on education *Emile* (1911) do not fall under today's framework of child development. Like Locke, Rousseau emphasized the distinctiveness of childhood as a phase in human life. He tells us that children have their "own ways of seeing, thinking and feeling" (p. 57). For instance, he tells us that

> from the first children hear spoken language; we speak to them before they can understand. Their vocal organs are still stiff, and only gradually lend themselves to the reproduction of the sounds heard; it is doubtful whether these sounds are heard distinctly as we hear them. (p. 37)

Both Locke's and Rousseau's remarks, however, are based on unsystematic observations of children, and not grounded in experimental studies. In *Emile*, Rousseau tells us that "we know not what nature allows us to be, none of us has *measured* [italics added] the possible difference between man and man" (p. 29). Perhaps, contemporary developmental research will show that children are much more able at various tasks than either Locke or Rousseau had supposed. Scientific research now grounds our understanding of children's development. However, individuals in general and children in particular were not yet objects of scientific knowledge at that time.[15] The view that there is a *rate* at which individuals developed and their development compared had not yet been advanced. Once that measure is acquired, development, as a norm, can be deployed in the detailed management of individuals. But the techniques and technologies for such knowledge would not be invented until the mid-nineteenth century.

The claim that childhood is a particularly modern invention is, of course, not new. Phillippe Ariés made such a claim in his landmark *Centuries of Childhood* (1962). But Ariés' analysis is flawed. He applied contemporary attitudes, assumptions and concerns about children to the past. Since present attitudes were not found in past societies, he concluded that such societies lacked a concept of childhood altogether. But all that he could have claimed was that they lacked *our* concept of childhood. By definition to be a child is to be not yet an adult, and all societies make such a distinction between those who are and those are not yet adults (Archard, 1993). My interest in this paper is in how the idea of development became a central organizing principle in the way we think about and interact with children, parents and care-providers and how such developmental thinking may pose unnecessary limitations on individuals. The emergence of that paradigm and its impact on children and their care-providers will be developed in the remainder of this article.

Knowledge

A key figure in the formation of knowledge of children's development was the Belgian astronomer and statistician Adolphe Quetelet. For him, just as there are laws governing the heavens and human societies, there are laws governing the development of man's various powers. And statistical thinking was the key to uncover such laws. Quetelet applied the 'Law of Error' used by astronomers at the time to human populations. Thus, the idea that there was a truth to be discovered about man's development which governed every aspect of his maturation could now be realized. Unlike Locke or Jean-Jacques Rousseau, who based their views on single or isolated observations, Quetelet used data from various anthropometric studies to find out what the average person would be like at various points in his or her development. In his view, the 'average man' (*l'homme moyen*) was the embodiment of the physical *and* moral attributes of his people. He claimed that the features of the 'average man' could be considered a 'type of perfection' for a group at a specific time, since extreme variations would cancel each other out. The features of the average man would serve as the standard against which an individual's development would be measured. Average features represent the normal, or healthy, state for individuals in a population (Hacking, 1990, chap. 19). Average values, as *norms*, are no mere arithmetic constructs. They have real effects in people's lives: normal connotes health, abnormal suggests deviance. People are motivated, then, to mould themselves according to such norms.

Educators and Evolutionary Thinking

Educators, too, had high hopes that anthropometric studies would yield knowledge about the laws of mental development in children. They had a practical interest in such studies. For them, the key in making pedagogy more effective was to understand how the child's mind unfolded. When educational practices are adapted to the natural developmental order of children's abilities and interests, such practices would finally be able to do what they were supposed to do: to mould these children into future citizens. The subject of mental development in children quickly became a hot topic for discussion in women's clubs and teachers' organizations in the mid-1800s. G. Stanley Hall of Clark University, a founding member of the American Psychological Association, tapped into this enthusiasm and put teachers and parents to work. Questionnaire after questionnaire about children's behaviour was filled out. It is as though the mere gathering of numbers and calculating of averages and presentation of tables and graphs guaranteed that their findings would reveal yet more laws governing children's development.

There was another reason for interest in children's mental development at the time. Those involved in natural history and 'evolutionary thinking' saw 'development' as *the* organizing principle in Nature. Robert Chambers, the author of the anonymously published popular work, *Vestiges of the Natural History of Creation* (1969), tells us that "the inorganic has one final comprehensive law GRAVITATION. The organic, the other great department of mundane things, rests in like manner on one law, and that is DEVELOPMENT" (p. 360, capitalized in original). The development of the mind was seen to separate human beings from the animal world. Children's mental development was of particular interest because the child was thought to be situated between the animal and the human. A number of papers on children's behaviour were published in the second-half of the Nineteenth Century. For instance, Charles Darwin's "A Biographical Sketch of the Infant" was published in *Mind* in 1877. The trickle of publications would soon become a flood.

Knowledge, Power, Ethics

The account just provided shows that developments in statistical and evolutionary thinking, worries about population health and education and much else, converged to create a space (conceptual and institutional) for the emergence of a science of child development. Hall's sloppy questionnaires would give way to more rigorous tests, such as Binet and Simon's intelligence test in 1904. Such tests provided a simple way to obtain knowledge about children's behaviour, scholastic or otherwise. They made it possible to reason objectively about children in developmental terms both physically and psychologically. For instance, claims such as 'a one-year-old boy should weigh 10 kg' or 'two-year-olds can use words such as I, me and you' are now taken to be true-or-false. More importantly, the various tests started to change the way in which research on child development was done. Children would be studied in controlled laboratory settings. Conceptual tools, techniques and instruments would be developed and refined to verify claims about children's development. Pediatrics and developmental psychology would become mature sciences, eventually providing us with now familiar claims such as 'children between the ages two and four have no real conception of abstract principles guiding classification.' Although modern societal relations of power are constitutive of the conditions for the possibility for knowledge of children's development (e.g., separation of childhood, concerns about populations and education, and so on.), they do not specify the true values of individual claims; rather, they provide the material and conceptual conditions for the possibility of such knowledge.

Knowledge of children's development also changed the way we think about and do things for children. Children are now seen as individuals who develop more or less normally, according to physical and psychological norms. Such knowledge had an immediate impact on parents. Parents were told by self-styled pundits, like James Sully, the Grote Professor of philosophy and psychology at the University of London (and a child-study enthusiast), that raising children was no longer

> a matter of instinct and unthinking rules of thumb [but] has become the subject of profound and perplexing discussion. Mothers—the right sort of mothers that is— feel they must know *au fond* this . . . creature which they are called upon to direct onto the safe road to manhood" (Sully, 1903, cited in Ross, 1972, p. 284).

The message was clear: good parents would seek out and learn the latest findings on how to raise their children. Parents, especially middle-class parents, sought out that knowledge in pamphlets and popular magazines, like *Parent's Magazine*. Development became part of their working vocabulary in their dealings with children and with one another. They willingly transformed their homes and *made* themselves into the kinds of persons that such knowledge required. Who wouldn't want their children to be healthy and normal? It may be true that, as the popular saying goes, 'it takes a village to raise a child,' but with the scientific notion of development, that a village had better include, or at least have access to, an expert or two.

Even if we moved away from the rigid thinking about development as reflected in various developmental charts as urged by popular writers like Dr. Benjamin Spock, and pediatricians themselves,[16] how could we today completely avoid thinking in terms of development in our interactions with children? Two recent British studies tracked the cognitive, social and emotional outcomes of children classified as small for their gestational age. These studies show that, although these children are less likely to excel academically, their social and emotional prognoses are good (Owens, 2001). But even earlier, long before the child is born, indicators have been established for the fetus marking it as a developing being. Today, parents, educators, healthcare providers and bureaucrats take for granted that it is in the nature of children that they 'develop' (i.e., their growth is governed by developmental norms). But *we* inculcate that belief in children and in ourselves. In the West, the first image a parent sees of her or his child is likely an ultrasound image of the fetus taken at a prescribed check-up of fetal development during pregnancy. Furthermore, think about the toys and games for children. They are designed with the aim of promoting developmentally appropriate skills. Consumers are very much aware of the age-appropriate recommendations of such games. Think about schools. The whole curriculum is based on fostering skills in a developmentally appropriate way. Such mundane practices and attitudes entrench the concept of development in our culture.

Recall the three kinds of questions examined by critical ontology: "How are we constituted as subjects of our own knowledge? How are we constituted as subjects who exercise or submit to power relations? How are we constituted as moral subjects of our own actions" (Foucault, 1984, p. 49)? In the previous discussion of childhood development, we have seen how individuals, in particular children, have become objects of knowledge, and how parents and other care-providers have willingly entered into various relations of power guiding their behaviour and that of children in their care. Such relations are informed by developmental thinking. That is knowledge and power of the three axes of knowledge, power and ethics. What about ethics? The relationship between children and parents, between children and experts, and parents and experts are all informed by the knowledge we have about development. And that knowledge has also shaped the way we think about our responsibilities in terms of caring for children (e.g., legislation on child abandonment, corporal punishment and so on). Such ethical demands have normalizing effects on individuals, which are asymmetrically borne. For instance, mothers, who are typically the primary care-providers of their children, bear the brunt of the burdens; and the hardships are multiplied for those in marginalized situations, such as single teenaged mothers.

Implications

What, then, are the implications of a practical critique for practices grounded in the model of childhood development? As the discussion in the previous sections illustrates, an analysis inspired by Foucault's notion of critical ontology shows how development itself became a central organizing principle in contemporary Western societies. Such reasoning about children has also penetrated other ways of thinking about children growing up in other traditions, such as the Native peoples of Canada's far north (e.g., formal schooling interrupts traditional communal practices, such as hunting. See Owens, 2001, and Roundtable, 1999). Yet, attention should be paid to these other child rearing practices since they may provide insights about children's growing up. The variability in child rearing practices provides a rich resource with which to understand Western child rearing practices. This is not a rejection of the vast body of knowledge now available on child development, but a call to take it seriously. Far from advocating anarchism, or worse nihilism, Foucault (1980b) himself tells us that his genealogical analyses do not "vindicate a lyrical right to ignorance or non-knowledge" (p. 84). Rather, they allow individuals to "question the truth on its effects of power and question power on its discourses on truth" (Foucault, 1997, p. 32). The point is *not* that we can do without knowledge, or truth. Foucault (1988a) adds that, "nothing has…proved that we could define a strategy exterior to [knowledge or truth]. It is indeed in this field of obligation to truth that we sometimes can avoid in one way or another the effects of a domination" (p. 15). In his view, changes can only be brought about "not by playing a game that was a complete stranger to the game of truth, but in playing it otherwise or in playing…other trumps in the game of truth" (ibid., p.15).

The historical inquiry into the development model shows that the idea of development cannot be neatly offered up in an either/or dilemma: either you accept development or you reject it. But, in grasping the workings of the normalizing effects of knowledge about child development on individuals, parents and other care-providers have a richer knowledge base to make judgements about children's growing up and child rearing practices. Knowledge of children's physical or psychological development can tell us when something has gone seriously wrong. But pursuing the standards set out by developmental schedules too single-mindedly could be disastrous for children. In choosing to use knowledge about child development, perhaps in conjunction with other models of how children grow up, these individuals are disrupting the normalizing effects of such knowledge. It is important not to overstate the claim however. Individual cases of resistance may not lead to a disruption in the practices and institutions of child development. Such 'macro-level' changes will require a great deal more, including the acceptance of other, including nonwestern accounts of child rearing.

As the case study of child development illustrates, the tasks laid out by critical ontology—demonstrating the historical contingency in our present ways of understanding and organizing ourselves and to imagine other possibilities—would seem to be key components in framing possible transformations. Such changes are, as noted earlier, provisional. They may or may not continue to contribute to the autonomy of individuals at some other juncture. Nonetheless, that they *now* remove some of the arbitrary constraints on a person's ability, or potential ability, to act would seem to suggest that increasing the capacity for autonomy in individuals is possible without a concomitant increase in the effects of disciplinary power on them.

Notes

1   An earlier version of the paper was published in the *Canadian Journal of Political Science*. I would like to thank the editors for permission to use materials from that article here, and to Professor Peters for inviting me to participate in this project.

2   The motto had already been adopted in 1736 by the Society of the Friends of Truth, an important group in the German Enlightenment (Kant, 1963).

3   Attitude is contrasted with 'analytics,' the latter is Foucault's term for formal theory (Habermas, 1986, p. 107).

4   Foucault's project also differs from Kant's. Whereas Kant gives a central role to autonomy in his critical philosophy, Foucault tells us that "the care for self implies also a relationship to the other to the extent that, in order to really care for self, one must listen to the teachings of a master. One needs a guide, a counsellor, a friend—someone who will tell you the truth. Thus, the problem of relationship with others is present all along this development of care for self" (1988a, p. 7).

5   According to James Tully (1999), limits are "any of the multiplicity of ways of speaking, thinking and acting, of being conscious of ourselves as human subjects" (p. 92). These limits are taken for granted, "functioning as the…horizon of [the subject's] questions and contests" (p. 93).

6   Foucault also gives 'critical ontology' the ironic name of 'historical ontology.' Of all the branches of philosophical inquiry, ontology would appear to be the least historical inclined.

7   Foucault was already aware in *Discipline and Punish* (1979) of the 'double bind' of the Enlightenment. He tells us that the "development and generalization of disciplinary mechanisms constituted the other, dark side of the process [of modernity]…The Enlightenment which discovered the liberties, also invented the disciplines" (p. 222).

8   James Tully (1999) tells us that, "the modification in practice provides in turn a test against which the original conceptual tools are assessed and reformulated and put into practice again, thereby forming a 'permanent critique'" (p. 99).

9   Michael Walzer (1986) writes, "Foucault makes no demand on us that we adopt this or that

critical principle or replace these disciplinary norms with some other set of norms. He is not an advocate" (p. 65). But what then are we to do, since "there may be some [positions] that we have 'good reasons' not to support" (ibid.)?

10   Foucault (1988a) claims that, "in the relations of power, there is necessarily the possibility of resistance, for if there were no possibility of resistance ... there would be no relations of power" (p. 12).

11   As such, the ethos of continual critique applies reflexively to Foucault's own project as well.

12   See also Vrinda Dalmiya and Linda Alcoff's (1995) discussion of midwives in relation to modern medical knowledge.

13   As Paul Rabinow (1984) points out, "critical ontology does not challenge whether or not a particular claim is true or false. If the discipline is a mature science, there would be well-established procedures by now to make that determination. Rather, it seeks to examine the conditions whereby certain statements were seen to be true or false, the concepts around which disciplines are organized" (p. 12).

14   Bradley (1989) is here commenting on Jerome Bruner's research on the interaction between adults and young infants.

15   On the science of the individual, see Foucault, 1979.

16   One pediatrician tells us that she uses "the growth charts with a grain of salt" (Owens, 2001, D1–2)

Bibliography

Alcoff, L. (1996). *Real knowing: New versions of the coherence theory.* Ithaca, NY: Cornell University Press.

Archard, D. (1993). *Children, rights and childhood.* London: Routledge.

————. (1998). John Locke's children. In S. Turner & G. Matthews (Eds.), *The Philosopher's child: Critical essays in the western tradition* (pp. 85–103). Rochester: University of Rochester Press.

Ariès, P. (1962). *Centuries of childhood.* (R. Baldick, Trans.). New York: Vintage Books.

Bradley, B. S. (1989). *Visions of infancy.* Oxford: Polity Press.

Chambers, R. (1969). *Vestiges of the natural history of creation.* Victorian Library Edition. New York: Humanities Press. (Original work published in 1844)

Code, L. (1995). Incredulity, experientialism, and the politics of knowledge. In *Rhetorical spaces: Essays on gendered locations* (pp. 58–82). New York: Routledge.

Dalmiya, V., and Alcoff, L. (1995). Are 'old wives' tales' justified? In E. Potter & L. M. Alcoff (Eds.), *Feminist epistemologies* (pp. 217–244). New York: Routledge.

Foucault, M. (1972). The Discourse on language. In *The archaeology of knowledge and the discourse on language* (R. Sawyer, Trans.), (pp. 215–237). New York: Harper Books.

————. (1979). *Discipline and punish: The birth of the prison* (A. Sheridan, Trans.). New York: Vintage Books.

————. (1980a). *The history of sexuality, Vol. I, Introduction* (R. Hurley, Trans.). New York: Vintage Books.

————. (1980b). Two lectures. In C. Gordon (Ed.), *Power/knowledge: Selected interviews and other writings, 1972–1977* (pp. 78–108). New York: Pantheon Books.

————. (1983). The subject and power. In H. L. Dreyfus & P. Rabinow (Eds.), *Michel Foucault: Beyond structuralism and hermeneutics* (2nd ed.) (pp. 208–226). Chicago: University of Chicago Press.

————. (1984). What is enlightenment? In P. Rabinow (Ed.), *The Foucault reader* (pp. 32–50). New York: Pantheon Books.

————. (1988a). The ethic of care for the self as a practice of freedom. In J. Bernauer & D. Rasmussen (Eds.), *The final Foucault* (pp. 1–20). Cambridge, MA: MIT University Press.

————. (1988b). Critical theory/intellectual history. In L. D. Kritzman (Ed.), *Michel Foucault: Politics, philosophy, culture* (pp. 17–46). New York: Routledge.

————. (1988c). Truth, power, self: An interview. In L. H. Martin, H. Gutman & P. H. Hutton (Eds.), *Technologies of the self* (pp. 9–15). Amherst, MA: University of Massachusetts Press.

————. (1988d). The concern for truth. In L. D. Kritzman (Ed.), *Michel Foucault: Politics, philosophy, culture* (pp. 255–267).New York: Routledge.

————. (1989). How much does it cost for reason to tell the truth? In S. Lotringer (Ed.), *Foucault live* (pp. 233–256), New York: Semiotext(e).

————. (1997). What is critique? In S. Lotringer & L. Hochroth (Eds.), *The Politics of truth* (pp. 23–82), New York: Semiotext(e).

Fricker, M. (1998). Rational authority and social power: Towards a truly social epistemology. *Proceedings of the Aristotelian Society*, XCVII, Part 2: 159–177.

Habermas, J. (1986). Taking aim at the heart of the present. In D. Couzens Hoy (Ed.), *Foucault: A critical reader* (pp. 103–108). New York: Basil Blackwell.

————. (1987). *The Philosophical discourse of modernity*. Cambridge, MA: MIT University Press.

Hacking, I. (1990). *The taming of chance*. Cambridge: Cambridge University Press.

Kant, I. (1963). What is enlightenment?" In L. White Beck (Ed.), *Kant on history* (pp. 3–10), Indianapolis: Bobbs-Merrill. (Original work published in 1784)

————. (1965). *Critique of pure reason* (N. Kemp Smith, Trans.) New York: St. Martins Press. (Original work published in 1781)

Locke, J. (1996). *Some thoughts concerning education*. In R. W. Grant & N. Tarcov (eds.). Indianapolis: Hackett. (Original work published in 1693)

Norris, C. (1994). What is enlightenment? Kant according to Foucault. In G. Gutting (Ed.), *The Cambridge companion to Foucault* (pp. 159–196). New York: Cambridge University Press.

Owens, A-M. (2001, February 12). A weighty dilemma. *The National Post*, pp. D1–2.

Rabinow, P. (1984). Introduction. In P. Rabinow (Ed.), *The Foucault Reader* (pp. 3–29). New York: Pantheon Books.

Rouse, J. (1994). Power/knowledge. In G. Gutting (Ed.), *The Cambridge companion to Foucault* (pp. 92–114). New York: Cambridge University Press

Ross, D. (1972). *G. Stanley Hall, the psychologist as prophet*. Chicago: University of Chicago Press.

Rousseau, J-J. (1911). *Emile, or on education*. (B. Foxley, Trans.). London: Dent. (Original work published in 1762)

"Roundtable" (1999). In J. Wong & D. Checkland (Eds.). *Teen pregnancy and parenting: Social and ethical issues* (pp. 151–175). Toronto: University of Toronto Press.

Shakespeare, W. (1994). *As You Like It* (A. Brissenden, Ed.). Oxford: Oxford University Press. (Original work published in 1600).

Tully, J. (1999). To think and act differently: Foucault's four reciprocal objections to Habermas' theory. In S. Ashenden & D. Owen (Eds.), *Foucault contra Habermas* (pp. 90–142). London: Sage.

Walzer, M. (1986). The politics of Michel Foucault. In D. Couzens Hoy (Ed.), *Foucault: A critical reader* (pp. 51–68). New York: Basil Blackwell.

Social Work as Government— A Power Analytical Perspective

Fabian Kessl

The Analysis of Power in Foucault

For those who are controlled, "[Power] invests them, is transmitted by them and through them; it exerts pressure upon them, just as they themselves, in their struggle against it, resist the grip it has on them" (Foucault, 1994a, p.27)[1] Michel Foucault's analyses of a "physics of power," as he presents them in his study *Discipline and Punish: The Birth of the Prison* (ibid., p. 229), are usually translated within socio-pedagogical debates into the question of whether, from such a perspective, all educational interventions should be exposed as mere acts for the stabilization of control. Available socio-pedagogic objections to approaches based on analyses of power are correspondingly marked by a clear unease. Micha Brumlik (1992), for example, writes: analyses of power subject "all of the modern humanities to the suspicion of control" (Brumlik, 1992, p. 163). Thomas Rauschenbach and Rainer Treptow (1984) ironically state that Foucault's analyses of power could, at most, be followed by a "radical non-intervention ('doing nothing is better than doing something')" (p. 60), and that would lead to a devastating consequence: the "career-strategic variety (is) the postulate of de-professionalizing" (ibid.). Thus, following Foucault would mean abandoning the project of social work, even the enlightening project of education.

Perspectives based on an analysis of power experience this type of massive rejection not only within the debates on social work. Socio-pedagogical grumblers also agree in a great chorus of German-speaking Foucault skeptics, whose common, adapted refrain was written by Jürgen Habermas and has been sung almost unchanged until the present day: influenced by Nietzsche, this French anti-enlightenment philosopher propagates against humanity (see Habermas 1998, p. 284). According to that suggestion, following Foucault would imply a complete and utter end to enlightenment. Current objections even aggravate these reproaches; Foucault is not only the Enlightenment's eulogist, but, likewise, a forerunner of neo-liberal theory formation (see Reitz, 2003).

Trapping One's Own Culture

Confusion in the reception of Foucault's works is generated mainly by the changes in perspective that he took on over the course of his writings and which he, in retrospect, in the introduction to *Use of Pleasure: The History of Sexuality, Vol. 2,* describes as the following "theoretical shift(s)": from the analysis of "forms of discourse practices" he moved to an analysis of the "open strategies and rational techniques…which articulate the practice of powers," in order to arrive at the analysis of "forms and…modalities of the relationship to itself… through which the individual constitutes and recognizes itself as a subject" (Foucault, 2000, p. 12). In his interpretation of Foucault, Wolfgang Detel (1998) consequently speaks of three phases: knowledge, power, and subjectivity, which are all determined by Foucault's occupation with the issue of specific historical "truth games" (p. 16). Already two years prior to the publication of *The Use of Pleasure,* Foucault wrote in the postscript to Hubert Dreyfus and Paul Rabinow's interpretation of his works, that he had been occupied with "three means of objectification, which transform people into subjects": the constitution of the sciences, the constitution of the regulation of the population, and the constitution of subject formation (Foucault 1994c, p. 243). "Not power, but the subject," (ibid.) is thus the theme of his research. And again, five years earlier, Foucault stated in an interview with Fontana and Pasquino (1978)—in light of his first genealogical studies at the beginning of the 1960s—"(I) wonder what it was that I spoke of then…if not about power" (p. 30). Finally, in the postscript to the quoted passage from the introduction to *The Use of Pleasure: The History of Sexuality, Vol. 2.,* Foucault (2000) wrote that, whereas he first looked at truth games in terms of their relationship to each other, he then subsequently turned to the study of truth mechanisms in their relationship to power relations in order to subsequently investigate "the study of the truth game in the relation of itself to itself and the constitution of itself as a subject" (p. 13).

Which perspective was at least chosen by Foucault? The way from the discourse to the subject or from the genealogy of the sciences to the genealogy of the subject? Or should we characterize Foucault in the line of subject theory, of power theory, or of an analysis of truth games? The obvious inability to classify the "work" of Foucault provides the base for both the fascination as well as contempt that his ideas seem to set off. On the one hand, when reading Habermas (1998), one suspects him almost at his wit's end, sweating at his desk, arguing as he writes of Foucault's "dramatic history of influence" and his "iconoclastic reputation" (p. 324) and at the same time, dedicates two chapters to him as the only reviewed author in *Der Philosophische Diskurs der Moderne* [The Philosophical Discourse of Modernity: Twelve Lectures]. On the other hand, the introduction by Thomas Lemke to what in recent years has become the most influential interpretation of Foucault in German reads like a religious creed of a convert, whose eyes have been opened by the rereading of the Foucauldian texts. Lemke (1997) begins his reaction to the German-language critique of Foucault by Habermas and others: "I had to go back to the beginning and start again" (p. 26). He continues, it is only this "turning back," that allowed the author, Thomas Lemke, to realize that the "critics of Foucault . . . had read less incorrectly and much more so 'correctly'" (p. 27). And although Lemke did not go so far, we could somewhat smugly add in for him...*only, they were not able to understand it, for they hadn't set out on the necessary path of "turning back."*

Regardless of whether now three phases (see Habermas, 1998; Detel, 1998) or "three axes" (see Fink-Eitel, 1997, pp.7-9.) are established within the Foucauldian works, almost all readers are irritated when faced with the question of whether the "work" of the French thinker is marked by "continuity" or "discontinuity." Foucault allows those who ask this question to continually run up against a wall, as Lemke's "turn around" action makes clear. It is not the question of consistency that can characterize Foucault's reconstructing and reflecting. Foucault refuses to ask this question. The confusion itself is actually his scientific desire. A little note which Foucault formulated in *Le Figaro Littéraire* at the time of his advance work on *Discipline and Punish,* with reference to Gaston Bachelard's scientific approach, is, to a certain extent, characteristic of his own approach:

> What especially amazes me about Bachelard is that he speaks against his own culture with his own culture, as it were...Bachelard liberates himself from this entire complex of values, and he liberates himself by reading everything and allowing everything to compete against everything else...And he does not do this because he wants to copy the great, broad culture of the Occident, Europe, or France. Not because he wants to show that it is always the same great spirit that lives everywhere and reigns and can be found the same everywhere; on the contrary, I have the impression that with his fissures, his deviations, his little interruptions, and his incorrect remarks, he is trying to trap his own culture" (Foucault 2002, p. 476f).

The analysis of discursive practices, the genealogy of knowledge forms, the reconstruction of means of subjectification and truth games, the analysis of power—Foucault's work is characterized by the search for analytical instruments in regard to each particular investigation he is working on. There is nothing like a "Foucauldian Theory", no such "system" of fixed analytical categories for an Analysis of Power. But Foucault's "tool box" stands ready for Power Analysis of that which can be seen and said. The works of Foucault leave us with no more and also no less than this tool box.

Social Work as Normalization

Foucault introduces education, public assistances, and social work alongside medicine and psychology as pillars of the "normalization mechanisms," existing since the early nineteenth century, and therefore as the heirs of the hitherto dominant "disciplinary mechanisms." In his opinion, education and public assistance are taking the place of the prison:

> As medicine, psychology, education, public assistance, 'social work' assume an ever greater share of the powers of supervision and assessment, the penal apparatus will be able, in turn, to become medicalized, psychologized, educationalized; and by the same token that turning-point represented by the prison becomes less useful when, through the gap between its penitentiary discourse and its effect of consolidating delinquency, it articulates the penal power and the disciplinary power. In the midst of all these mechanisms of normalization, which are becoming ever more rigorous in their application, the specificity of the prison and its role as link are losing something of their purpose" (Foucault 1994a, p. 306).

Are socio-pedagogic institutions the heirs of the prison? Is the capitalist industrial modernity for this reason a phase of "socio-pedagogical reformation of the disciplinary system" (Rehmann, 2003, p. 79)? Is the objection justified, as formulated, for example, by the historian Detlev Peukert: that the "vision of historians from the Foucauldian school, [who states] that modern society is becoming an ever more perfect prison world, is disproportionate" (Peukert, 1986, p. 67)?

Countering this, I present here the thesis that with these types of assessments—still widespread today in German educational sciences and social work—a theory of power assumption as a repressive force is reproduced. Many authors in the educational sciences await the liberation of the individual (*subject*) as the result of successful pedagogic intervention. In this sense, Michael Winkler states in his *Theorie der Sozialpädagogik (Theory of Social Pedagogy)*: The subject "learns to decide what to do with itself, to formulate its own perspectives and to follow them; becomes capable of educating itself" (Winkler, 1988, p. 335). Likewise, the materialist educational theorist Joachim Heydorn states at the end of his polemical treatise *Über den Widerspruch von Bildung und Herrschaft (On the contradiction of education and control)*: "[P]eople should leave their undoing behind, truly experience the light that is within them, sensually, tangibly, as a transformed world" (Heydorn, 1970, p. 337). Within German language debates on social work, it is described, against the backdrop of these types of ideas, as an anti-State or countersocietal institution—without taking into account the constitutive state-forming structuring of social work (see Kessl, 2005). Taking that conception seriously, social work has to be meant to make available places *beyond* power and control.

Analyses of power, on the contrary, make clear that historically specific means of governing can only be appropriately decoded when the idea of an "outside" of power relations is abandoned. The disciplinary power of the eighteenth century was transformed to a "integrated system", as Foucault describes the logic of early welfare arrangements (see Krasmann 2003). That integrated system is under siege in the so called OECD-states since the 1970s and strengthened since the 1990s: "The Social", as Robert Castel takes it (2003), is constantly in a transformation process since then: the welfare arrangement are focusing the population of a nation state. The post-welfare-arrangements are focusing smaller groups of neighborhood-, family- or ethnic communities, which are (re)called to take over self responsibility for their daily life conduct. An inclusive system displaces the integrated system, we could conclude. It is not possible to adequately grasp these recent shifts in the power-knowledge complex as they are discussed and implemented in many instances with reference to the design of social work with a power-theoretical investigation (see Kessl & Otto, 2003).

New control measures propagate, for example, the democratization of supporting structures through "flat hierarchies," "employee participation," or "self evaluation," thus offering at least a semantic "less control" and "more freedom." The analysis of the achieved gain in liberty for the participating actors, however, is radically curtailed without consideration of the phenomenon that such renditions of self-management measures do not overcome relations of power and control, but instead, "merely" readjust the relationship between foreign- and self-management. Works dealing with the analysis of power, such as the studies of governmentality, present the analysis of making relational, the relations of historically specific social forms. These types of works are concerned with concretizing what it might mean when Foucault (2002), with reference to Bachelard's methods, makes the claim, of "trapping one's own culture" (p. 476).

At the end of *The History of Sexuality: The Will to Knowledge Vol. I*, Foucault (1999) writes that a "power technology aimed at life" has characterized the arrangement of social life in central Europe since the eighteenth century (p. 172). In conjunction with the Enlightenment, disciplinary societies became normalization societies, one could conclude from Foucault—although in an almost unseemly sequential straightening—that institutions of medicine, psychology, education, and public assistance arise for the regulation of the *body* of the *individual* and the *population*. In his ninth lecture of the academic year 1974/1975, which dealt with population groups designated as socially abnormal in the context of the study published in the same year, *Discipline and Punish*, Foucault (2003) quotes from the scholastic and pedagogic program of the philanthropies in the second half of the eighteenth century: "We need your children, it is said. Give them to us. We, like you, need these children to be normally formed. So, entrust them to us so that we may form them according to certain *norms* [italics added]" (p. 256). Children are the people who do not (yet) correspond with the arranged norms. Philanthropists thus, consistently and explicitly identify the *training* of norms as their educational program. Sociopedagogic measures have been conceived in the same manner since the onset of their institutionalization and professionalization in the nineteenth century: the goals of their interventionist measures are identified as norms. Hermann Nohl's comment with regard to the design of relations between the generations already aims at this, when in 1930, he added at the conclusion to his thoughts that he was concerned with the "continuity of the spirit" (p. 120). Consequently, several years later available for this purpose, with the implementation of the *Reichsjugendwohlfahrtsgesetzes (RJWG)* [German child welfare law], was the "Jugendfürsorge" (youth public assistance) and its current beneficiaries: primarily, the available programs in the area of educational assistance and youth social work. Until the present day, they are assigned with the task of performing sociopedagogic normalization. The Weimar ministerial advisor in the Ministry of the Interior, and parliamentary representative of the German Democratic Party (DDP) Gertrud Bäumer (1929) distinguishes in this sense between youth public assistance and youth social services:

> Understood as youth social services are all measures for *normal* children, for whom the state and society participate to facilitate the family's tasks. ... On the contrary, the term youth public assistance comprises such measures that in one way or another are concerned with abnormal situations and are to be implemented in a preventative, protective, or healing capacity. (p. 18).

Here, Bäumer makes tangible the program of a chronological hierarchical categorization of foreign and self-management as the *hierarchical ordering of homogenization and individualization strategies:* only when a certain degree of homogeneity is achieved is the growing generation also allowed a measure of individuality. At the same time, however, the "normalized" children and youth are allowed a certain measure of de-normalizing, a thus controlled game with "normality."

Youth Assistance as a Component of Governing the Social

The implementation of social work since the second third of the nineteenth century in the German confederacy and subsequently in the German empire is part of a governmental disposal that has been implemented in European nation states as "social policy" at various time periods and under different forms since the eighteenth century. The protagonists in sociopolitical programs were so successful in thematizing the concretization gaps between a structure based on a division of labor and different future models, that, consequently, state regulation of the identified social problems, and thereby constructed, found a base as a necessary measure for stabilization of civil society. According to Kevin Stenson (1993), professional social work can therefore be described as "an element of productive governmental practises which create and operate within regimes of truth" (p. 42).

Yet, when social work carries out governmental actions, or to put it differently, stages and administers normalization processes, is there anything that can be done beyond a submission into the structure of power? Do power analytical reflections therefore lead us to resignation with regard to a project of social work, for example as Thomas Rauschenbach and Rainer Treptow assume?

The communication theory perspective, which is anchored in the German language theory through the tradition of the explicit and also implicit reception of Habermas's *Theorie Kommunikativen Handelns* [Theory of Communicative Action] and the associated discourse ethics do not allow for reflection from an analysis of power.[2] Harmonizing models of consensual negotiation ("roundtables," "district conferences," "citizen forums," or "interdisciplinary case study conferences") dominate debates in an area that is not only permanently confronted by what are in part radical social stratification and marginalization processes, but is also first granted legitimacy through the manufacture and symbolization of such social problem areas. The *lines of conflict* that run through these types of arrangements can thus first be made visible when they are understood as interaction situations, conflict-laden because heterogeneous in terms of interest and stratified through the historically specific relations of power and control. In his inimitable, almost sarcastic manner, in *Politics and Ethics*, Foucault (1994b) replies to the question of the stipulations for consensus: " I would go so far as to say that perhaps one should not be for mutual consent, but instead against non-consent" (p. 707).

The task in putting together sociopedagogical arrangements is to make it possible to see the logic of structuring underlying professional sociopedagogical (governmental) actions that permanently reproduce it. The convictions on which this conduct is based are the result of historically specific, thus particular agreements for the arranging of the social realm. In other words, dominant interpretations display a certain ethical filling of universal gaps. The sociopedagogical challenge comprises realizing an inevitable particular content and its connection to an equally inevitable intangible universality. It could be pointed out: Power and control analytical perspectives rather than perspectives from communication theory, are inevitable. Social work does not escape from the structures of power. It is a constitutive part of the governing of the social. Nonetheless, from this perspective, the conclusion is not that it has to submit to the structures of power. Instead, it must help its users to become as independent as possible—yet, *within* the structure of power. For in the end, it is about the skill of not governing and not being governed in such a sociopedagogic way.

[Translation: Lisa Rosenblatt]

Notes

1   All quotes from Foucault are translated from German.
2   A definitional attempt still effective today describes social work as an intermediary institution between system and environment.

Bibliography

Bäumer, G. (1929). Das Jugendwohlfahrtswesen. In N. Hermann & L. Pallat (Eds.), *Handbuch der Pädagogik, Fünfter Band,* (pp. 18–26). Langensalza: Beltz.

Brumlik, M. (1992). *Advokatorische Ethik: zur Legitimation pädagogischer Eingriffe.* Bielefeld: Karin Böllert.

Castel, R. (2003) *L'insécurité sociale. Qu'est ce qu'être protégé?.* Paris: La République des Idées/Seuil.

Detel, W. (1998). *Macht, Moral, Wissen: Foucault und die klassische Antike.* Frankfurt: Suhrkamp.

Fink-Eitel, H. (1997). *Michel Foucault zur Einführung,* (3rd ed.). Hamburg: Junius.

Foucault, M. (1978). Wahrheit und Macht. In M. Foucault, *Dispositive der Macht* (pp. 21–54). Berlin: Merve.

————. (1994a) *Discipline and punish: The birth of the prison* (A. Sheridan, Transl.). New York: Vintage Books (Original work published in 1979).

————. (1994b). Politik und Ethik. *Deutsche Zeitschrift für Philosophie,* 42(4), 703–708.

————. (1994c). Das Subjekt und die Macht. In H. Dreyfus & P. Rabinow (Eds.), *Michel Foucault: jenseits von Strukturalismus und Hermeneutik* (pp. 243–261), (2nd ed.). Frankfurt a.M.: Beltz Athenäum.

————. (1999). Der Wille zum Wissen: Sexualität und Wahrheit, Band 1.Frankfurt a.M.: Suhrkamp.

————. (2000). Der Gebrauch der Lüste: Sexualität und Wahrheit, Band 2, (6th ed.). Frankfurt a.M.: Suhrkamp.

————. (2002). Seine eigene Kultur in die Falle locken. In M. Foucault, *Schriften in vier Bänden. Dits et Ecrits.* Band II, 1970–1975, 476–477. Frankfurt a.M.: Suhrkamp.

————. (2003). *Abnormal, lectures at the College de France (1974–1975)* (G. Burchell, Transl.). New York: Picador.

Habermas, J. (1998). *Der philosophische Diskurs der Moderne* (6th ed.). Frankfurt a.M.: Suhrkamp.

Heydorn, H-J. (1970). *Über den Widerspruch von Bildung und Herrschaft.* Frankfurt a.M.: Suhrkamp.

Kessl, F. (2005). *Der Gebrauch der eigenen Kräfte: eine Gouvernementalität Sozialer Arbeit,* Weinheim/Munich: Juventa.

Kessl, F., and Otto, H-U. (2003). Freed to pursue a new illusion? The new privatization of social services [retrieved on December 19th, 2005 from] *http://www.uni-bielefeld.de/paedagogik/agn/ag8/Freed%20to%20pursue%20a%20new%20illusion.pdf*

Krasmann, S. (2003). *Die Kriminalität der Gesellschaft. Zur Gouvernementalität der Gegenwart,* Konstanz: UVK.

Lemke, T. (1997). *Eine Kritik der politischen Vernunft: Foucault Analyse der modernen Gouvernementalität.* Berlin, Hamburg: Argument.

Nohl, H. (1930). Das Verhältnis der Generationen in der Pädagogik. In H. Nohl, *Pädagogische Aufsäatze* (pp. 111–120) (2nd ed.). Langensalza: Beltz (Original work published in 1914).

Peukert, D. J-K. (1986). *Grenzen der Sozialdisziplinierung: Aufstieg und Krise der deutschen Jugendfürsorge von 1878 bis 1932,* Cologne: Bund.

Rauschenbach, T., and Treptow, R. (1984). Sozialpädagogische Reflexivität und gesellschaftliche Rationalität. Überlegungen zur Konstitution sozialpädagogischen Handelns. In S. Müller, H-U. Otto, H. Peter & H. Sünker (Eds.), *Handlungskompetenz in der Sozialarbeit/Sozialpädagogik II: theoretische Konzepte und gesellschaftliche Strukturen* (pp. 21–71). Bielefeld: AJZ.

Rehmann, J. (2003). Vom Gefängnis zur moderne Seele: Foucaults 'Überwachen und Strafen' neu besichtigt. *Das Argument,* Vol. 45(249), 63–81.

Reitz, T. (2003). Die Sorge um sich und niemand anderen. *Das Argument,* Vol. 45(249), 82–97.

Stenson, K. (1993). Social work discourse and the social work interview. *Economy and Society,* Vol. 22(1), 42–76.

Winkler, M. (1988). *Eine Theorie der Sozialpädagogik: über Erziehung als Rekonstruktion der Subjektivität.* Stuttgart: Klett-Cotta.

❧ Chapter 8 ❧

The "Intrapreneur" and the "Mother": Strategies of "Fostering" and "Developing" the Entrepreneur of the Self in Organizational Development and Affirmative Action

Susanne Maria Weber

Introduction

In the German private industry organizational development and affirmative action for women are current concepts of institutional change. This article[1] offers a perspective which focuses on the practice of normalization of subjects as well as the reconstruction of organizational cultures. "PowerKnowledge" becomes the central category. With the logic of "loosely coupled systems" a link between discourse analysis and organizational development is made (Weber, 1998; Weber, 2000). Whereas the rationality found in organizational development creates the intrapreneur as the in-company entrepreneur, the currently dominating initiatives of affirmative action for women in Germany see women as "entrepreneurs of the family." Both concepts stress the principle of "support and development" of human resources.

Different organizations use the possibilities of both concepts in different ways. Organization-specific varieties of screenplay knowledge, that is, of the rationality current concepts are based on, are established. Specific strategies for each company become apparent. The organizations deal in their specific ways with this knowledge, and they can be integrated in the typology of "market," "clan" and "bureaucracy."

In concepts of organizational development and their realization, entrepreneurial rationality can be analyzed in an educational mode of betterment. Therefore, educational knowledge has to be questioned: In which way and through which practical intervention can it have normalizing effects? It has the task to optimize the efficiency of human resources. It constructs the life-long learning "entrepreneur of himself" in strategies of organizational development. At the same time, we see the strategy of "fostering and developing" human resources in the mother as "entrepreneur of the family," who is responsible for the optimization of the child's qualities through education. This knowledge is strategic knowledge because it forms the nexus between the economy and the population (Weber 2006a). In this way, educational knowledge can be described as normalizing knowledge within a dispositive of power (Foucault 1978a,b,c). This dispositive of power is no longer equal to the pyramidal form of the mechanical "bureaucracy" but equals instead the net-shaped model of power of the "market." At the level of a discourse analytic constructivism the organization possesses the status of a scenery where the "norm" can display itself (Weber 2006b). The concept of 'human resource" assigns a new position to subject and gender difference. In the structure of the "market," difference is no longer a deficit as it was within the logic of the organizational structure of the "bureaucracy"; it is also no longer a border as in the concept of the "clan." In fact, it is a resource within the scope of a "management of diversity" (Weber 1999).

The organizational form and rationality of the "net" is all around. In his book "The Corrosion of Character" ("Der flexible Mensch") Richard Sennett (1998) impressively describes a new organizational model that becomes clear through the following example of work organization in economy. Let us imagine the mile long Ford factory: on the left, the incoming raw material in front of the factory gate, then miles of construction and assembly streets, and on the right, the finished product, a car. The foreman gives instructions, the construction is divided into parts, every person performs one movement and hands the partly finished product down the line. The time schedule is strictly rhythmic, the organizational structure of the work is the same every day. In contrast to this, we find the organizational model of the network. In Bill Gates' programming center various teams work in parallel on the development of a new program. They work late nights. No hierarchies, no sequentially organized work, no clocks on the wall: everybody runs against time and in-house competition. Only the best one of the teams wins the contract—the others lose the game.

This organizational model of competitive networks is not only present in the economy. The net as a new basic pattern appears in many fields like global political science, technology and social debate as well as in the natural sciences. Everywhere it becomes the basis for interpretations of "world explanations" (Weber, 1999). How is this to be regarded and evaluated? Are new concepts of management, new concepts of deliberative models of politics, of shaping social life only a new fashion, a new myth? And which status does this knowledge possess in the context of global modernization dynamics? Will there be a global tendency of the homogenization of management concepts?

Within the German contexts I searched for the rationalities behind the concepts and models of organization. I found the reinforced thesis that the "bureaucracy" and "net" models are based on rationalities that oppose each other and that the "net" seems to become more and more the dominating rationality of social behavior. The following results are based on an empirical study in which the new concepts of management were researched as knowledge repertoires in an epistemological sense. Using Foucault's method of discourse analysis (1992), they were analyzed as "surfaces of a discourse", which become sociologically relevant. Combining the methodological approach of discourse analysis with grounded theory (Strauss 1991), the empirical application of this discursive practice in different types of businesses in the private economy was analyzed.

I first found that the new organizational model of the net dispositive represents a new type of power. Such knowledge goes along with subjectivating effects of power. This makes it obvious that it is not enough to stay within an affirmative or ideologically critical argumentation. It is necessary to ask for rationalities. According to Foucault (1988), this is the only effective criticism:

> The criticism of power enforced on lunatics can not be limited to psychiatric institutions: those who question the right to punish cannot be satisfied with denouncing prisons as totalitarian institutions. The question is how such power relationships are rationalized, as this is the only way to prevent other institutions with equal goals and to the same effects from taking their place. (p. 66)

The analysis of operating power is an analysis of strategic operations. It examines in which way knowledge interacts with new concepts of change and how it is able to re-actualize its meaning. Closely connected to this are questions about how specific power-knowledge becomes successful, how it reaches hegemonic position and how power-knowledge secures its existence. Similarly, one has to examine which knowledge supplies lose the battle for definition power (Hörster, 1993).

Therefore, Foucault (1978b) searches for the "tactics" of knowledge and its "games" (p. 65). By doing so he replaces a juridical (law-oriented) and negative (failing) matrix with a strategic, polycentric and process-oriented model of power (Foucault, 1978c). The analytical method as well as Foucault's model of power allows learning more about the relationship between economic, educational and cultural knowledge supplies. The method of discourse analysis systematically uses the "foreign view" on the obvious, the self-evident, on the myth of everyday life (Barthes, 1964). Foucault´s perspective on the "surfaces", where a discourse appears, allows to look as well for "identified problems" as for "identified solutions" (Weber 1998). We find both not only in organizational development debates, but as well in comments on the state of the family. So it will be shown, that power knowledge creates two different positions of subjects – "intrapreneur" and "mother". As we will see, problems are diverse and can be met in the organization – and in the family.

Diagnosis of Problems: Risk, Increase of Complexity, and Failure of Control

In current diagnoses the world looks extremely complicated. The current social debate for example, is about the increasing risk of a modernization dynamic that becomes independent and uncontrollable. The solutions of the past are the problems of today. Institutional strategies of problem solving create new problems which are barely calculable, accountable and adjustable. In the face of growing side effects of instrumental action, failure of control and increasing complexity are diagnosed. Research and practice deal with the questions of *if* and *how* the unpredictable can become predictable.

Risk

Risk has to be calculated even if it can no longer be limited and foreseeable. From this point of view, Society has become a "risk society" (Beck 1986)

> The entrance into risk society takes place in the very moment when socially decided and therefore socially produced dangers dissolve the valid security systems of already existing risk calculations of the welfare state: atomic, chemical, ecological and genetic engineering risks are, unlike the risk of the early industrial age, a) neither to be delimited locally or temporarily, b) incalculable according to the rules of causality, guilt and liability, c) irreparable and uninsurable (Beck, 1993, p. 451).

The category of risk refers to the life of subjects and their identity, to institutional change, to nation state strategies as well as to global development. Every strategy of action turns into a risky project holding creative powers as well as the possibility of failure. Problems expand into existence-threatening risks. Risk is not only crucial at national level – in sociological debate, the world itself turns into a world risk society (Beck, 1997). Risk is being identified as well at organizational level as in families.

Increase of Complexity

In this debate, risks are no longer limitable or under control. In this context, the discussion about "unintended consequences" which are no longer foreseeable and calculable, about the so-called "paradoxes of instrumental activism," has started. This leads to the confrontation with the fact that partial, reductive strategies do not provide solutions but only create new problems. Institutional action suffers from public distrust; Beck describes this as organized irresponsibility.

The situation is marked by the fast increase of social problems and challenges as well as by the recognition of the fact that 5 to 6 billion human beings are touched by these problems (Gruppe Von Lissabon 1997; 20). They affect all areas: politics, economy, culture and ecology. "The new environmental dangers are global, they have effects far away from their place of origin and are sometimes invisible: large scale destruction, the hole in the ozone layer, polar melting, pollution of the oceans" (Beck 1997; 9). Problematic situations cannot be solved by using the causal logic strategies of instrumental action anymore. The aim is not to think in cause-effect relations but to reach an understanding of effect chains. In organizational development like in affirmative action programs, increase of complexity is regarded as a problem.

Failure of Control

A third aspect becomes apparent: failure of control. It is a pattern of perception concerning global development as well as organizational action. This problem produces categories of loss of controllability at different levels of action. For Messner (1998), there is a danger of "downward spirals intensifying each other" (p. 35) in the drifting apart of rich and poor in economical integration and social out-casting: "Worldwide tax cut cycles and financial crises of states resulting from that, deregulation races, wage dumping, social and environmental dumping" (ibid.) increasingly narrow the scope of action for structuring social politics. The world seems to go haywire. Are the risks of a continuing increase of complex interrelations still controllable? If so, how? Between apocalyptic scenarios and euphoric descriptions of the future there is an agreement that the old control mechanisms do not work anymore. A fast-changing world—so the "common sense"—needs control mechanisms which are different from the established bureaucratic routines.

Businesses are discussed as more and more often at risk of being exposed to public politics. In an increasingly insecure world even industrial projects become a political undertaking (Beck, 1997b). They are forced to communicate (Münch, 1992). Beck sees the institutions of the nation state of the modern industrial age in a deep crisis (reflexive modernization). The old coalition for progress loses the trust it enjoyed before (Beck, 1997b).

Risks, increase of complexity and failure of control in discourse and as problems are equally relevant on the level of local, world and organizational action. On the organizational level the risk is seen as the inability to compete because of rigid and bureaucratic organizational structures. In a world of rapid change the one-sided orientation towards securing the "status quo" is regarded as dysfunctional. "Bureaucracy" is more and more seen as static, hierarchic and segmented. Looking at the families´ side, the traditional model of a hierarchical and patriarchal relationships is not acceptable any more. The ideal of the egalitarian couple and the egalitarian relationship between children and parents arises – as well in privacy, traditional forms of control seem to loose terrain.

Old and New Power-Knowledge of Control: "Bureaucracy" and "Market"

Bureaucracy and market are two organizational models and with them two rationalities that are diametrically opposed to each other. The organization typology according to Ouchi et al (1993) differentiates between "bureaucracy," "market" and "clan." Whereas bureaucracy is based on official channels, promotion, specialization and hierarchy, the clan focuses on involvement, profit-sharing, counseling, consensus, seniority and lifelong employment. The market, on the other hand, bases the involvement of its employees on a pronounced achievement-orientation, a hiring and firing practice according to its momentary needs, a payment system based on achievement and jobs for a single person or a team.

In the scientific as well practitioners´ debate about organizational development the ideal cases of bureaucracy and market contrast with each other. The bureaucratic apparatus is criticized for being overly controlled, innovatively weak, rigid, overcomplicated and overstabilized. Because of their "following the rules" policies, their orientation towards security and the calculated achievement willingness of their employees, organizations are seen as unable to fulfill today's requirements. Public bureaucracies, in particular, are accused of political failure. Their institutionalized state power is perceived as obstructive and foiling (Jaenicke, 1986). They are criticized for their oversized staff and administrative machineries, the doubling of working procedures and excessive precision and control. By separating theoretical and practical work, the specific knowledge and innovative power of their subordinates seem to be left unused, their efficiency prevented to unfold (Bosetzky & Heinrich, 1980).

The organizational structure of bureaucracy is criticized to gear decisions and abilities to the top and relations to be linear. Bureaucracy is said to function regardless of people, because it sees human beings as a factor of insecurity that needs to be controlled. It is criticized to slow down human initiative: any independence of mind is immediately drawn back on the track of regulations and procedures. Bureaucracy prevents any self-initiated movement of the employ-ees. This "undemocratic quality" of employees' treatment is questioned. Bu-reaucracy is said to be about order and obedience; to be also about fellowship but only in an impersonal and abstract way. It is said, that it forms a complex formal frame of regulations with defined responsibilities, division of labor, refined job descriptions and given channels of procedure. Operations are "arti-ficially fixed, repeatable, calculable and can be taken over by others" (Kühl, 1994, p. 28). The tasks are fragmented and segmented and all procedures are formalized. Bureaucracy focuses on calculability, precision, reliability and abso-lute expectancy security. Routine dominates the daily business. In the "me-chanical bureaucracy" no space exists for exceptions and "extra tours." It links human beings like gears in mechanical procedures. The mechanical bureaucracy operates, it does not fight. It is designed for stability, not for change. It is static and stays like it is, regardless of profit and loss.

A new flexible organizational model is set up against this hierarchic, seg-menting and static practice. It is regarded as suitable to encounter the risks of increasing complexity and uncontrollability and is propagated as an emergency anchor for the effectiveness of institutional action. The logic of production and organization has changed. Now, subjects are supposed to act autonomously, to be team-oriented and to structure organizational action in a process-oriented way. The changed concepts of production are said to arise from the organiza-tional need of qualitatively different mechanisms of coordination (Esser, 1992). It is no longer about quantity but about quality at the lowest cost. This is to be achieved by organizing structures flexibly and integrating functions instead of segmenting them (Boyer, 1992).

Quality control should therefore no longer take place at the end but has to be integrated in production process. The organizational ideal is no longer py-ramidal but net-shaped. The obedience to the order of hierarchic structures is confronted with an "entrepreneur of himself." The old department borders are confronted with the border crossing structures of teams and the bureaucratic form of organization focused on keeping up the "status quo" has to compete against the "continuous process of improvement."

Economic Networks: Intrapreneurs, Teams and the Continuous Process of Improvement

When searching the current management literature about organizational devel-opment it is impossible to avoid "net" figure (Weber, 1998). There is a demand for open and flexible organizational structures which determine as few things as possible in advance. Or as the organization consultant Kühl (1994) puts it: "Communication processes have to be organized in a network of feedback loops. The final consequence of this is that organizations are no longer formed structures but turn into an ever-changing process of feedback and improvement" (p. 133).

According to this the old organizational model of bureaucracy has to step down; and the "market" model based on the net principle is celebrated. This model relies on complete competition and does not aim at keeping up the status quo. The organization of work is oriented towards holistically defined tasks and self-coordination within groups (Staehle, 1988).

People ideally have to be entrepreneurs (intrapreneurs) in a market. This market exists inside as well as outside the company. The in-company market transforms former colleagues into "service providers" and "clients" (Moldaschl & Schultz-Wild, 1994, p. 23). This market model modifies also the functions of departments and their interaction with each other. Departments are restructured into profit-centers. The concept of profit-centers is based on decentralization and the localization of management. Each unit is autonomous and economically responsible for itself.

The American sociologist Richard Sennett (1998) notes:

> A cornerstone of modern management is the belief that loosely linked networks are more open to fundamental restructuring than the pyramidal hierarchies which dominated the Ford era. The connection between the central points is loose, you can remove parts without destroying other parts, at least in theory. The system is fragmented, this provides a possibility for intervention (p. 60). The basic principle of the net is flexibility. The campaign for institutional change is led under the guiding term of flexibility. (p. 62)

Sennett marks flexibility as belonging to a system of power, which consists of the elements of discontinuous restructuring of institutions, flexible differentiation of production and the concentration of power without centralization.

Here the two models confront each other at the conceptual level. This leaves the question of *if* and *how* the new rationality of management is realized in institutional contexts and which relevance it can claim by doing so. In the following section three examples of organization will clarify the variance of the net rationality. They are not singular examples or cases that can be transferred to the models of bureaucracy, clan, and market. The three categories cannot be limited to the social sector: all of them can also be found in state, economy and civic society sectors. Nevertheless, they stand for different qualities and resources with regard to marketability and the resources of solidarity and equality. In a governmentality perspective, they belong to different regimes of power –

state reason, "policy" and "market". As it will be shown, they go along with positionings of subjects along sex (Weber 2006a).

Organizational Models Bureaucracy, Clan and Market

In bureaucracy all procedures are organized formally through formal channels and are independent of the flow of information. They are based on habit, predictability and dependability. Procedures and decisions should be calculable and transparent.

The 1980s and 1990s saw the development of new aims and guiding principles for bureaucratic organizations as well. Concepts like "total quality management" were designed to increase the competitive capacity of businesses. They needed to adapt to the market and improve their marketing and "striking power." The functional apparatus of bureaucracies is now seen as "blown up" and in need of a "trim down." Former departments are turned into profit-centers and even the upper management must change their self-conception. They have the task to become supporters of their employees: before the door was held open for the "boss," because of his seniority. Now, he is a service provider for his employees. The duration of employment is less important, and in case of a promotion seniority is less relevant. Orientation towards efficiency is considered to be of high priority. The especially talented are to be supported. Evaluation of employees, an instrument that had worked exclusively top-down, is now used from down below to the top. Even the management has to prove its capability.

Balanced cooperation between equals is on demand but the newly created internal entrepreneurs politicize in order to support their own interest. Executives use restructuring measures for their own ends. Instead of team-work and cooperation the principle of competition takes effect. The focus is not on the interest of the organization but on the interest of one's own department. Instead of leveling off hierarchies' rationalization, intensification of work and outsourcing take place. The aim of orientation towards development remains unfulfilled. There is no time left over for the active participation of the employees in the processes of change or in job related continuing education.

The clan organizational model is often found in family businesses or in specialized high-performance organizations (e.g., in the computer industry). As already implied in the name, clan is based on familiarity and personal relationships. It is, therefore, the counterpart to bureaucracy. The clan model deals not with formalized procedures and clear definitions of tasks, but with improvisation, situational decision making, "management by muddling through." Since there are hardly any formal regulations, the clan can operate in the market very fast and *ad hoc*. The clan deals with increased profit through enacting the community. The clan aims at offering its employees a home and a family and works with solidarity as a resource. Peace within the company, harmony between employees and a good social climate matter greatly.

Formal legal grounds form the bases for employment contracts, yet individual solutions win over the collectively organized employee representation. The employer acts in value-oriented ways towards actual situations and people. He controls his business through "management by wandering around." The "boss" sees himself as "father." The clan model stresses the principle of "shepherd and herd." The shepherd pays constant attention and escorts his herd at all time. He corrects deviations and looks out for lost sheep. He keeps his flock together.

Whereas the clan is based on the principle of loyalty and care, of shepherd and herd, the market is about total competition. In this system nobody is equal and top performances are reached: high individual performance equals higher individual profit. Organizational development is not introduced by chance and *ad hoc* decisions, but is instead practiced systematically. A steady increase of the general business performance is to be reached through organizational counseling. Employees integrate this system in a different way than in the clan. The structure of the clan distributes the company's needs equally to all employees; the market on the contrary, focuses on employees' abilities and individual resources. Everybody has to contribute something. One does not look for individuals' weaknesses, but for each persons' strengths to support and develop them.

The net forms the organizational model of the market. Aims are set and pursued strategically. All factors of success are systematically examined and included in the plans: in the service sector, for example, location, shop fittings, uniforms, smiling employees, etc. are seen as important success factors. The client should feel comfortable. The feel of small trade or handicraft is gone: the logo, the designer equipment, employee's clothing and the style of advertisement signalizes professionalization.

The concept works. Support of human resources, accompaniment of processes, increasing competition and provision of incentives in combination with technical control is the secret of success of the expanding "market". The ideas and the feedback of the employees are integrated in a continuous process of improvement. Recognition of employees and appreciation of achievement are of high importance. At the same time there is high pressure of success.

The market model focuses on what is useful and employable. Leadership is an emancipatory process where management becomes the service provider for its employees. The market supports and develops the potentials of its employees to increase company's success. Continuing education has to impart "process competence" and "extra-functional qualifications." Employees should develop a self-perception as lifelong learning personalities. They constantly monitor themselves and work on their continuing improvement. Yet, in this model, there is no time left over for a life outside of work.

Educational Knowledge, the Self-Improving Subject and the Position of Norm

The following matrix shows the position of educational knowledge within the discourse of optimization and betterment and the positioning of the "intrapreneur" and the "mother". The bureaucracy, market and clan "deal" represent different modes of power-knowledge and its institutional representations. Bureaucracy is still based on hierarchy, segmentation and static structures and it works with the formalization and the separation of public and private. The clan is based on a principle of low formalization. It integrates the working subject in a kind of "family-based" education, in a homogenous "entrepreneurial unity." The market on the other hand, favors the self-improving subject left to the educational knowledge of support and development.

These three organizational models represent different forms of power which oppose each other diametrically: the rationality of the pyramidal power and the rationality of the power of the "net" (Weber 1998), in which the educational knowledge of support and development gains a central function. In the third organizational model, the market, a new model of control appears, described by Sennett (1998) as flexible capitalism.

The educational knowledge has the task to generate this so-called self-improving subject. Yet, the control rationality described here is not to be handled in an affirmative or ideology-critical way. This rationality has a subjectivating quality and "passes the inner parts of the body" (Foucault 1978c). It does not enact a repressive model of power, but one, which activates human capital.

Organizat- ional Model	Practice	Modus	Form	Pedagogical Aspect	Difference and Position of Women	Position of the Subject
Bureaucracy	Order	formalism and law	pyramid	execution	marginalization and outsourcing	Receptor of orders
Clan	Advice	community and moral	circle	inclusion	Integration / marginalization	member of a community

Market	Incentive	competition and profit	net	support and development	Defining, employing / using	Entrepreneurial subject

Approaches of "management" arise as pendants to the possibilities of extensive technological control and systematical networking. In this way, the focus of new executive concepts shifts from case-oriented towards subject-oriented management. To the degree to which control functions are covered by technological means, personnel management becomes primarily a communicative task. Control is combined with material incentives based on achievement-oriented payment. In personal relationships the creation of incentives can be crucial. The de-individualization opens up space for human warmth, for primary pedagogical relations in which trust becomes an employable resource. Preventive management is therefore based on communication and process-oriented control. This applies to the level of subjects as well as to the levels of teams and organizational units. As "inner communities of achievement" teams are economical and social units of achievement at the same time. Applying such an understanding of organization, management becomes a task of development and support. While the manager becomes a "supporter and developer" and "service provider" to his staff, a mentor of personal development, the employee becomes an "entrepreneur of his own development" while competing with others.

This practice of power is pedagogical, supportive, connecting and demonstrative. It makes non-communication a high risk. Therefore, preventive management has to be designed as a continuous monitoring of processes. Through the concept of lifelong learning the subject becomes the self-improving subject that has to emancipate and develop itself constantly. Thus, the subject is seen as a "pedagogical subject." Through the appeal "Success is within you!" the subject becomes an "authentic subject in process." At the same time, the actually contradictory imperatives of "invent yourself" and "know thyself" come into action. They can be characterized as a practice of self-definition and self-examination, which is at the same time constructive and investigative. In this sense business develops into a learning laboratory. In the pedagogical knowledge of support and development the old practice of confession in both its religious and secular meaning comes in. The development of the personality serves the creation of insights into the inner self. Belief is secularized and focused on the subject which now—being divine— has to create itself in regard to self-realization and success. Therefore, educational knowledge becomes knowledge of creation.

The self-perception of such an entrepreneur-employee relationship is socially enacted through the educational knowledge, the norm of lifelong learning, and is offered as a concept of identity. Here the norm displays itself. It does not only have an influence on business but becomes relevant as a general social pattern of behavior as well as an option and appeal for new concepts of identity. Thus, educational knowledge takes over a systemical and strategic position in the power-knowledge complex of the current knowledge of change. It is regulating knowledge within a new "knowledge repertoire" or "dispositive of power."

The Tactics: Self-Organization, Trust and Learning

The pedagogical knowledge of the market functions within the power dispositive of the net. Its mechanisms are self-organization, trust and learning. This pedagogical knowledge embodies itself in the figure of the intrapreneur as the self-organized learning personality, and in the relationship between employee and manager as a pedagogical relationship. The intrapreneur is able to survive the competition in the market. Such an employee becomes a human resource and no longer receives orders. He counts as company "capital," which could not develop its full potentials within inflexible hierarchies and narrow rules (Fuchs & Besier, 1996). All employees are included in a constant process of improvement. They are subjects to lifelong learning. The conception of personality applied here uses the basic pattern of a "flexible self" (Sennett, 1998). This is based on the picture that a person is generally able to change throught his life, as long as he just gets enough chances to do so (Türk, 1981). Increasingly, subjects as well as organizations are labeled as learning systems. Learning and working no longer separate nor are they sequential phases. Instead, they merge into one another: working is learning (Sülzer & Zimmermann, 1996).

In considering growing risks, increase of complexity and failure of control, learning becomes a new coping strategy as well as a new control mechanism. As the following section shows, the concept of "support and development" turns into control knowledge and a mode of action for institutional strategies, in order to increase efficiency.

The Tactic of Self-Organization

The self-organizing "entrepreneur of the self" is no longer in the position of an alienated subject. He "realizes himself" through aspiration and self-perception.

In the network organization autonomous units and profit-centers are loosely linked together. They can act flexibly and independently from other parts of the system. Through inherent activity and far-reaching self-regulation of all relatively independent units regulation is optimized. The needs of each situation can not only highly expedite but shape the ability of the whole system to react and act proactively. Thus, the system is less guided through rules and regulations and works in a process-oriented way instead.

In the context of an organization this autonomy is ambivalent. According to the principle of the net, decentralization and de-hierarchization create a power shift from a centralized to a polycentric pattern. Because of this polycentric structure the system becomes more efficient and vulnerable at the same time. The inherent activity can quickly change into an inherent dynamic where the intrapreneur could start to represent his own interests instead of those of the organization, thereby becoming political and incalculable (A classical example are the sudden moves of managers and scientists to the "competitor"). Men become a risk for the system. The whole organization grows into a world of conflicting interests. Therefore, net strategies hold many structural sources of conflict within them.

In this respect, solution strategies can equally be causes for problems: they add to the increase of incalculability and complexity as they carry their specific risks and new needs of regulation within them.

The Tactic of Trust

Preventive action can limit risks most efficiently as shown in what follows.

In order not to become a risk the apparent freedom has to be bound through mechanism of soft control.

> Whereas the creation of "profit-centers" is a strategy to increase organizational flexibility, networks are an approach of businesses to organize an insecure surrounding and stabilize it. Put differently, it deals with the integration of stabilizing organizational elements into turbulent and unstable surrounding relations. (Kühl, 1994, p. 52).

Teams, in practitioners´ managerial discourse visualized as sailing crews or jazz bands, build the corrective for the intrapreneur. Here, the binding powers of groups and teams act as a resource. The usefulness of teamwork is in the emotional quality of "localization," the resources of solidarity, but also in the dimension of avoidance of anonymity and therefore of social control. The new community concepts are not to be confused with "the old business ideology of the company as a family" (Esser, 1992, p. 158). The difference lies in the consistent orientation of the intrapreneur and of the group as a whole towards the mutual business' aim. Employees are links of a chain and not isolated "bearers of achievement" (Sommerlatte, 1996, p. 120). In this discourse, Teams should create solidarity, trust and social control.

Solidarity, trust and social control become control mechanisms which help to reduce the risk of control failure as found in the current literature about organizational development: "Everyday we try to be guided by the following: network instead of hierarchies, regulatory and feedback loops instead of rules, change instead of inflexibility, responsibility instead of jurisdiction, participation instead of control" (Ploenzke, 1996, p. 158f).

The company is designed as a "village community". Freedom and commitment have to be brought into a sensible balance. "How is it possible to make business a hierarchy-free area/space? How is it possible to become a home for creative people?" (Ploenzke, 1996, p. 155f). The protagonists of the "world society" also demand the team and cooperation principle. Problems are only regarded as solvable if the protagonists orientate themselves toward a common solution (Messner, 1994, 1998). Neither the self-organization of the intrapreneurs and their integration in "loosely coupled" teams nor the preventive securing of their functional behavior for the organization via the "trust" resource can take into account process orientation and systemic securing. Those demands are met by the "learning" factor.

The Tactic of Learning

Subjects as well as organizations need to become the designers of their lives, their identity and their image. The possibility to shape creates a pressure to give shape. Facing high risks, increasing complexity and loss of control, the question of "which way is the best?" becomes more and more important. Under the pressure of rapid change and unpredictable developments linear structures turn out to be more and more suboptimal. Therefore, strategies have to be flexible and need to adapt situatively and temporarily. They follow the principle of process orientation and temporality.

Learning facilitates the shaping and optimization of processes. Teams connect achievement with learning (Katzenbach & Smith, 1993). Characteristics of learning are open-mindedness, non-linearity, information processing, integration of errors and feedback loops. Learning seems to be a net-shaped, holistic process of information in the brain. Capra (1996) explicitly describes the relation between the net paradigm and learning:

> Because communication networks are able to create feedback loops, they are also able
> to generate the ability of self-regulation. For example a community which keeps up an
> active net of communication will be able to learn from errors, because consequences
> will spread through the net and return to the starting point. This enables the commu-
> nity to correct errors and to arrange and organize itself. (p. 101)

However, it becomes apparent that learning has a much more comprehensive significance. For example, the performance of every single unit is important for a successful general outcome. The performance of each single "cell of
an organism," of each subject or protagonist within a network, of each business
in a strategic alliance becomes important and is object to optimization. Closely
connected with the subject of networking is the question of competencies. "In
order to reach optimal results, we have to support creativity and communication" (Ploenzke, 1996, p. 153). The guiding principle is that of the self-
organized, net-able and learning individual. It is a

> player with a new kind of reason. Individuals and organizations who are ready to de-
> velop this kind of spirit, are those who participate in a new kind of game after their de-
> cision. And it is individuals and organizations which allow all of us to make the profit
> usable for everyone, which means to take home the marbles, when the world is chang-
> ing fast. (Lynch & Kordis, 1992, p. 25).

In connection with the competence of networking and doing it to the right
degree, learning is of special significance. Considering systems where learning is
not a risk, it can become a partly complementary strategy. Learning at the level
of subjects, organizations and organizational networks can take remedial action
against such risks. For example, in connection with networking of organizations there is a demand for "cooperation instead of competition" or put differently for "co-opetition". This new kind of relationship becomes a learning
object for subjects and organizations and a comprehensive strategy of systemic
securing, based on a rationality of prevention and "loosely coupled systems."

Strategies of "Freedom" "Loosely Coupled Systems" and "Systemic Securing"

The self-driven activity of the intrapreneur, the organization linked through
powerful teams, the permanently learning employees and the constantly self-
optimizing organization are elements of a discourse-strategy.

The Strategy of Prevention

What type of rationality is prevention based on? Prevention defines types of risks and presumes that they worsen if no intervention takes place. Early and/or timely interventions promise to reduce risks. In preventive strategies measures are established and conceptualized as "aids." Such standard problem is institutionalized and urges other organizations to develop similar measures. Thus, the interests and "real needs" of those who are affected are accounted for (Hellerich & Wambach, 1983). Prevention develops into a form of interaction that aims at delimiting the incalculable and preventing possible ills through social measures and a practice of insurance. Prevention as meta-interaction aims at deciding on the process of interaction for oneself (Schülein, 1983).

Which role does the rationality of prevention play in organizational concepts? The integration of intrapreneurs into highly binding teams, the continuous learning of intrapreneurs and increased innovative powers of organization through learning are strategies of prevention. Also, process regulation, monitoring and controlling are preventive, thus during the whole process. They work with feedback loops, the permanent processing of information and the optimized knowledge supplies in order to handle the risks of increasing complexity and control failure.

The Strategy of Loosely Coupled Systems

What is the rationality of loosely coupled systems? The control model of rigid linkage does no longer function for systems of high complexity, because of high degrees of dependence. "The more rigid the parts of a system are linked together, the higher is the possibility that local disorders affect additional parts of the system" (Perrow, 1987, p. XI). The principle of loosely coupled systems proves to be superior to the principle of rigidly coupled systems, because the former can occur independently from each other. It is built on self-controlling units, which participate in the process together, but without being in a cause-effect relation (Perrow, 1987). The principle of networking is itself the principle of loose linkage of parts of the system that are independent from each other.

How is the principle of loosely coupled systems applied in concepts of organizational development? New strategies strictly avoid inflexible structures (Weber, 1998) as shown with the example of tools of behavior control.

> The soft method of behavior control through myth (mental programs) takes into account, that goals as well as acting conditions in organizations are ambiguous, complex, and contradictory, which leads to the introduction of vague blanket clauses like 'discre-

tionary powers', 'intuition', 'common sense', 'taking chances' etc. to ensure capability of action in cases of norm collisions. (Neuberger, as cited in Weber 1998, p. 133).

Strong ties are always created through pictures whether in the discourse about networking in small nets in the social field, or the "company as village community," or whether the team business is pictured as a jazz band or sailing crew. The "fleeting procedure" of images corresponds with the principle of loosely coupled systems. The discoursively created images neither impose social norms nor moral rules. They act in regulated ways by letting images "flow," which has normalizing effects. "The power of relationship technologies is based on imposing nothing, neither new social norms nor old moral rules. It allows both to fleet against each other until a point of balance is reached" (Donzelot, 1979, p. 220).

The Strategy of Systemic Securing

The strategy of systemic securing integrates the tactics of freedom, commitment and learning. In this comprehensive securing strategy learning turns into an individual right. "Rights" correspond with "free choice"—you can claim them, they provide options for the subject. So, for example, at subjects's level this is called the right to continuing education. Through organizational learning complex systems are supposed to reflect and optimize their patterns of action (Weber, 1998). Systemic strategies work with comprehensive and totalitarian effects of power and control authorities. With optimization as orientation during the process the subject as well as the organization and the network must decipher their selves—to find their authentic self—and to get to know themselves. This approach draws near the old techniques of confession and to the Christian practice of reflection and confession. The subject, the organization and the network have to tell the truth about themselves. Communication has to be authentic and symmetric. Resources and tools of cooperation like trust, discoursive communication, negotiating and consensus come into action (Weber, 1998). They ensure transparence and trust, they serve the monitoring proc ess, supply the systemic point of view, the love for details and the possibility of correction through the feedback loops of learning systems. The dispositive of the net and its functional mechanisms can be displayed as shown in the following matrix.

Knowledge figure	Autonomy	Group	Development of the self
Identified problems	Hierarchy	Segmentation	static
Organizational development as institutional solution	Intrapreneur	team	continuous process of improvement
Identified risks	Politiciziation	loss of control	failure of control
Practice of knowledge tactics	self-organization and free will	trust and guiding models in social-economical networks	learning, support and development
Practice of knowledge: strategies	Prevention	loosely coupled systems	systemic securing

Management of Gender and Diversity in Economic Networks?

When searching the positions of "difference" and the "gender" category in the different models of organization, three different localizations become apparent: exclusion, marginalization and use. The discourse about differences equally contains gender, cultural and physical differences. Three positions appear here.

Negation and Exclusion of the Female: the "Bureaucracy"

Bureaucracy takes places in public space. Allegedly neutral, public space proves to be a men' s club where female authority is not symbolized. There is no space for "privacy" which is connected with femininity. What part do supportive measures for women play in this? Whereas concepts of "total quality management" supposedly help the highly rigid bureaucracy to become more flexible and efficient, affirmative action for women remains the same. They still count as sociopolitical, therefore, as low priority strategies, a negligible burden when costs need to be reduced. On the contrary, especially during the reorganization of business procedures and/or with politics of rationalization female employees have to step back. Affirmative action for women turns into a tool for integrating women into the family and to exclude them from the job market. Women who take a "paid leave for new parents" are compensated with premiums in exchange for the right to return to their former job after the leave. Even though the new model of management asks for qualities like communication skills and the ability to work in teams, it does not include female managers, but is meant for junior male staff members. Such organizational development reinforces old gender relations. Women are not envisioned as intrapreneurs within the company but as "mothers." A women is most economic as a mother, because she provides the support of the next generation and secures "quality" of the children in the family. In organizational terms, gender identifies as deficit, absence and problem.

Marginalization of the Female: the "Clan"

Which position women and femininity take in the analyzed discourse and the organizational model of the "clan"? The clan has a head: it is male and self-understood as a "father" or a patriarch. Mostly, he personally decides whether women have a chance in his business or not. In a traditionally oriented clan, no female trainees are accepted or the whole management department is male. Affirmative action for women is seen as a classical supportive structure for families and not to support women's ascension in the company. And the highly professionalized clans in the computer industry represent a brotherhood of male experts.

Organizational development does not take place systematically but *ad hoc*. Neither is affirmative action for women seen as a substantial part of organizational development in the clan where gender difference is seen "God's will." The family is the basic unit of competition. Economic life relies on the survival of the fittest, where men succeed. Women are the indispensable "recharging station" for the entrepreneur and the energy reserve behind the scene. But the principle of the clan does not exclude women altogether. The system integrates them in marginal and subordinate positions.

Use of Female Business Resources: the "Market"

The third type of organization, the "market," uses resources. The market model only supports the "capable." Here, only achievement counts. Supportive measures for women and personnel development are one thing. Women (are said to) own "female abilities" such as communication skills and talent for selling and female employees are seen as a business resource. The market model works towards achievement and is, therefore, less discriminating than the bureaucracy or clan models. However, it defines what is female using all traits and characteristics. For example, friendliness and a smiling attitude integrate the selling act as "service qualities."

Here, difference is no longer a risk for economical, political or educational action. Neither is it simply the horizon and matrix of a subjective being. Together with the expansion of the dispositive of the net and the operationalization of power knowledge, difference turns into cultural diversity. Diversity replaces the ignorant and know-all simplicity. It is multi-voiced against single-voiced, dialogue versus order, unified search for solution against top-down recipes. During the seventies the figures of self-organization, of networking and creation of processes could be found in the political discourse of resistance. Nowadays, they hold their place in the economical discourse about increased efficiency and achievement (Weber, 1998). The self-organization of cultural protagonists puts up complexity and process orientation against simplification and static systems. The multi-perspective found in the concept of "management of diversity" corresponds with the demands of complexity-oriented and situative models of regulation. Through the influence of the dispositive of the net and the extension of economic rationality, cultural diversity becomes a usable resource.

Notes

1   It is based on my dissertation "Organisationsentwicklung und Frauenförderung. Eine empirische Untersuchung in drei Organisationstypen der privaten Wirtschaft" (1998).

Bibliography

Barthes, R. (1964): Mythen des Alltags. Frankfurt a. M: Suhrkamp.

Beck, U. (1986). Risikogesellschaft. Frankfurt a. M: Suhrkamp.

————. (1993). Risikogesellschaft und Vorsorgestaaat—Zwischenbilanz einer Diskussion. Nachwort. In F. Ewald, *DerVorsorgestaat* (pp. 535–558). Frankfurt a.M.: Suhrkamp.

————. (1997). *Weltrisikogesellschaft, Weltöffentlichkeit und globale Subpolitik.* Wien: Picus.

Bosetzky, H., & Heinrich, P. (1980). Mensch und Organisation. Aspekte bürokratischer Sozialisation. Köln: Kohlhammer.

Boyer, R. (1992). Neue Richtungen von Managementpraktiken und Arbeitsorganisation. Allgemeine Prinzipien und nationale Entwicklungspfade. In A. Demirovic, H-P. Krebs & T. Sablowski (Eds.)., *Hegemonie und Staat. Kapitalistische Regulation als Projekt und Prozeß* (pp. 55–103). Münster: Westfälisches Dampfboot.

Capra, F. (1996). *Lebensnetz. Ein neues Verständnis der lebendigen Welt.* Bern.: Scherz.

Donzelot, J. (1979). *Die Ordnung der Familie.* Frankfurt a.M.: Suhrkamp.

Esser, U. (1992). *Gruppenarbeit. Theorie und Praxis betrieblicher Problemlösegruppen.* Opladen.: Westdeutscher Verlag.

Foucault, M. (1978a). Wahrheit und Macht. Interview mit Michel Foucault von Allessandro Fontana und Pasquale Pasquino. In: Foucault, Michel, *Dispositive der Macht. Michel Foucault über Sexualität, Wissen und Wahrheit* (pp. 21–54). Berlin: Merve.

————. (1978b). Historisches Wissen der Kämpfe und Macht. Vorlesung vom 7. Januar 1976. In Foucault, Michel, *Dispositive der Macht. Michel Foucault über Sexualität, Wissen und Wahrheit* (pp. 55–74). Berlin. Merve.

————. (1978c). Die Machtverhältnisse durchziehen das Körperinnere. Gespräch mit Lucette Finas. In Foucault, Michel, *Dispositive der Macht. Michel Foucault über Sexualität, Wissen und Wahrheit* (pp. 104–117). Berlin: Merve.

————. 1988, Für eine Kritik der politischen Vernunft. In: lettre international. Sommerausgabe (pp.58–66). Berlin: Verlagsgesellschaft Lettre International.

————. (1991). *Sexualität und Wahrheit, Bd. 1. Der Wille zum Wissen.* Frankfurt a.M.: Suhrkamp. (Original work published in 1976)

————. 1992, Archäologie des Wissens. Frankfurt a.M. Suhrkamp. (Original work published in 1973)

Fuchs, J., & Besier, K. (1996). Personalentwicklung mit Perspektive. In J. Fuchs (Ed.), *Das biokybernetische Modell. Unternehmen als Organismen* (pp. 181–204). Wiesbaden: Gabler.

Gruppe Von Lissabon (1997). Grenzen des Wettbewerbs. Die Globalisierung der Wirtschaft und die Zukunft der Menschheit. München.: Luchterhand.

Hellerich, G., & Wambach, M. M. (1983). Risikoprognose als Prävention. In M. M. Wambach (Ed.), *Der Mensch als Risiko* (pp. 126–136. Frankfurt a.M.: Suhrkamp.

Hoerster, R. (1993): Normale Regulierung der Delinquenz und Sozialpädagogik. Methodologisch Überlegungen zurr Analyse einer diskursiven Praxis in pädagogischer Absicht. Frankfurt/Main. (unveröffentlichte Habilitationsfassung).

Jaenicke, M. (1986). Staatsversagen. *Die Ohnmacht der Politiker in der Industriegesellschaft.* München: Piper.

Katzenbach, J. R., & Smith, D. K. (1993). *Teams. Der Schlüssel zur Hochleistungsorganisation.* Wien: Ueberreuther.

Kühl, S. (1994). *Wenn die Affen den Zoo regieren. Die Tücken der flachen Hierarchien.* Frankfurt a.M.: Campus.

Lynch, D. & Kordis, P. (1992)· *Delphin-Strategien. Management-Strategien in chaotischen Systemen.* Fulda: Paidia.

Messner, D. (1994). Fallstricke und Grenzen der Netzwerksteuerung. *PROKLA. Zeitschrift für kritische Sozialwissenschaft, 97*(24), 563–596. Münster: Westfälisches Dampfboot.

————. (1998). Die Transformation von Staat und Politik im Globalisierungsprozess. *Entwicklungspolitik Heft 13*, 31–40. Frankfurt a.M.: Evangelischer Pressedienst.

Münch, R. (1992). *Dialektik der Kommunikationsgesellschaft.* Frankfurt a.M.: Suhrkamp.

Moldaschl, M., & Schultz-Wild, R. (Eds.). (1994). *Arbeitsorientierte Rationalisierung. Fertigungsinseln und Gruppenarbeit im Maschinenbau.* Frankfurt/New York: Campus.

Ouchi, W.; Johnson, J.B.; (1978): Types of organizational control and their relationship to emotional well-being. *In: Administrative Science Quarterly, June, Vol. 23, Ithaka; New York,* 293–317.

Perrow, C. (1987). *Normale Katastrophen.* Frankfurt a.M.: Campus.

Ploenzke, K. C. (1996). Führen in Netzwerken—Der Manager als Dienstleister. In J. Fuchs (Ed.), *Das biokybernetische Modell. Unternehmen als Organismen* (pp. 149–160). Wiesbaden: Gabler.

Schülein, J. A. (1983). Gesellschaftliche Entwicklung und Prävention. In M. M. Wambach (Ed.), *Der Mensch als Risiko* (pp. 13–28). Frankfurt a.M.: Suhrkamp.

Sennett, R. (1998). *Der flexible Mensch. Die Kultur des neuen Kapitalismus.* Berlin: Berlin.

Staehle, W. H. (1988). Human Resources Management (HRM). Eine neue Managementrichtung in den USA? *Zeitschrift für Betriebswirtschaft, 58*(5/6), 576–587. Wiesbaden: Gabler.

Strauss, A. (1991). Grundlagen empirischer Sozialforschung. *Datenanalyse und Theoriebildung in der empirischen soziologischen Forschung.* München. Fink.

Sommerlatte, T. (1996). Lernende Organisationen. In J. Fuchs (Ed.), *Das biokybernetische Modell. Unternehmen als Organismen* (pp. 113–122). Wiesbaden: Gabler.

Sülzer, R., & Zimmermann, A. (1996). *Organisieren und Organisationen verstehen. Wege der internationalen Zusammenarbeit.* Opladen: Westdeutscher Verlag.

Türk, K. (1981). *Personalführung und soziale Kontrolle.* Stuttgart: Enke.

Weber, S. (1998). *Organisationsentwicklung und Frauenförderung. Eine empirische Untersuchung in drei Organisationstypen der privaten Wirtschaft.* Königstein/Taunus: Ulrike Helmer.

———. (1999). Dispositive der Macht: Von der „Pyramide" zum „Netz". In V. Aithal, N. Schirilla, H. Schürings & S. Weber (Eds.), *Wissen, Macht, Transformation. Interkulturelle und internationale Perspektiven* (pp. 165–184). Frankfurt: IKO.

———. (2000). Fördern und Entwickeln: Institutionelle Veränderungsstrategien und normalisierendes Wissen. *Zeitschrift für Erziehungswissenschaft 3,* 411–428. Wiesbaden: VS Verlag.

———. (2006a). Der „Intrapreneur" und die „Mutter". Pädagogische Gouvernementalität am Kreuzungspunkt von Ökonomie und Bevölkerung. In S. Weber, S. Maurer (Eds.), *Gouvernementalität und Erziehungswissenschaft. Wissen – Macht – Transformation Transformation.* (pp. 139–162). Wiesbaden: [VS Verlag].

———. (2006b). Gouvernementalität der „Schulgemeinde". Zwischen experimenteller Demokratie und Improvisationstechnologie. In S. Weber, S. Maurer (Eds.), *Gouvernementalität und Erziehungswissenschaft. Wissen – Macht – Transformation Transformation.* (pp. 77–100). Wiesbaden: [VS Verlag].

❧ Chapter 9 ☙

Thinking Governmentality 'from below': Social Work and Social Movements as (Collective) Actors in Movable/Mobile Orders

Susanne Maurer

The considerations in this chapter are trying to explore the Foucauldian notion of governmentality related to self-understandings, perspectives and collective experiences in the context of critical/"radical" social work which is historically connected with social movements, (e.g., "social action"). The term "movable/mobile orders" appearing in the title refers to processes of radical transformation which affect the notion of society as a whole—the concept (and collective experience) of nation states as welfare states. Against that background I am asking how this is also affecting movements of critique (social movements) and practices of care (social work). Finally, I put forward the open question: Do we, after its deconstruction, need another "turn" towards "identity"—in the sense of (self)-localization and be-longing?

For a quick review of the "history of my present thinking" related to governmentality, I would like to mention a few points: Having been an activist and also a "historian," a "thinker" in the context of German feminist movements, I am also doing research and teaching in the field of social work. At the same time, I am interested in relations between gender, memory and democracy in a transnational context. My reflections in this chapter will surely develop towards those points of reference. Theoretically, I feel inspired by Foucauldian thinking—and still by critical theory in the tradition of the Frankfurter School, and how it has been further developed by feminist thinkers like Seyla Benhabib or others (see for example Benhabib, 1992).

First, I want to introduce social work—"product" and actor of social change following the industrial revolution, developing with(in) the (late) 19th century, representing both a "soothing" response to social conflicts and struggle, and giving voice to the human experience of misery and neediness. In my perspective, social work—beside (and along with) its subjectivating and normalizing practices and effects which are usually more focused by Foucauldian reflections—can also be considered as an actor of problematizing social conflicts.

Speaking of social work as product and actor within a profound process of dynamization of society, the same can be said about social movements: They represent different attempts of transformation—be it in the perspective of "security" (concerning existential needs and risks which are historically new, see Ewald, 1993), or in the perspective of opening the framework of people's lives for new possibilities (like education and democratic participation). The most important qualities of social movements—apart from certain ideologies and programmes—are (about)

- expressing/"voicing"/representing rebellion against received and experienced restrictions or demands (*Zumutungen*),
- aiming at transformation of society as a whole,
- formulating an (utopian) horizon of hope, of "a better life in a better society," where human needs and desires will be met in a more adequate, "better" way.

However, social movements are "products" of specific experiences of "life in society" and are producing/creating/constituting new contexts (and cultures) of such experiences. To clarify the here addressed connection between social work and social movements, I would now like to "step aside" and go back to the turn of the 19th century.

Social Movements and Social Work in Imperial Germany

The following is about two different, though also comparable, "streams" in the historical process that has made the rising of modern social work in Germany both necessary and possible: the working class movement and the feminist movement in imperial Germany in relation to social policy and social work. I want to stress how both social movements did develop a certain perception and perspective, and last but not least did develop practical politics to deal with the social changes and conflicts related to the process of industrialization and arising modern bourgeois society. In other words, I am interested in the "power of problematizing" which is connected with social movements, according to the Foucauldian notion of a "history of problematizing" (i.e., making a topic out of something which is then acknowledged as relevant and meaningful), here, making a topic out of social inequality and raising the question of social justice.

Here is a sketch of the historical "background": In Western Europe the transition from a feudal to a capitalist society during the 18th and 19th century brought radical political, social and cultural change. A new order of society emerged—a working class formed in a new way, an ambitious *bourgeoisie* as the rising socio-cultural force, a modern ("scientific") bureaucracy and a new set of disciplines (especially the human and social sciences). The thoughts of Enlightenment and Romanticism (*Aufklärung* and *Romantik*) as well as the civil revolution of 1848 (though not very successful in Germany), had an important impact and, last but not least, the debates concerning "social reforms" reflect ambivalent feelings about the thoroughly rationalized—and rationalizing!—*"Dampfmaschinenkapitalismus"* (steam engine capitalism).

Familiar concepts and ways of living, community as well as family orders broke up (at least they were "disturbed" or "troubled"), and new patterns of behaviour, new qualifications for working and new social orientations had to be found. (This long lasting transformation process is historically and ideologically connected with the evolvement of the "enlightened subject", the "working subject"—both "naturally" conceptualized as male.)

"Die Soziale Frage" (the social problem) of the time referred to new phenomena of poverty and neediness then caused by wars, crop failures, economic deprivation as well as a new kind of forced mobility and an enormous growth of population. This multi-facetted misery made new forms of *"Hilfe"* (help/aid/assistance) necessary and was also a challenge to new ideas of educational reforms. Thus, education and help would become central motives of social debates and controversies during the 18th and 19th century.

The turn of the century (1900) appears as an especially ambiguous period of radical change: The social atmosphere is, so to say, oscillating between a romanticizing critique of technology and a steadfast/undiminished/undaunted trust in the myth of progress. This period is somehow shaped by polarized qualities like war and peace, young and old, city and rural area, baroque traditionalism and expressionism, democratic verve and monarchist standstill. Cultural and social conflicts evolve dynamically and provoke new responses—getting them for example, by the quasi-parallel banning of socialist organizations and national insurance put by Reichskanzler Bismarck (*Sozialistengesetze und Sozialversicherung*).

"Sinnkrisen and Kulturkritik" (crises of meaning and the critique of culture) become a big challenge for education—and suggest a variety of social pedagogies (*soziale Pädagogiken*). Here I would like to mention for example the idea of social pedagogy in the context of society as a whole ("the changing of persons in processes of learning and the changing of social situations by social policy," see Salomon, 1926).

Now, why do I emphasize the working class as well as the feminist movements in Germany in relation to the developing of social pedagogy, social policy and social work in the new modern sense of the rising 20th century? The two represent a different but structurally connected approach towards the *"Soziale Frage"* (the social problem of inequality, poverty and social justice). They repre-

sent a prototypical experience of reality, a prototypical focus on the social conflicts of the time, and a prototypical strategy of politics and social practise.

Here is not the place to point out the complex and multi-layered realities of
those two social movements. They are controversial and ambiguous in themselves (as is the social situation as a whole). Their very own spectrum includes a
lot of different positions and perspectives, fighting each other sometimes
fiercely. I have to sketch the picture very roughly then—taking into account that
social movements are neither homogenous entities nor very clear where to start
and where to end, their character being more of a fluid kind.

Both working class and feminist movement are initiated by the reality of
poverty and exclusion (while they perceive and experience poverty and exclusion in quite different ways). Both develop or are inspired by a profound critique of the status quo and both unfold visions of a better future society
(utopia). This means that both deal with problems of inequality and with the
question of participation and government. Their main difference lies in their
how they fundamentally deal with it.

It could be said that the working class movement first of all wants "to
change the situation" (more or less the society as a whole) while the feminist
movement emphasizes the change (and "personal growth") of the person (as to
change the situation!). I make this point not in order to depreciate the feminist
movement. "Being a feminist" myself I am obviously interested in the acknowledgement of its contributions. I would rather like to offer analytical ideas that
hopefully may lead to a better systematic understanding of that feminist part of
history. Like I mentioned before, Michel Foucault teaches us that it is worth
paying attention to the history of problematizing itself while reconstructing
historically processes of social change and the—as obviously as subtle—
establishment of new social (and mental!) orders. Therefore, I am very much
interested in patterns of perception and interpretation of social experience that
structure (and create) theories as well as practises of different social movements.
Within my own studies the following could be explored (see Maurer, 2004): The
specific focus of the working class movement allows us to perceive power relations in connection with a certain kind of economy; it allows us to perceive class
contradictions and diverging political and economic interests of the different
social groups. The relevant "social position" is the class position, and the metaphor of choice related to social transformation is "fight" or "struggle" (fighting
for justice/struggle for freedom)—and if not "struggle," at least, "policy" or
"politics."

The specific focus of the feminist movement allows us to perceive relations
of dependency "right into the finest fibre of the soul"; it lets us perceive power
relations not only connected with the economy but also with morality and iden-

tity. (Here is where education comes in.) The relevant "social position" (which will often be interpreted as quite a "natural"/biological position) is the gender position. The metaphor of choice related to social transformation is "contribution" ("the specific female contribution," especially in education and social work), and in "politics" they tend to be "maternalist" (*siehe "geistige Mütterlichkeit"*)—at least, or mainly, concerning the more moderate protagonists of the movement.

Still, the difference indicated here that can only be roughly characterized at this point, is not a result/effect of "insight" or "decision" which could be better or worse, less or more adequate. Rather, it is influenced by social experience related to very different (possible subject) positions in the context of society as a whole which is structured not only by class contradictions but also by a specifically gendered social order. Here is an illustration: The working class movement as a whole does not seem to have much (discursive) trouble of legitimation—the heroic fight for freedom and justice may suffice itself. The feminist movement, however, does (has to?) invest a lot of discursive energies in legitimating its own demand of being fully integrated into the evolvement of the modern social system. While the idea of class, and therefore of class position, allows (and also forces!) the experience of "collective identity," the gender position remains connected to the individual experience. Although "collective" in many ways, it is specific to 19th century Western Europe, or more precisely, the German *bourgeois* version that continuously privatizes, individualizes and naturalizes the gender position—even in the context of (and by!) the feminist movement itself.

However, the importance of individual experience is exactly where feminist social work comes in: Starting from the experience and reality of individual misery, feminist social workers and educationalists in imperial Germany could develop complex and far-reaching concepts of social practises. They not only became founders and practitioners of many organizations which created local social cultures and provided concrete help where needed. They also researched and elaborated analysis in the context of early sociology and national economy. So, the impact of their social contribution cannot only be described as 'moderating social conflicts' or 'class appeasement/reconciliation,' but must also be perceived and acknowledged as 'making use of their specific power to problematize structural problems of capitalism'—in terms of class and gender. (The fact that the often claimed and widely practised maternalist politics lead into new traps of the persisting gender system is part of the story but has to be told in another context. See Maurer, 2004).

The working class movement, however, could—at least at the very radical wings of its spectrum—not really integrate dimensions of individual experience.

The cooperative movement, with its idea of mutual/reciprocal help, with the idea of collective organization of reproductive work, were tolerated, and became practically important. However, politically as well as theoretically it often remained depreciated.

Emancipation Movements of the Late 20th Century and the Seduction of Neoliberalism

New social movements like the New Left, the civil rights and student movements of the 1960s, the anti-authoritarian impulse of the "extra-parliamentary opposition" APO in Western Germany, created and formed new concepts of politics, thus, in a certain way, responding to other tendencies of re-opening and de-structuring political sphere(s). The new feminist movements, among others, contributed to politicize "the private" sphere (life and self). Thus, "the political" lost its boundaries—was recognized, conceptualised and practised as a shifting framework, and appeared, along the same process, as de-localized and ever-present, as always and never reachable (or distinctive).

On the other hand, the late 20th century new social movements transformed former notions of emancipation (in a more juridical or formal sense) into "subjectivity"—understood as an internal and external process of self-liberation and self-realization. This is where the Foucauldian notion of governmentality comes in. Nicolas Rose and others showed how governing in the new sense of neoliberalism meets "emancipation" (see Rose, 2000).

Michel Foucault speaks about tricky aspects of "power" which are dis-/attracting receptions as well as fighting energies of oppositional forces towards forms/modes of governing which have historically already lost their weight. The even trickiest aspect here seems to be the fact that this will happen with the help and/or by means of critical theory (see Foucault 1977).

In another context lately I worked out thoughts on seductive aspects of neoliberalism for critical/radical social workers—encouraged by Foucault, and always interested in how government works (in both senses!).[1] It was interesting for me to realize that, apparently almost every aspect within emancipative concepts of social work is somehow met by a neoliberal "promise." A few examples follow:

- the promise of "freedom," (e.g., of movement and mobility) in a "land of possibilities without borders or limits," also the concept of the "entrepreneur self" meets the desire for autonomy;

- the promise of self-determination meets the longing for (and is connected with the attraction of) the power of definition, shaping/designing, and controlling;
- the challenge to move and change constantly, the demand of flexibility meets the desire to break out of petrified structures or stuck situations;
- the discourse about (and promise of) quality, in the social work context connected with the notion of process-oriented and cooperative evolution and controlling/categorizing procedures at the same time, meets the desire to make quality which is created in one's own working context more recognizable, visible, performable, "fit for competition";
- along the new forms/modes of documenting, evaluating and categorizing social work there is a promise of simplicity which meets the desire for clarity, control, even solution of complex problems.[2]

In a nutshell, the very connection between "emancipation" and neoliberal orientations refers to the specific "cocktail" typical for the latter—the mixture out of fantasies of omnipotence and, on the other hand, the evocation of self-responsibility (such as "conduct by self-conduct"…).

But, like Richard Sennett (2002) or Zygmunt Baumann (1999) have made very clear, the resources and options for playing the neoliberal game of "freedom" and "flexibility" are distributed very unequally. And Lisa Adkins and Celia Lury have argued in a feminist perspective of social theory that, for example, gender inequality is still at work and reproduced anew when it comes to chances to relate to identity as a performative resource (see Adkins & Lury, 1999; see also Soiland, 2005).

In the neoliberal logic/"world" you have to be strong (strength, competence or power is one of its seductions!), energetic and highly effective in your performance. There is no real space for weakness, need, burn-out or despair. For example, being aware of new reflections on the notion of "networks" (which are no longer emerging out of or created by grass roots initiatives but will be more and more a normative and forcing strategy of organization), I suddenly realized the "cruelty of relationality" (like networks forcing people to perform non-stop, because you have "to show up," be active, and never stop to "deserve" your being part of that specific context).

This is a crucial moment where social (especially feminist) movement expertise on the one hand, and social work expertise on the other could be productive and subversive at the same time. Let me develop that argument from a, maybe, unusual angle.

Social Work as Society's Memory of Social Conflicts

Here I would like to draw attention to one rarely addressed dimension of social work: its function as a "Place (or Site) of Memory" concerning social conflicts of the past and present. Given the fact that social work can be considered as one specific answer to social problems of the time, its institutions, concepts, methods as well as every day routines can be understood as "traces" which have been inscribed on society's surface documenting former societal struggles. They can be read as effects of political actions, as condensed, "materialized," institutionalized practises (i.e., in the context of governance strategies, social movements or developments in science and education). Thus, the actual appearances/performances or "shapes" of "social work" in each society represent controversial debates about inequality, injustice, and exclusion. They represent certain perceptions as well as specific perspectives and last but not least practical politics to deal with the social changes and conflicts related to transformation processes (see the passage related to Imperial Germany).

With no intention to simply ride "the memory wave" in order to (re)construct and stabilize a profession's or discipline's "identity," I am interested in the political potential of historical (re)construction in relation to social work. Even more: Are processes of remembrance (which also include counterremembrance) one productive way to develop an analytical perspective related to social work and "power-knowledge"?

Now what is the (research and analytical, political) background of my argument that "social work can analytically be considered as society's memory of social conflicts"? Firstly, the research on the "history of social work," reconstructing social problems (in their relations to social movements) as well as the creation and development of social work "landscapes" and concepts, here especially done in a gender sensible perspective (see Maurer, 2004; Kessl & Maurer, 2005). Secondly, the research on the "history of feminist movements," reconstructing historical connections between feminism and the development of modern social work in a German context, generation relationships within feminist movements, the nexus/problematic of collective memory and gender and, in that very context, possibilities of "building tradition" in a critical sense referring to "collective experience" and "movement knowledge." Thirdly, political action and critical theory, "inside and outside" social work as well as "inside and outside" the academic sphere, trying to be aware of the complex dynamic of

thematizing and de-thematizing while analyzing the characteristics of oppositional movements and oppositional thinking. And finally, the focus on power
related theories and analysis of social work, not at least following the studies
and thinking of Michel Foucault.

As I have already mentioned, this refers to the concepts, procedures and
every-day practises of social work; the theoretical and methodical instruments of
social work; the institutions and "actors" (professionals as well as volunteers) of
social work. Any of these aspects and "given realities" has a specific story linked
to specific receptions of social problems or conflicts as well as to specific attempts to work on them/to "solve" them or, at least, respond to them. Should
this historical knowledge get lost, so I want to state, the political, also (self-
)critical dimension of social work tends to get neutralized. At the same time, I
do not want to state that any kind of historical knowledge is functioning as
"critical memory" of social conflicts. It has to be asked which kind of memory
is needed if the "explosive" (political) potential of social work should be "laid
bare."

Thus, what is meant and what is not meant when I speak of "social work as
society's memory of social conflicts" needs to be further defined. Four different
aspects developed this notion: firstly, "collective memory" and "collective processes of remembrance" (Halbwachs, 1985); secondly, "cultural memory" (Assmann & Assmann, 1995) and "processes of trans-generational cultural
transmission" which are organized by certain (i.e., hegemonial) narratives;
thirdly, "Places of Memory" ("Lieux de mémoire," Nora, 1998) which
can/mean to represent "collective experience" in a certain national or cultural
context; fourthly, "social memory" (Burke, 1991; Welzer, 2001) referring to all
different kinds and practises of remembering in a social, every-day context—
those modes of remembrance which are more ephemeral, almost not-noticeable
but, nevertheless, effective.

Each of these different, though connected approaches nears the dimension
of conflict, and there is always a power-related notion about it. Each of them
also deals not so much with "real events of the past" but more so with actual
social and political practises referring to those events. Thus, they share a certain
interest in the "use of the past," an interest in "struggles about the past." With
Foucault it could be said that this is about the "spheres of truth."

In contrast to the concepts of "social, cultural or collective memory," I
would further stress the qualities of dissent, diversity and multitude, taking especially into account hegemonic dynamics and their inherent strategies. In a
German context, reflections about the "use of the past" cannot be disassociated
from the "politics of remembrance" concerning the Nazi-Regime in "the German past" (!). A lot of my theoretical references are linked to that special his-

tory. But the same authors and texts make also clear that we can learn a lot about societies' dealing with their past in a very general and structural way, too. Studies on the "politics of remembrance" in different states and societies start from the need of creating a common history ("Imagined communities," see Anderson, 1983) as to give themselves a weight also measurable in the "space of time."

This, so I want to argue, is also relevant to a field like "social work." It refers to its self-understandings and its claims for being the legitimate "force" in society that deals with certain tasks concerning social problems and conflicts. Accepting this could also mean to build and establish a non-critical tradition as to "simply" confirm and stabilize a discipline's and profession's "identity." This is surely not the point I want to make. On the contrary, I am convinced that the contested and questioned field of social work can get some self-consciousness and strength not by neutralizing contradiction, tension and fragmentary states of being but by cultivating vivid processes of controversial reflection and re-membrance.

Memories and counter-memories are circulating in the field of social work. Traces of past conflicts are often multi-layered and contradictory. Such "disturbing" memories can irritate the process of building a "tradition," they can also lighten it up in a critical way. My notion of "social work as society's memory of social conflicts" does build on the latter, assuming that a "place of memory" does have the potential to function also as a place of new political debate, thus "re-opening the past," not petrifying it.

Adding focus to the multi-layered processes of "inventing traditions" (and also forgetting them, maybe at the same time) in their very specific functions for certain social "actors" (professionals, activists, projects, institutions etc.), for "participants" in the "social-work-complex", the more structural view of "memory" will be also opened to a more dynamic view by the notion of "re-membrance." "Remembrance" allows to look at the diverse struggles about the past, at the diverse and controversial attempts of cultural transmission in order to build some kind of "tradition," in order to build or (re)stabilize an "imagined community" (consciously or unconsciously).

Because "struggles about the past" are making "difference/s" visible and accessible, they are potentially reopening them to politics. In other words, historical (re)construction can (re)open social work to politics/political debate as long as there remains something disturbing, something irritating about it.

Perspectives

Finally, I would like to sketch how perspectives of critique could be thought or conceptualized—taking into account Foucault's analysis of governmentality.

First of all, social movements and movements of theorizing in a critical perspective have to be recognized in their rhythmic quality/aspects—steps of "opening" are often followed, or even accompanied by steps of "closing"—as to establish, "secure" and also "conserve" experiences and "successes" of social struggles (see here again the meaning and function of re-membering and re-minding!). This relates to what Seyla Benhabib attempted to show referring to critical theory (see Benhabib, 1992), and what I tried to develop further seeking to reconstruct and analyze "individual-collective" experiences related to political practise, "self-conduct" and ways of living and oppositional thinking within my own studies on feminist movements in the early and late 20th century (see Maurer, 1996; 2004).

Inspired by Foucault I sought to reconceptualize my own notion of dynamics concerning critical thought and oppositional movements (see Maurer, 2005). Very disturbing was especially the sudden awareness that my, at least theoretically preferred, accent on fluidity, openness, heterogeneity and relationality of thought (see for example Flax, 1990) and political concepts could easily turn into an instrument or welcome resource in the sense of neoliberal deregulation. Thus, I re-minded myself of an older insight which could lead "out of that trap." In my own research, as to de-totalize, it turned out to be productive to reconstruct very precisely the "movements within movements"—the very complex search of/seeking for new orientations, perspectives, points of reference; the longing "to break out," "to break through" the experienced restrictions within the social movement itself and its ideology (see Maurer, 1997), to reach out for something else; the exploration of new perspectives which is, hopefully, an ongoing process in the context of social movements. Thus, taking seriously again the notion of fluidity and heterogeneity but within the collective social movement framing, and taking care for experiences with such/those "movements within movements" brought up another question: Where are those experiences "saved/stored" and how can they get evaluated and worked on in a future perspective?

A certain space or place where memories of restriction and struggles with and against those restrictions can be "saved/stored" needs to be created. There has to be a place where processes of re-membering/re-minding will be cultivated in a critical sense—not at least to become aware of the subjective involvement into/with that "network of power relations." From there, new impulses for critical movements of change could emerge. (See also the above section on "social work as society's memory of conflicts")

Surely, no critical political strategy can just be "subversive"—it needs to always be understood as deriving from specific historical and socio-cultural constellations. Still, I want to stress the more abstract quality of transformative intention. When Foucault points out that social movements, with their activities and attempts "towards liberation" and all their visions and concepts of freedom are still (and/or will become again) part of the whole framework which is creating (and created by) power relations as well as governing in more effective ways (according to the "needs of time"), he does stress the quality of *"Zumutung"* (demand) when he shows how conducting by self-conducting works, and how the ethics and aesthetics, those practises of the self could be thought (and practised) in a way which is connected with freedom. The very passage between the individual and the collective dimension has still not been enough focused on.

Notes

1   Having done some research on the attraction of the Nazi-Ideology/-Movement (!), on the many ways in which men and women could and would attach themselves "subjectively" with not only the promises and visions but also experiences the Nazi-Regime would (and had to) offer. See Dörr, Kaschuba, Maurer 1999.

2   At the same time, facing that scenario, there can be received a variety of practises which could be characterized as, more or less passive or "conservative", "practises of resistance" – trying to survive the new trends by ignoring them, by living in "niches".

Bibliography

Adkins, L., & Lury, C. (1999). The Labour of Identity: Performing Identities, Performing Economies. *Economy and Society*, 28(4), 598–615.

Anderson, B. (1983). *Imagined Communities*. London: Verso.

Assmann, J., & Assmann, A. (1994). Das Gestern im Heute. Medien und soziale Gedächtnis. In K. Merten (Ed.), *Die Wirklichkeit der Medien* (pp. 114–140). Opladen: Westdeutscher Verlag.

Baumann, Z. (1999). *Unbehagen in der Postmoderne*. Hamburg: Hamburger Edition.

Benhabib, S. (1992). *Kritik, Norm und Utopie. Die normativen Grundlagen der Kritischen Theorie*. Frankfurt a. M.: Fischer- Taschenbuch Verlag.

Burke, P. (1991). Geschichte als soziales Gedächtnis. A. Assmann & D. Harth (Eds.), *Mnemosyne. Formen und Funktionen der kulturellen Erinnerung* (pp. 289–304). Frankfurt a. M.: Fischer-Taschenbuch Verlag.

Dörr, B., Kaschuba, G., & Maurer, S. (1999). *"Endlich habe ich einen Platz für meine Erinnerungen gefunden"—Kollektives Erinnern von Frauen in Erzählcafés zum Nationalsozialismus.* Pfaffenweiler: Centaurus.

Ewald, F. (1993). *Der Vorsorgestaat.* Frankfurt a. M.: Suhrkamp.

Flax, Jane (1990): *Thinking Fragments. Psychoanalysis, Feminism and Postmodernism in the Contemporary West.* Oxford: University of California Press.

Foucault, M. (1977): Der Wille zum Wissen. Sexualität und Wahrheit 1, Frankfurt a.M.: Suhrkamp.

Halbwachs, M. (1985). *Das kollektive Gedächtnis.* Frankfurt a. M.: Fischer.

Kessl, F., & Maurer, S. (2005). Soziale Arbeit. In F. Kessl et al. (Eds.), *Handbuch Sozialraum* (pp. 111–128). Wiesbaden: VS Verlag für Sozialwissenschaften.

Maurer, S. (1996). *Zwischen Zuschreibung und Selbstgestaltung. Feministische Identitätspolitiken im Kräftefeld von Kritik, Norm und Utopie.* Tübingen: edition discord.

————. (1997, July). *Dogmatism in Feminism? Or How Feminists Succeed in Dissenting.* Paper presented at the Women's Studies Network Association Conference, Women, Policy and Politics, London.

————. (2002, August). *Social Movements and Social Work in Imperial Germany.* Paper presented at the German-Japanese Conference Sozialpädagogik in Japan und Deutschland: Historische Wurzeln, Theoriebezüge und Praxisprobleme, Tokyo Metropolitan University.

————. (2004). *Zum Verhältnis von Frauenbewegungen und Sozialer Arbeit um 1900—Versuch einer historisch-systematischen (Re-)Kontextualisierung nebst Überlegungen zu einer reflexiven Historiographie in der Sozialpädagogik.* Hildesheim: Habilitationsschrift.

————. (2005): Soziale Bewegung. In F. Kessl et al. (Eds.), Handbuch Sozialraum (pp. 629–648). Wiesbaden: VS Verlag für Sozialwissenschaften.

Nora, P. (Ed.) (1984–92). *Les lieux de mémoire.* Paris: Gallimard.

————. (1998). *Zwischen Geschichte und Gedächtnis.* Frankfurt a. M.: (Fischer-Taschenbuch Verlag)

Rose, N. (2000). Tod des Sozialen? Eine Neubestimmung der Grenzen des Regierens. In U. Bröckling, S. Krasmann & T. Lemke (Eds.), *Die Gouvernementalität der Gegenwart* (pp. 72–109). Frankfurt a. M.: Suhrkamp.

Salomon, A. (1926). *Soziale Diagnose.* Berlin: Heymann.

Sennett, R. (2002). Respekt im Zeitalter der Ungleichheit, Berlin: Berlin-Verlag.

Soiland, T. (2005). Kritische Anmerkungen zum Machtbegriff in der Gender-Theorie auf dem Hintergrund von Michel Foucaults Gouvernementalitätsanalyse. *Widersprüche*, 25(1), 7–25.

Welzer, H. (Ed.). (2001). Das soziale Gedächtnis—Geschichte, Erinnerung, Tradierung. Hamburg: Hamburger Edition.

ဆာ Chapter 10 ∞

Only Love for the Truth Can Save Us:
Truth-Telling at the (World)university?

Maarten Simons and Jan Masschelein[1]

Of course there is no time—we are facing important challenges and are confronted with large transformations of our universities. What is at stake is our survival. Our survival as university, as research group, as individual lecturer and researcher. What is needed is accountability. Economic but also scientific tribunals are extremely active and are suing as never before. Being obsessed with quality and excellence is the only way to guarantee our survival. Since we do not have time, however, we will hurry up to take some time and to formulate an idea.[2]

For sure, the old idea of the university is dead. And meanwhile, the 'last academics' have finished their mourning—we have confessed ourselves to the community of the entrepreneurial academic staff being focused on quality and excellence. But let us be honest about this: although this community offers us a lot of chances, we feel ill at ease being part of it; her future is not ours; her ethos of work is becoming less and less self-evident. And since we think this unease is not just a matter of a personal attitude, we would like to look at this situation as an opportunity to bring a new idea about the university into the world, an idea to which we feel ourselves attracted. This idea is strongly inspired by Foucault and foremost by his ethos as a truth-teller—Foucault as we experience him.

Before we express this idea, we will first investigate past and present conceptions about the university focusing on the orientation and on truth-telling at this institution. Therefore, our main interest is not epistemological (truth related to the theory and her concepts), but the way scientific truth-telling is being practised and being distinguished from nonscientific speech. It is about the ethics (and not the epistemology) of truth-telling. And it is at this level, (i.e., the level of the ethos), that we would like to present another idea of the university.

Orientations of the University and Scientific Truth-Telling

The Orientation of the Modern University

We use the term 'modern university' here to refer to the university as it is conceptualised at the end of the eighteenth century. Exemplary for this conceptualisation is the famous proposal of Humboldt (1810) for the university of Berlin. It is not our aim however, to discuss this proposal and other proposals during that period in detail, but to point in a general way at basic elements of this way of thinking. This way of thinking was not only influential in Germany, but in many other European countries as well as parts of the Anglo-Saxon world. Our main interest is in the orientation of this 'modern university'.

The modern university is conceived as an institution for science, (i.e., science through research). This scientific research is an activity that incarnates the scientific search for unity of the truth (the one truth). The 'spirit of truth' guides this activity that points towards the universal principles of the truth in its totality (as a kind of regulative principle). Anrich (1960) reflects upon this guidance as being the submission to the 'law of scholarship' and used expressions such as the "Hippocratic Oath at the university" or the "duty to follow the method" (p. 5). Due to this orientation the practice of research at the university is regarded as a practice of general edification (*'Allgemeine Bildung,'* 'general education'). Through a submission to the law of scholarship and thus, in an orientation towards the universal, the research takes part in a process of self-edification. In other words, research acts as a practice to shape a force within human beings that is directed towards unity—the latter being the anthropological premise in this conception (*'Formung seines innersten Wesens, der Formung seines Charakter'*) (Ibid, p. 5). These considerations about scholarship, research and general edification enable us to understand how education at the university is regarded and how society gives a particular meaning to the university.

Scientific education at the university is general edification through participation in research. This participation enables students to be submitted to the law of scholarship and to educate themselves by being oriented towards the universal. Or to use Habermas' (1990) more recent terminology: the procedures of communicative rationality (structuring the so-called internal public spheres of scientific disciplines) are part of research (researchers submit themselves to the claims of an argumentative discussion) and imply an orientation to (universal) consensus. Thus, students' participation in these scientific discussions implies that they submit themselves to the tribunal of communicative rationality and that they take part in a process of general edification because of this universal orientation. According to Habermas (1990) this is the case because learning processes at the university are held together through the communicative forms of scientific argument.

Therefore, the claim is that scientific research and scientific education are one and that this kind of education should be distinguished from other (lower) forms of education (for pupils). At the university, according to Humboldt (1810), the researcher is not there for the student, but both are there for the sake of scholarship (also Riedel, 1977). In a more general way, we could say that for these authors research and education are orientated towards the universal and that to speak at the university implies a submission to the tribunal of scholarship (or the scientific tribunal). Of course, different formulations of the laws of this tribunal have existed during the nineteenth and twentieth century (universal reason, the method, a fundamental theoretical rationality, the communicative procedures, and so on).[3] However, the idea of research-based truth-telling involving a submission to a tribunal remained.

Based upon this point of orientation and this kind of tribunal, the meaning of the university and its academics for society is argued, or the other way around: society reflects upon the meaning of the university on this basis. The modern university looks at the state as a guarantee for its autonomy, (i.e., the law of scholarship as the condition for free or autonomous research and education) and the state should ensure that the university can institutionalise this autonomy.[4] The German tradition concerning (public) financing of the university and the (neutral) appointment of professors illustrate this external organisation (Ash, 1999; Nybom, 2003). However, a question appeared: why should the state finance this kind of institution (or even allow it to exist)? For the modern university claims that it is not an institution of higher vocational education and that it does not offer immediate returns for civil society. Moreover, professors in the German tradition distance themselves form direct political and state-related issues in their disinterested striving for the truth. And yet, the modern university has a meaning.

As intellectuals, academics enter the public domain in the name of truth and their speech depends upon the submission to the scientific tribunal. What they are doing is addressing society in the name of something to which they have access and that is based upon the laws of the tribunal they know well. This transcends the actual organisation of society. In other words, as intellectuals academics are inhabiting the "kingdom of truth" and they address the "civil kingdom" and their inhabitants (Hunter, 2000). Precisely, because the scientific tribunal of truth is enlightening for the civil order, the scientific truth-telling of the researcher—when she addresses civil society—is a kind of judgement. Scientific truth-telling allows the academic to judge as an intellectual when he speaks within society (outside the university). In other words, the scientific verisdiction (truth-telling based upon the law of scientific scholarship) results in an intellectual jurisdiction within civil society. Following Foucault (2001), we could argue therefore, that the position of the intellectual as universal intellectual or as intellectual orienting herself to the universal is related (from a genealogical perspective) to the figure of the jurist (Foucault, 2001). In the name of a fundamental right (and their access to that right) these jurists judged the power of the state and its illegitimate activities. In the same way, the academic is enlightening (or emancipating, humanising) society as a universal intellectual by judgments based on the laws of the scientific tribunal.

What we would like to emphasize here is that this judging truth-telling is both an addressed and pedagogical speech. It is an addressed speech since the tribunal to which one positions oneself also defines the public. The public are those who have not (not yet, or not enough) submitted themselves to the laws of the "kingdom of truth," (i.e., those who do not (yet) orient themselves towards the universal but towards what others, what the state or what the market is prescribing), or who live a disoriented life, those who are not (yet) edified. Thus, the universal intellectual addresses universal mankind. Or more specifically, mankind is the addressee that appears when the intellectual looks at civil society in the name of her scientific tribunal. Mankind, and the potential and promise of real humanity, is the subject that can realise herself in an orientation towards the universal. Without this orientation, and without the university, civil society lacks an orientation and/or a direction towards the universal. Or to use Habermas' (1990) argument: what is present in an exemplary way at the university and within the scientific procedures of research is what is needed for society to have a (common) understanding of itself. The intellectual is playing the 'mediating role of the interpreter' in a differentiated society looking for a general orientation and directed towards mutual understanding (Habermas, 1989). This clarifies immediately why a particular pedagogical (edifying) dimension is part of this truth-telling. From the very beginning the aim of the universal intellectual is to guide people towards the 'kingdom of truth' and to educate them. And as Lyotard (1984) claims: intellectuals address everyone as a carrier or embryo of a human entity that should be realised. As an intellectual the academic sees her task within society and for the sake of her inhabitants in helping to bring about the right orientation. Or at least, she considers her task to give a direction to a society which she regards as blind (i.e., lacking all light), or in which, for example, mankind is being sacrificed on the altar of state citizenship and/or of the economy.

But does the university still have this meaning for society today? Is research and education at the university still oriented towards the universal and is the academic submitting herself to the law of scientific scholarship? Is the duty to follow the method still meaningful here and is the academic positioning herself as a truth-teller who judges (from within) society? It is not our aim to answer these questions in a principled or theoretical way, but to answer them indirectly. A general description of the actual conception of the role of the university expressed in European policy documents allows us to show that the university, within the actual knowledge society, has other points of orientation—or at least, that it is asked to take these as guiding ideas.

The University Today: Orienting Oneself in the Knowledge Society

A reference with growing importance for the university today is the knowledge society and knowledge economy. Europe and the member states have formulated the strategic goal to reform Europe into one of the strongest knowledge societies and economies in the world (the Lisbon-strategy). Against this background, a recent communication of the European Commission (2003) claims that universities have a unique role to play in this kind of society and economy. This unique role refers to the combination of three activities by universities which are functional for the knowledge society: the production of knowledge (research), the transmission of knowledge (education), and the additional training and regional development (service).[5] However, in order to be functional, universities have to deal with challenges. We will present a short overview of these challenges for each of the functions.[6]

With regard to the research function, it is crucial to understand that the university produces knowledge among other producers such as private (and public) research centres and research and development units of private companies. It is argued that this new, international/European positioning of the university results in challenges with regards to competition, collaboration and financial issues. Furthermore, as an international/European institution for higher education, the university plays an important role in the training of new 'professional researchers'. In that regard, the university aims to offer research competencies that enable people to produce knowledge in autonomous ways. And since professionals in a knowledge society also need research competencies, the training of research professionals is another challenge for education at the university. In the service function challenges occur at different levels. First, universities could play a role in the development of local knowledge platforms. Secondly, they can also offer their expertise as a service for social and economic development in a region. And finally, they are challenged to offer adequate training in adult education. An important question then arises: how should the university, while taking these challenges seriously, orient herself? What direction is available for the multi-functional university in the knowledge society?

The understanding of the university via the concept of functions no longer grounds the orientation of the university in an idea (of humanity) that transcends society. However, this preliminary remark does not imply that the multi-functional university no longer orients itself.[7] The new point of orientation is excellence, (i.e., the university strives for excellence for each of its functions: excellent research, education and service) (see also Readings, 1996). However, to understand what excellence actually means, it could be useful to focus on the attitude or on the gaze out of which the university appears as something that could be approached in terms of excellence. In other words, excellence is about a judgement but foremost also about a vision on what needs to be judged.

In a competitive environment the university has no such thing as a fixed norm for good research, good education and good service. Instead, the point of departure is that knowledge society holds some functions and that some organisations receive the financial resources to 'take up' these functions. Quality indicators (i.e., to judge whether something is functional for the knowledge society whereby this functionality could be operationalized in different ways) assess this accreditation. However, being functional for the knowledge society remains the background or horizon for this operationalization. In a way, everything could be chosen as an indication for quality as long as there is a consensus that it implies an income for society. This way of thinking about the university and its task implies that the university submits itself to (or is being submitted to) a kind of permanent quality tribunal. Furthermore, this submission is the condition under which excellence can receive the importance it has today. In other words, excellence has an almost absolute meaning against the background of these relative quality indicators.

Excellence does not just mean that a university is functional. In a way this functionality is already taken for granted. Instead, excellence refers to the fact that a university performs a function (or a group of functions) better than other organisations. Therefore, the quality tribunal obsessed with excellence links up with the dictates of comparison and optimisation. The excellent university, given a set of quality indicators, performs better than other institutions. For a university to remain excellent (or to become excellent) it is of strategic importance to optimise each of its functions. Excellent universities evaluate themselves on a permanent basis (before outside organisations do it). These dictates of comparison (and comparability) and optimisation do not only apply in relation with other universities but also inside the organisation of the university as illustrated by the development of 'poles of excellence' in research.

Here, we emphasize that this comparison (and the competition implied) is also a steering mechanism between the university (with its three functions) and organisations outside the university that focus on one of these functions. In fact, for each of its functions the university deals with organisations that perform one particular function. In the research function, the university competes with research centres (and research in private companies). Competition with regard to education occurs with institutions of higher (vocational) education. Also, these institutions orient themselves to the knowledge society and try to offer an education that stimulates research skills. Indeed, the growing attention given to 'research based teaching' (and for education that stimulates research) is foremost developed at higher education institutions other than universities (and with a limited 'real' research function) (Brown & McCartney, 1998; Jenkins & Zetter, 2003). Within the knowledge society, the university finally offers services such as public and private centres for consultancy, regional development, and for training.

This competition, or at least the fact that we can reflect upon theses issues in terms of competition and comparison, implies that each of the functions of a university is also performed by other institutions. One could argue at this point that the education of new researchers (professional researchers) is exclusively a university function. In official documents, this right to offer PhDs indeed serves as a kind of (formal) definition for a university (see for example, the European University Association, 2003). But also, other institutions perform this function, such as specialised 'graduate schools' (in the United States and increasingly in Europe). They focus explicitly on the training of new researchers and detach themselves from the broader university. Moreover, there is the training of professional researchers in collaboration with private companies. Thus, since other or new organizations perform this function, the following question becomes even more urgent: what makes a university a university?

According to official documents, the uniqueness of the university lies in its simultaneous combination of three functions within one organisation. Thus, the university excellence should relate to how well it combines these three functions. However, why is it necessary to combine these functions? Is the combination itself functional for the knowledge society? Or should we not claim that this combination is rather inefficient? Why do we still need universities when other mono-functional institutions can possibly perform more efficiently (more excellently) each of its functions? Has the university become a kind of ridiculous organisation self-causing 'unfair' competition for itself? And couldn't we say that the academic staff is exploited (in a classical Marxist sense) being forced to perform three different functions, while in other organisations one staff member performs one function? Should we agree with Max Weber (1991), who long argued: "*Innerlich ebenso wie äußerlich ist die alte Universitätsverfassung fiktiv geworden*" (Both regarding its content and as an institutional form, the university has become fictional—our translation) (p. 240).

Habermas also raised these questions, not to answer them positively in a direct way, but to argue that there exist reasons why the expected functional differentiation is not completed and why the university does not dismantle itself. According to Habermas (1990), the persistent 'integrative consciousness' of the university and its academics (the consciousness that research, education and critique belong together) is rooted in the life-world and in the communicative procedures oriented towards mutual understanding. As long as research at the university is embedded in the life-world (and thus, not determined completely by the laws of the economic system and of the power apparatus and by the logic of functional differentiation), there is an orientation towards the universal (understanding), and the university is more than a multi-functional organisation. According to Habermas, this orientation within research guarantees that participation is a process of general edification, (i.e., that research equals for both the researcher and the student a process of edification). In addition, this orientation gives the researcher a foundation for her 'juridical' speech in society.

According to others, Habermas holds on in a stubborn way to principles and distinctions without any value of reality. System theorists see it as inadequate to take the distinction between the life-world and functional systems as a point of departure and to ground the meaning of the university for society on that basis.[8] They consider 'integrative consciousness' (the internal relation of research, education and service) as a kind of nostalgic remembrance without any factual meaning, influence or orienting potential. The actual steering instead, is systemic in nature. The university is still a multi-functional organisation because its subsystems more or less work for each other (for example, due to their proximity). It will remain multi-functional as long as that combination is functional itself. But as argued, the creation of the European knowledge society implies the development and optimisation of these three functions independently with their optimal performance resting on competition. Within this focus, the challenges offered by the knowledge society could be understood as the beginning of the end of the multi-functional university and its integrative dream.

Proposals for a Re-Orientation of Truth-Telling at the University

In 'our' knowledge society the university needs apparently to orient (and differentiate) itself in such a way that it is at the same time forced to dismantle itself. Therefore, we ask whether the university still has or could have another meaning for society than the current one in knowledge society today. To argue that this meaning does not relate to a new orientation (and to a submission to a new tribunal), we first discuss recent attempts to re-orient the university.

Mittelstrass (1989, 1994, 2001, 2002, and 2003) for example, emphasizes the necessity of an edifying rationality within scientific research, but similarly argues that we try to re-shape the scientific ethos. In his view, science should not only offer a kind of '*Verfügungswissen*' (positive knowledge about causes or a know-how to solve problems) but also an '*Oriëntierungswissen*' (knowledge about the orientation) (1989, p. 9; 2003, p. 12ff). The latter could guide our actions, focuses on goals and tries to answer the question 'what should we do?' The former kind of knowledge is a 'positive knowledge' while the latter is 'regulative knowledge.' According to Mittelstrass, this orienting, regulating knowledge is what misses in our technical, scientific culture. Without this knowledge human self-realisation has no orientation, any destination and does not relate to a kind of general edification ('*Bildung*').

Mittelstrass (2002) argues that the condition for this orienting knowledge is a particular scientific ethos or form of life. Bringing about this ethos requires that we transcend the disciplinarian organisation (at the level of research and education) and the specialised, disciplinarian ethos of science. This is possible since the organisation of science based on disciplines results from a historical development and has itself no theoretical foundation. Moreover, it is a necessity since this disciplinarian ethos (related to the specialised disciplines) does not allow an orientation to the universal. Mittelstrass is straightforward about this: "Experts, as we define them today, do not have any 'education' ('Edification' or '*Bildung*')" (As cited in Kopetz, 2002, p. 99, our translation). Against this background he proposes trans-disciplinary research (and not interdisciplinary research where the disciplines remain the point of departure). In trans-disciplinary research the starting point are questions and problem domains as they appear in society in a general way (and not as they appear within the limited scope of separate disciplines). This type of research implies a kind of general orientation and offers the university a new potential for general edification (Mittelstrass, 2002).

Mittelstrass' aim therefore, is to re-think the university (in the German tradition) as a research university in which trans-disciplinary research and the correlating ethos have an edifying potential. In other words, it is an argument for a 're-direction' of the scientific ethos in the name of an idea of general edification orienting itself towards universality. By this, he wants to re-assess the orientation towards excellence. However, and as a consequence of his reformulation truth-telling at the university has once again a dimension of addressing and enlightenment. A human being is regarded as someone who can get 'lost' in her attempt for self-realisation and who is in need of, according to Mittelstrass (2001, p.3), a 'competence of orientation'. Truth-telling at this kind of university is not only orienting, but tells us first and foremost that "Only as a form of 'edified' self-realisation the reasonable nature of human beings is being realised" (Ibid., p. 11, own translation). And while the expert offers society her services focused on application, the academic as intellectual can judge within society according to the laws of reason. Although Mittelstrass rethinks the traditional university and takes into account actual challenges, his proposal reintroduces the idea that truth-telling at the university is about orientation, addressing and jurisdiction.

From quite a different angle, Derrida (2001)[9] offers in *Université sans Condition* a perspective to re-orient the university. A characteristic of scientific speech (within the *Humanities*) is that it creates a reality. However, this performative dimension of scientific speech does not imply that academics create something *ex nihilo*. Instead, scientific speech could and should be regarded as a kind of committed speech. This commitment however, cannot be reduced to a free or personal choice of the academic. Scientific speech is a kind of answer or response, (i.e., it refers to a demand from outside and is therefore a kind of duty). Furthermore, this demand from outside can only articulate itself throughout scientific speech. It is important to stress that according to Derrida this 'demand' is ethical. However, ethics do not refer to general norms or rules but are about doing justice to the Other. In this perspective, the duty of truth-telling has an ethical foundation and truth-telling still is juridical speech, which should be understood in a rather particular way.

For Derrida, juridical speech is not a kind of autonomous speech that implies that the academic sets a law for herself and judges accordingly. In Derrida's perspective, the law is heteronomous, therefore able to orient us and to ask us to do justice. Justice here is not what is right (according to laws) in a certain context. Justice precedes the law or the rights (although rights are needed for justice to have meaning) (Derrida, 1994). This idea of justice (and the question to do justice) implies that truth-telling at the university does not find the ground for the truth in itself but in the Other (and in that sense, it is a kind of speech without conditions). A demand from outside (the Other) directs our speaking and thinking and gives them their ethical dimension or dimension of responsibility. Scientific truth-telling therefore, does not only involve a kind of attitude but also a kind of obligation or duty (to do justice to…). And according to Derrida (2001), this has important consequences for the organisation of scientific research and education.

Disciplinary-based science and education prevent that certain challenges and demands from the outside enter the university. In a way, the disciplines become prisoners of their own discourses. Therefore, Derrida proposes to orient the university towards alterity. In other words, he points into the direction of a truth-telling that is 'grounded' on a duty that precedes every kind of responsibility and engagement that one has chosen oneself. [10] And exactly for that reason speaking at the university remains an addressed speech with educational and/or ethical implications. Within and for society, the academic offers a testimony of the demand to be responsible and to do justice (i.e., in public her personal position or testimony (a kind of 'profession') demonstrates to others that justice is not being realised in the (actual, concrete) rights or law).

In summary, we claim that for Derrida the ethos of truth-telling at the university implies a kind of pathos (i.e., it is a kind of passionate speaking and thinking contaminated by demands coming from the outside that are loyal to a unspeakable inclination, see Laermans, 2001). Truth-telling at the 'university without condition' is a kind of passionate, ethical speech that submits itself to a law (beyond the law, justice beyond the actual law). It is a speech before a tribunal although this tribunal is what should be looked for over and over again. This tribunal transforms the academic into a "processing subject" (Jans, 2002) who submits herself to a tribunal and law (and thus involved in a process) and also judges ('juridical') herself. It is a subject that permanently searches for an orientation and is in an 'accused' (responsible) position. Therefore, we could argue that in Derrida's modified perspective, truth-telling is still an addressing, juridical speech that has an educational force since it aims at an initiation into the kingdom of justice/truth or points at least, towards that kingdom.[11]

Another Idea: A Worldly University Without Orientation

The current university no longer orients itself towards an idea (of universal humanity or rationality) that transcends itself. Instead, it moves towards excellence and quality (i.e., what is functional for the knowledge society). However, in this position the death sentence of this university seems to be signed when other (mono-functional) organisations perform its functions (research, education, service) and when the combination of these functions is no longer functional. While quality and excellence are regarded as the condition for our survival, this orientation in fact, seems to be the beginning of the end of the (modern) university. Therefore, it is possible to ask whether we still need universities in the era of globalisation with a growing differentiation and specialisation of functions. In other words, is it still possible for the university to have a meaning? This question does not focus on whether research is still possible (or whether we should make the distinction between applied and fundamental research, for example), whether education is possible (and whether a difference exists between research-based education and 'other' education) or whether service is still possible (or the distinction between experts at the university and other experts). *The question instead is whether education, research and service could be linked in such a way that it is possible to label a kind of research and truth-telling as typical for the university?*[12] Some agree it is. However, in their proposals the meaning of research and truth-telling at the university correspond with modern conceptions (i.e., offering a new kind of (ethical) orientation). Research here directs itself towards an (orienting) tribunal and research-based truth-telling is both addressing and juridical. In these conceptions, the ethos of truth-telling at the university relates to a law (a norm or '*nomos*') and is regarded as a kind of submission with an orienting potential (even if this orientation has to be looked for over and over again).

Are these alternative options realistic? With this question we do not want to discuss whether they can be realised or whether they are effective, but we want to challenge the ethos itself. Maybe the willingness to speak in the name of a kingdom (of truth or justice and its laws or principles) is a sign of decadence (as Nietzsche uses the word) (i.e., a willingness to live under a protecting and immunising monopoly and thus to think that one can impose oneself the conditions of life). Don't we then behave ourselves as 'shipwrecked persons' who try to impose their conditions to the sea? (Sloterdijk, 2000a) However, in our view, we should rather accept that it is not at all about orientation. We should not try to find a new orientation and leave behind the willingness to behave as people who want to judge. Maybe it is possible to formulate another research, another form of truth-telling and another meaning for the university? Could enlightenment have another meaning? We believe it is possible—and the following part therefore, is a kind of confession.

Drawing upon Foucault (and foremost his ethos), there is another idea of the university if we are prepared to disconnect the meaning of the university from the obsessive search for orientation and if we disconnect truth-telling at the university (i.e., verisdiction) form judgement or jurisdiction. To propose another idea of the university implies that we first give up the comfort of having a position (a position defined in relation to a kind of tribunal and its laws). To propose this idea is to send an invitation to practice another ethos (i.e., an 'experimental' ethos characterized by a un-comfortable exposition towards the present).

Research of the Present[13] and the Experimental Ethos

What is at stake is to abandon the comfort of the protection by a tribunal and to ask the question of the present (instead of bringing the present (society) to trial). This implies that we ask what is happening in 'our' present, what is happening with 'us,' through 'us' and by 'us' today and what 'we' experience. This 'we' could become the focus of the research and of our thinking. In other words, as inhabitants of the university (in our idea) we cannot avoid the present and our involvement in the present. It is not our involvement in a doctrine or tradition, neither our belonging to a community or humanity in general, but our belonging to the present, to a 'we.' Therefore, the question is: what are 'we' today and what is happening to 'us'?

Of course, it could be argued that research in modern university was/is also concerned with the present. But it was/is a rather particular concern. The background of this concern was/is to be able to judge the present (in relation to laws or principles). Therefore, this caring attitude has no interest in the present as such. It is an attitude in which one looks at the present from the perspective of a particular future (based upon the criteria of reason or humanity, for example), as something that needs orientation, judgement, foundations and thus, limitation and guidance. Research of the present instead leaves behind this attitude of wanting to orient the present. It involves an experimental attitude in the full meaning of the word: exposition to the present and thus, accepting to be touched, infected or even intoxicated,[14] accepting to think and become otherwise—without immunizing oneself in advance. Such research implies to give up the comfort of a position (an established place, a foundation, a ground) and to expose oneself (and one's thoughts) to one's own limits. What is needed therefore, is an 'ascesis', putting oneself to the test or an exercise in thinking.

This exposition to the present is uncomfortable because of the lack of a tribunal and of criteria, but also because one belongs to the present and one's own position is at stake. The aim cannot be limited to gaining insight in or to acquiring expertise. Foremost, putting oneself to the test is a practice of self-transformation without the promise of a better position in the future.

Truth-Telling: Asceticism and Experience

The university is a place for scientific truth-telling that is foremost a practice. With practice we do not refer to the idea that speech as such has an effect or is productive and performative. Truth-telling as practice means that who tells the truth does something with herself and should do this to be able to tell the truth. Truth-telling implies work upon self and a particular relation to self and to others. This is what we meant with ethos. Thus, truth-telling has an ethical dimension because as a practice it implies a particular ethos (and not because it could have ethical consequences).

In the modern university, as well as in the current one and Derrida and Mittelstrass' university, truth-telling is a kind of comfortable speech that implies a well-defined position constituted and authorized by a tribunal and its laws. This relation to a law results of course, in depending on its sanctions (and exclusion as a final solution), but offers a kind of comfort of a promised 'home-land' or kingdom. This speech defines its public in relation to this kingdom and tribunal and addresses this public in an orienting way in the name of this kingdom. It seems as though we do not want to give up this position, although the idea of an orientation (and a kingdom) seems to be lost today. In other words, it seems that there is still the willingness to have or find a comfortable position in which we do not have to put ourselves to the test.

However, in our idea the researcher and truth-teller at the university no longer have a mandate of a kind of kingdom. In a certain way, they only have the mandate of our present, of our time. Research therefore, should not be concerned with the problem of legitimisation and of lost or new foundations, neither with finding or defending positions, but with 'experience' in a literal sense (i.e., what is happening to us today). In order to have to say something, the researcher should infect herself with her own time and problems, with today's diseases and events.[15] It is about listening to the present or being 'present in the present.' In this sense, the mandate of truth-telling at the university relates to 'one's personal experience' and therefore, always has an existential dimension. As Sloterdijk (2000a) reminds us, one could refer to the old formula of the six-ties: 'science in the first person.' The first person however is not the 'I', but re-fers instead to a vocative. It refers to someone whose is being talked to or who is affected. And as Wittgenstein has argued, we should leave behind the formula 'I think' instead say 'this is a thought,' and find out how we can relate to this thought. Truth-telling also implies a passionate, feverish speech. But it is an-other passivity, another hijacking than the ones implied in the duty in relation to the law. This passion involves being grasped or hijacked by the present in a per-sonal experience.

However, 'personal experience' has nothing to do with a personal opinion, but involves using oneself (both in a psychic and somatic way) as a kind of 'me-dium' in which something can be recorded or inscribed and through which something can be expressed or articulated. The university, then, is the place for experimental thinking and research captured by the present that is being hi-jacked by 'worldly problems' that it has to carry or sustain and communicate. Two elements are required: a direct contact with the present or being affected and preparatory practices and exercises, or asceticism.

Here, we can situate the meaning of 'education' at the university. The uni-versity is not educational in the sense of initiating students into a kingdom or transmitting skills and knowledge, but in the sense of offering the opportunity to shape and transform one's own existence through study and experimental research. This study[16] and research ask for attention (i.e., being present in the present in order to be captured by the present and to communicate it (to share it, in the different meanings of to share)). Again, this study and attitude imply an attentive attitude that is both passive and un-flattering. As a result, education at the university aims at making people attentive and thus to make possible that there is a kind of affection, pawing and eventually experience. As argued before, two elements matter to achieve this: to literally bring together (implying among other things, to move oneself, to look, to travel,…) and an 'athletic training' to use the formula of Sloterdijk (2000b). The latter could be labelled as prepara-tory, e-ducational practices or as asceticism.

Activities such as exercise, reading (classics), write (and/or copy by hand), listen, repeat, recite, etc. can be considered as disciplinary e-ducational practices that bring students and teachers in a condition where something can happen, in which an experience becomes possible and in which they (their relation to the self and others) can be transformed. These e-ducational practices therefore, are also always a kind of de-immunisation (leaving behind a position and the submission to a tribunal). On the other hand, these practices offer the opportunity of e-ducational moments. These moments are, as the etymology of the Latin verb 'e-ducere' shows, in a literal sense moments by which we are being led out of ourselves, outside or into the 'world' or 'no-man's land' in which we are exposed, without the protection of a position (within a kingdom of truth). E-ducational moments are when the student and the teacher are exposed to each other and to 'the text' or to the present. At these moments something could be noticed or said that was not being expected or foreseen, moments at which words could receive a new meaning. There is no need for these moments and they do not have a place, but they can take place, they can happen. At these moments people are standing with empty hands and they cannot cover themselves in the illusion of autonomy neither of heteronomy. These moments do not know 'clients' or 'suppliers' and are not the result of an investment.

These e-educational practices and moments require time, a lot of time. But it is not a time that results in a profit. Maybe, it is a school time in the sense of the Greek word '*scholè*,' (i.e., free time or time that is not occupied with the necessity of survival, excellence or added value). It is a time we call worldly time, time of the world or time of an exposition to the present. Instead of being leisure time, school time is a difficult, hard time (i.e., a time to deal with the question of the present and of living together, of being with the words, the texts, things, with others). What appears in this time is a world that confronts us with questions (and not with solutions). At school and during school time we carry a burden and we are not involved in the process of knowledge production and transmission. Being part of the world therefore, is having no position and being exposed and confronted with a question. And e-ducational practices exactly offer the opportunity to enter the world or to become affected.

This explains why we stick to our idea of the modern conception of the university as the place and time of a particular type of truth-telling (i.e., a truth-telling based upon a particular type of research or research of the present that has a potential for edification since it implies a particular ethos). This experimental ethos combines an 'asceticism' (e-ducation, exercise) and a pathos, a pathos of love for the truth or of curiosity (in the Foucauldian sense) and not a pathos of duty (towards a law). This asceticism and pathos constitute the subject of truth or the truth-teller, not the memory of timeless ideas, the election by a god or the initiation in a tradition or school. Furthermore, the source for the authority (although undermining itself time and again) of this truth-telling lies in the experience itself (and not in the mandate of a kingdom). To tell the truth in this way is not without risk (a characteristic that has always been related to truth-telling) and requires courage.[17] In short, truth-telling links up with an attitude to risk one's life or to experience: to be prepared to expose oneself, to be attentive to the present, to be in a world where our soul and body can be hurt, to become passionate (and the story goes that one of Plato's academy super-scriptions was that those who do not want to have erotic relations should not sign on).

A Non-Addressed Speech: A Matter of Love?

Truth-telling at the world-university is not directed towards a culture, a nation or a state, neither to mankind as such. What is at stake is to address the world or, paradoxically stated, to address what could not be addressed. Nobody is being addressed or nobody in the sense of no-one in particular. In this way, the aim of the world-university is to tell the truth and telling the truth means that who needs the truth is not defined in advance. This truth-telling does not address the inhabitants of the knowledge society (offering them productive knowledge). Instead, worldly truth-telling opens up the world in the knowledge society. And therefore, speaking at the world university is always a kind of untimely truth-telling.

A timely or addressed truth-telling is always a kind of focused and directed speech: directed towards students (in a classroom), other researchers (in journals) or practitioners (in lectures). A main characteristic here is the presence of a tribunal: an educational regime (curricula, examinations), the tribunal of the scientific community, the tribunal of application. Speaking in a classroom, in journals, in the domain of labor is not about making something public, but is related to privatisation. Of course, with regard to these places and these populations the term public is equally being used, but it refers then to bringing something (knowledge, learning material, research results) into a condition where it can be appropriated. Public means that everyone can make use of it, it is of no-one, it is no one's property, no one can appropriate it for herself exclusively. The horizon of this conception is that something can be appropriated, can be made proper. In this way, public truth-telling is from the very beginning an addressed speech or speaking with a well-defined public of users in mind.

Worldly truth-telling or non-addressed speech is not about property or appropriation.[18] Speaking at the world-university takes the idea that in the world no one or nobody is special seriously, and that this opinion or assumption concerning equity asks for a rather particular kind of truth. The world 'asks' to speak the truth without addressing someone in particular, and 'asks' for ideas, words, gestures that are universal in a certain way. They are not universal because everyone at every place should understand them, but because they answer to the question of being-with, of living-together, of being exposed and being inspired by the opinion of equity. In this way, it is through worldly truth-telling that we speak about the world. Or to reformulate this idea, the act of making something public or worldly does not stress issues of addressing or accessibility, but the fact of pure communication. In truth-telling and based upon research of the present an idea or a thought is being communicated.

The non-addressed character of this speech implies that the truth-teller at the university is not a wise man/woman.[19] A wise (wo)man takes the position of someone who remains mostly silent and speaks publicly only when asked. Due to his exposition to the present, the truth-teller at the world-university cannot be silent. Instead, she is 'unable to keep thoughts for herself' and therefore, she puts her own life (and relations) at stake (Arendt, 1994). The non-addressed speech also implies that it is neither a speech of riddles (i.e., prophetic speech that reveals the future), nor a speech that uncovers the true 'being' of the world. This speech says 'what is.' [20] However, saying 'what is' is neither a constative speech act nor a per- formative speech act (in the Austinian sense). The former implies the possibility of legitimisation and therefore, a kind of judgement. Also, the latter could imply a legitimisation (i.e., criteria with regard to the effect and to a defined public). Since truth-telling based on research of the present also studies and brings into play the criteria of what can be thought and what can be said (the criteria of science, for example) and the limits of the present (the limits of the acknowledged disciplines and domains for example), this speech does not know in advance who is being addressed, who will be its judge and on what criteria it will be judged. It is truth-telling without knowing who needs or expects this truth. And therefore, this experimental speech, as Lyotard (1984) claims, always remains something like "shouting in the desert" (pp. 69–70).

Again, we emphasize that such a truth-telling is only possible on the basis of an exposition or a being out of position. In a certain way, it is a speaking in one's own name, or more precisely a speaking without name or face and thus, an exposed speaking, a speaking in and out of an exposition (in and out of the world as public space). This speaking is not a kind of judgement. It is a verisdiction that is not at the same time a jurisdiction. But still, it can have a meaning. Worldly speech enlightens in a literal sense: it brings light, it makes visible and thus, it exposes what is. Exposition—and to make public in this meaning—implies that it can be touched and that it can touch (us) for itself (transforms 'us' as being 'subjects'). We remind that this kind of enlightenment is not the one offered by reason, but by experience. Therefore, non-addressed truth-telling is not an irresponsible speech and could have indeed meaning for society.

Concluding Remarks

With these thoughts about truth-telling at the university, we have first and foremost put our own position at stake: who are we as truth-tellers? Based upon this we expressed an idea and communicated it. However, this idea does not ask us to judge upon our university today. This does not mean that it is just an idea. Therefore, we will mention very briefly specific points of attention and practices that articulate this idea.[21]

The universities in the knowledge society are expected to organise poles of excellence: excellent research based upon a particular system of indicators. The research of the present and worldly truth-telling asks for 'worldly poles of attention' concerning worldly problems. An example is maybe that scarcity (of food, energy) places states in a rather particular position towards each other. This does not ask from a university a kind of jurisdiction or a tribunal (accusing nations or bringing nations to the court because they would fail in this respect) but a verisdiction: a world-university can show what is at stake, what nation-based sovereignty implies. It cannot be the intention of worldly speech to submit nations to a new, more fundamental sovereignty (of a kingdom of truth and its laws), but to show that sovereignty of nations results in certain problems. The world 'asks' from the university that it communicates this, that it shows it and that it focuses attention on these uses.

In this conception the academic community is not defined (or defining itself) in the confession to the same methodology or the same tribunal (the scientific tribunal, the quality tribunal, the tribunal of truth), but it is a community of people sharing the exposition towards the present. Their speaking together is not a kind of jurisdiction, no exchange of judgements (and convictions), and their discussions are not imitations of war with other means. It is a community of curious people that is taking care of the present.[22] What they share or have in common is not a language (or a particular code), but an ethos and thoughts. They do not form schools into which people should become initiated (and whose entrance gates and hierarchies should be defended). Being part of this community is edifying because the community invites to bring oneself to the test, it invites to 'experience' and it is itself a kind of laboratory of experience and of thinking in the sense of bringing thoughts to or in the world, that can put something to the limits and that can play with 'us' (instead of the other way around).

The modern and current academic world as a kingdom of truth cannot be disconnected from an activity of control on the access. People can pass the entrance gate if they submit themselves to the laws of the tribunal of truth (a judgement on the basis of the number of publications in peer-reviewed journals, for example). From an academic perspective auto-nomous refers to the submission under a law (*nomos*). The idea of worldly truth-telling instead, could be connected to a kind of profession (in this sense we refer again to the idea of the Hippocratic Oath).[23] The members of the university community, the academics, maybe could relate to Cicero's (1980) following advice:

> We, the academics, we live from day to day. We express everything which touches us by its convincing character and in this way we are the only ones who are really free. We enjoy a larger freedom and are more independent; our capacity to judge knows no constraints, we don't have to follow any prescription, we don't have to carry out any order, I would almost say that nothing obliges us to defend a case just like that (V, 11, 33; our translation).

Academics are there for nobody, nobody in particular.

Notes

1 The naming order is a pure strategic option.
2 See also Derrida, 2001, p. 59.
3 For these other conceptions, see Jaspers & Rosmann 1961, Schelsky, 1963.
4 The title of Humboldt's proposal—"Über die innere und äussere Organisation der Höhere wissenschaftlichen   Anstalten"—clarifies this conception (Humboldt, 1810).
5 The translation of the critical meaning of the university into the function of service in the modern/actual university is already an indication of a transformation in the self-understanding of the university.
6 This part is based on the report of the Strata-etan expert group on the relation research-education at the European universities (2003).
7 Already in the sixties, Kerr (1963) refers to the university as a 'multi-versity' because there is an expansion of the number of functions and because the university has an new meaning for the new 'knowledge society.'
8 For this kind of argumentation (although not explicitly dealing with Habermas) see Luhmann, 1992; Gutu, 1998; Laermans, 1999.

9   We do not focus on his earlier publications on the university (see Derrida, 2004).

10 In his study 'The university in ruins,' Readings (1996) ends up with a similar idea of an ethos of duty.

11 Also Foucault's comment on Derrida's work is instructive: "… je dirai que c'est une petite pédagogie historiquement bien déterminée qui, de manière très visible se manifeste. Pédagogie qui enseigne à l'élève qu'il n'y a rien hors du texte, mais qu'en lui, en ses interstices, dans ses blancs et ses non-dits, règne la réserve de l'origine ; qu'il n'est donc point nécessaire d'aller chercher ailleurs, mais qu'ici même, non point dans les mots certes, mais dans les mots comme ratures, dans leur grille, se dit 'le sens de l'être'. Pédagogie qui inversement donne la voix des maîtres cette souveraineté sans limites qui lui permet indéfiniment de re-dire le texte" (Foucault, 1972, p. 267)

12 As we will elaborate we believe that such a link is still possible. However, within the framework of this paper we are able to pursue our proposal into the question whether such a link is itself bound to a certain physical 'place.'

13 This does not imply that we should not read 'old' texts. Quite the contrary. It does not mean that the present should become a kind of tribunal or a totality of 'being.'

14 See Sloterdijk, 2000a.

15 This is based upon Sloterdijk, 2003

16 Education at the university is centred around study which is not the same as student-centred. Therefore, we agree with the idea of Humboldt that teachers (professors) are not at the university for students, but that both are there for the truth.

17 This theme is discussed in: Arendt, 1994.

18 The idea of non-addressed speech is also discussed in: Walser, 2000.

19 Foucault is elaborating this analysis of truth-telling according to four 'types' (the wise men, the prophet, the teacher, the parresiast) in his last, unpublished, lectures at the Collège de France (see recordings to be consulted at IMEC in Caen).

20 According to Arendt (1994), no world can survive without people who are ready to do what Herodotus has done for the first time in a conscious way: to say what is (*'legein ta eonta'*), or to testify of what is and what appears to be since it is.

21 The problem of the institutionalisation of the idea will not be discussed as it deserves a separate discussion.

22 See also the dream of Foucault: "I dream of the intellectual destroyer of evidence and universalities, the one who, in the inertias and constraints of the present, locates and marks the weak points, the openings, the lines of power, who incessantly displaces himself, doesn't know exactly where he is heading nor what he'll think tomorrow because he is too attentive to the present. (Foucault, 1989, p.155).

23 In contrast to the actual procedures of jurisdiction a profession and an oath are rather uncomfortable since we put ourselves to the test.

Bibliography

Anrich, E. (1960). *Die Idee der Deutschen Universität und die Reform DeutschenUniversitäten.* Darmstadt: Wissenschaftliche Buchgesellschaft.

————. (1994) Waarheid en politiek. In: *Tussen verleden en toekomst* (pp. 125–162).Leuven: Garant. (Original work published in 1967)

Ash, M. G. (Ed.). (1999). *Mythos Humboldt. Vergangenheit und Zukunft der deutschen Universitäten.* Wien: Böhlau.

Brown, R. B., & McCartney, S. (1998). The link between research and teaching: Its purpose and implications. *Innovations in Education and Training International, 35*(2), 117–129.

Cicero, Marcus Tullius (1980). *Gesprekken in Tusculum (Tusculum Disputationes)* (Vertaling C. Verhoeven). Baarn: Ambo.

Derrida, J. (1994). *Kracht van wet. Het 'mystieke fundament van het gezag'.* Kampen: Agora/Pelckmans.

————. (2001). *Université sans condition.* Paris: Galilée.

————. (2004). *Eyes of the university. Right to philosophy 2.* Stanford: Stanford University Press.

European Commision, Strata-Etan Expert Group, (2002). *Developing foresight for the development of higher education/research relations in the perspective of the European research area (ERA).* (E. Bourgeois, Rapporteur)

————. (2003, February). *The role of the universities in the Europe of knowledge.*

European University Association (EUA) (2003, may). *Response to the communication from the commission. The role of the universities in the Europe of knowledge.*

Foucault, M. (1972). Mon corps, ce papier, ce feu. In D. Defert, F. Ewald & J. Lagrange (Eds.), *Dits et écrits II 1970–1975* (pp. 245–268). Paris: Gallimard.

————. (1989) The end of the monarchy of sex. In S. Lotringer (Ed.) *Foucault live: Interviews, 1966–1984* (pp. 137–155) (D. M. Marchi, Trans.), New York: Semiotext(e). (Original work published in 1984)

————. (2001) Entretien avec Michel Foucault (With A.Fontana & P.Pasquino). In D. Defert, F. Ewald & J. Lagrange (Eds.), *Dits et écrits. II: 1977–1988* (pp.140–160). Paris: Gallimard Quarto. (Original work published in 1977)

Gutu, G. (1998). Zu Fragen der universitären Forschung. Mit Blick auf den philologischen Bereich an rumänischen Hochschulen. *Internet-Zeitschrift für Kulturwissenschaften, 3* http://www.inst.at/trans/3Nr/gutu.htm

Habermas, J. (1989). *De nieuwe onoverzichtelijkheid en andere opstellen.* Amsterdam: Boom.

————. (1990). De idee van de universiteit—leerprocessen. *Comenius, 38* (10), 166–168.

Humboldt, von W. (1810). Über die innere und äussere Organisation der Höheren Wissenschaftlichen Anstalten in Berlin. In H. Weinstock (Ed.) (1957), *Wilhelm von Humboldt* (pp. 126–134). Frankfurt a.M: Suhrkamp. (Original work published in 1810)

Hunter, I. (2000). *Rival enlightenments: Civil and metaphysical philosophy in early modern Germany* Cambridge: Cambridge University Press.

Jans, E. (2002). Kritische Intoxicaties. Over cultuur, crisis en explosies. *Etcetera, 20* (80), 5–9.

Jaspers, K., & Rosmann, K. (1961). *Die Idee der Universität: für die gegenwärtige Situation entworfen.* Berlin: Springer.

Jenkins, A., & Zetter, R. (2003). *Linking teaching with research in departments.* York: Generic Centre/Learning and Teaching Support Network.

Lyotard, J. F. (1984). *Tombeau de l'intellectuel et autres papiers.* Paris: Galilée.

Laermans, R. (1999). *Communicatie zonder mensen. Een systeem-theoretische inleiding in de sociologie.* Amsterdam: Boom.

————. (2001). *Ruimten van cultuur. Van de straat over de markt naar het podium.* Leuven: Van Halewijck.

Luhmann, N. (1992). System und Absicht der Erziehung. In N. Luhmann & K. E. Schorr (Eds.), *Zwischen Absicht und Person: Fragen an die Pädagogik* (pp. 109–124). Frankfurt a.M.: Surhkamp:

Kerr, C. (1963). *The uses of the university.* New York: Harper & Raw.

Kopetz, H. (2002). *Forschung und Lehre. Die Idee der Universität bei Humboldt, Jaspers, Schelsky and Mittelstrass.* Wien: Böhlau Verlag.

Mittelstrass, J. (1989). *Glanz und Elend der Geisteswissenschaften.* Oldenburg: Bis Verlag. Retreived from *http://www.uni-konstanz.de/FuF/Philo/Philosophie/Mitarbeiter/mittelstrass/liste.htm*

————. (1994). *Die unzeitgemässe Universität.* Frankfurt a.M: Suhrkamp.

————. (2001). *Bildung und ethische Masse.* Paper presented at McKinsey Bildet, Hamburg, Gallerie der Gegenwart. *http://www.mckinsey-bildet.de/downloads/02_idee/ w2_vortrag_mittelstrass.pdf*

————. (2002). *Die Modernität der klassischen Universität.* Marburg: Marburger Universitätsreden. Retrieved from *http://www.uni-konstanz.de/FuF/Philo/Philosophie/ Mitarbeiter/mittelstrass/Marburg-2002.htm*

————. (2003). *Das Mass des Fortschritts. Mensch und Wissenschaft in der'Leonardo-Welt.'* Köln: Karl Rahner Akademie.

Nybom, T. (2003). The von Humboldt legacy and the contemporary European university. In E. De Corte (Ed.), *Excellence in higher education* (pp. 17–32). London: Portland Press.

Readings, B. (1996). *The university in ruins.* Cambridge: Harvard University Press.

Riedel, M. (1977). Wilhelm von Humboldts Begründung der 'Einheit von Forschung und Lehre' als Leitidee der Universität. *Zeitschrift für Pädagogik*, 14, 231–247.

Schelsky, H. (1963). *Einsamkeit und Freiheit; Idee und Gestalt der deutschen Universität und Ihrer Reformen.* Reinbek bei Hamburg: Rowohlt.

Sloterdijk, P. (2000a). *Essai d'intoxication volontaire. Conversation avec Carlos Oliveira.* Paris: Calman-Lévy.

————. (2000b) *Le penseur sur scène.* Paris : Christian Bourgeois.

————. (2003). *Ni le soleil ni la mort. Jeu de piste sous forme de dialogues avec Hans-Jürgen Heinrichs.* Paris: Pauvert.

Walser, M. (2000) *Über das Selbstgespräch. Ein Flagranter Versuch.* Die Zeit, 13 January, 42–43.

Weber, M. (1991) *Wissenschaft als Beruf.* In M. Sukale (ed.), Max Weber. Schriften zur Wissenschaftslehre (pp. 237–273). Stuttgart: Philipp Reclam. (Original work published in 1919)

ஐ Chapter 11 ையை

Foucault: The Ethics of Self-Creation and the Future of Education

Kenneth Wain

Ethics and Morality

The last phase of Foucault's work, covered by his last two books and late essays, is often described as 'ethical.' Which means that, in general terms, he became less concerned to describe the workings of disciplinary power in modern society, as he had been in his earlier writings, and more concerned with defining the spaces for freedom such a society permits its members both in the political and in the ethical sphere. A society that, in his earlier accounts, he described as obsessed with its own security and with the efficient policing of its members, rather than with their freedom or education. The learning society he described in *Discipline and Punish* (1991) was one where individuals pass from under one form of domination into another;[1] a society that employs a spectrum of disciplinary technologies, an arsenal of repressive pedagogical techniques that it puts to work in its institutions, and not just its corrective ones. A panopticon society that is obsessed with the general procedures and practices of policing and surveillance in their various forms that it collects under the general rubric of governance, and which it defines in terms of bio- and disciplinary power. Foucault described the modern-postmodern learning society in such asphyxiating terms that it led to a chorus of well-known objections by a variety of critics that it had squeezed freedom out of the reckoning completely, conceding it no space at all in our daily life rendering the word meaningless. Rendering meaningless the word education also. This is still a common perception about Foucault. For those who know his work, however, it needs no saying that freedom was not something he set in contrast with power, at least not in his later work. To the contrary, he wanted to describe freedom *in terms* of power, or better still power relations, as he described everything else, including his ethics which he perceived as the practice of freedom or liberty. This is how he summarizes the relation between liberty and ethics: "Liberty is the ontological condition of ethics. But ethics is the deliberate form assumed by liberty" (Bernauer & Rasmussen, 1994, p. 4). In simpler terms, it means that there is no ethics without liberty, indeed that ethics is the form one gives to the practice of one's freedom.

Let me elaborate on this account of ethics and on the relationship between ethics, conceived of in this way, and morality. In an autumn 1983 interview with Stephen Riggins, Foucault further defined ethics as "the relationship you have to yourself when you act," (Kritzman, 1990, p. 15), thereby distinguishing it from morality which has to do with the relationship you have with others, with codes of behaviour prescribed for all, and which deals in imperatives, rules of conduct, or commands. Habermas (1994) makes a roughly similar distinction between ethical questions where we "want to get clear on who we are and who we want to be, and 'moral' questions where we want to know what is equally good for all" (p. 104). In contrast with ethics, which has to do with freedom, morality has to do with truth, with 'games of truth' as Foucault calls them. It therefore, plays a very different sort of language game from that of ethics, that of governance and control, which is the same language game as that of politics. Foucault places a certain kind of ethics and conventional morality among the essentially repressive technologies of power, referred to earlier, where one is made "subject to someone else by control and dependence, and tied to his own identity by a conscience of self-knowledge." Both kinds of technology suggest "a form of power which subjugates and makes subject to," or, to use Foucault's own word, subjectivates (Dreyfus & Rabinow, 1983, p. 212). The language game in both games of power play has *normality* as its central concern. In both, *truth* is represented as the expression of a normality, as a matter of abiding with established norms, and falsehood as the departure from or the betrayal of those same norms. To subjectivate is to impose norms; to "categorize the individual, mark him by his individuality, attach him to his identity, impose a law of truth on him which he must recognize and which others have to recognize in him." (Ibid., p. 212). In other words, it is to impose an ethics on one, a relationship one has with oneself that corresponds with a conventional morality that one recognises as true, and to act in ways that are recognisably approved by that same morality. Conventional morality subjectivates most subtly and effectively by cultivating confessional practices that encourage the subject to tell the truth about herself, to work on her morality through her conscience.

Some further explanation of the Foucaultian understanding of the relation of ethics to morality may be required at this point for the sake of clarity. O'Leary (2002) points out that Foucault defined conventional morality according to a threefold schema according to which it is

first a moral code which may be more or less explicitly formulated; second, the actual behaviour of those who are 'subject' to this code; and, third, the way individuals constitute themselves as moral subjects of the code—that is, the way they 'conduct themselves' and 'bring themselves' (*se conduire*) to obey (or disobey) a set of prescriptions. (p. 11)

The last aspect is how Foucault understands ethics. It differs from the other aspects of morality in that, it is not a field of rules, principles or precepts, it is the field of our self-constitution as subjects." [It consists of] the set of attitudes, practices and goals by which we guide our moral self-understanding. In this schema, ethics is a sub-set of the category of 'morality.' [This is where Foucault locates] the aspect of 'subjectivation.' (p. 11)

But subjectivation needs not mean the cancellation of freedom or the total loss of power, unless it takes the form of domination. One needs to understand how Foucault sees the relation of freedom with power; not as something antithetical to it but, to the contrary, as something necessary to it. There is no freedom without power but equally there is no power without freedom; each is a condition for the other. The matter is similar with power and knowledge. As O'Leary (2002) puts it, for Foucault "freedom…is not a state for which we strive, it is a condition of our striving" (p. 159). It is also the condition of one's ethical self-expression and of one's education. To be without power is to be without freedom and vice-versa. It is to be dominated by the will of another; to lack power-freedom utterly. It is to be in a relationship where power is blocked, it does not circulate; where the relationship with a teacher takes the violent form of indoctrination (Bernauer & Rasmussen, 1994). Enculturation needs not take that form, and it does not do so, in theory at least, in the modern liberal societies Foucault studies.

In liberal societies both enculturation and indoctrination are distinguished from education, which is identified with an ethics of rationally autonomous. According to Kant what distinguishes autonomy from enculturation, in this respect, is not the absence of rules in the former as distinct from the latter but the provenience of the rules. An autonomous ethics involves imperatives, yes, but it implies a form of governance of the will not by the external laws or maxims of a conventional morality that govern a heteronymous will, but by laws of reason that are universal. Foucault, of course, dismisses the Kantian idea of a universal law of reason but retains the idea of autonomy as a sign of moral and intellectual maturity,[2] and invites us, more radically than Kant, to create "new forms of subjectivity through the refusal of this kind of individuality which has been imposed on us for several centuries," (Dreyfus & Rabinow, 1983, p. 216) which include the subjectivation of our conscience by conventional morality. He continues:

Maybe the target today is not to discover what we are, but to refuse what we are. We have to imagine and to build up what we could be to get rid of the kind of political 'double-bind', which is the simultaneous individualization and totalization of modern power structures. (Ibid., p. 216)

Self-refusal and self-creation are essentially Nietzschean tasks, not Kantian. They require a radical reading of the Socratic exhortation to 'know oneself' which Socrates regarded as indispensable to ethics as the art of living, whereby knowing oneself is not *examining* one's life, looking *inside* oneself, through the lense of one's socialized conscience, but knowing how one is constituted a subject, subjectivated, by the different economies of power, the processes and practices that constitute one's self as an encultured self, including how one's conscience is constituted by a conventional morality—an undertaking for which genealogies provide appropriate tools.

Foucault's rejection of conventional morality connects his ethics with Nietzsche's famous, and notorious, immoralism; Nietzsche's understanding of ethics as a trans-valuation of values; his well-known undertaking to cast his ethics beyond good and evil. O'Leary (2002) quotes Nietzsche's view that morality will perish over "the next two centuries" (p. 7) and remarks that Foucault believed this event was inevitable, and that, to some extent, it has already happened, raising the question how we are to fill the void created thereby, how we can live without morality. But self-creation is not the only way. In *After Virtue* (1981) Alasdair MacIntyre narrates the same loss, echoes Nietzsche's view that the death of God threatens us with nihilism, but responds to the challenge this situation creates differently from either Foucault or Nietzsche. MacIntyre's conclusion that morality is in a state of crisis stems from his account of the state of our moral language today and, in particular, our inability to resolve moral disagreement often rendering it interminable and aggressive, a situation which, he believes, bewilders ordinary people who want guidance for their moral lives and know not where to find it. Like Nietzsche, MacIntyre locates the cause of this state of disorientation deep within modernist culture which he describes as *emotivist* in its essence.[3] His response to it is to resituate an Aristotelian virtue morality in the modern world that would give people's lives a sense of purpose and direction. Elsewhere, MacIntyre (1987) also complains about a loss of education in the modern world which he also puts down to our modernist culture. He puts it down to the chronic inability of modern schools to resolve the tension between the simultaneous tasks they are entrusted with of socializing the young into roles their society requires and making them individuals. This is because, he argues, our pluralist modernist culture proscribes the notion of an educated public such as was found in eighteenth century Scotland; a public with a 'single mind' adhering to a common philosophy of common sense. Education today requires the reconstitution of such a public which, like the Scottish public, would operate with a single philosophy and morality.

MacIntyre describes the modernist culture as one that is bureaucratic and manipulative in the public realm and chaotically permissive in the private, in the sphere of ethics. Foucault shares this assessment of the modern world but rejects the politics of the educated public, of which there is a liberal Kantian version endorsed and propagated by Habermas and others, which is different from MacIntyre's Scottish version.[4] His answer to the permissiveness of modern ethics is, as we shall see, different. This is because, against MacIntyre, Foucault supports the Enlightenment project that also set ethics up against morality in the form of the Kantian doctrine of an autonomous will, parting company with it, as I said earlier, when it proposes that should express itself in conformity with a universal law of Reason. Or, to put it more generally, that it needs to be expressed in conformity with *a* morality. In this respect, while he commends the maturity of the Enlightenment he wants to go beyond. But that does not mean that he conceives of ethics nihilistically; as the absence of any morality at all. Indeed, though like Nietzsche, he wants to cut off the king's head by dispensing with *universal* moralities completely, he does not, any more than Nietzsche, suggest dispensing with morality, as the obedience to rules, as such; he just sites it differently than Kant, not in Reason but in a different place, in the individual herself, and the same is true of education.

Ethics in the Private Sphere

For both Nietzsche and Foucault, ethics as the work one does on oneself, and education, are one and the same thing. Nietzsche defines both as self-creation, thereby locating them in both the moral and the aesthetic sphere. And the same is true with some important differences, with Foucault. According to this definition education is *self-education*, but that does not mean that it does not require teachers, great educators, as Nietzsche calls them. But these are only exemplars to follow. Nietzsche contemptuously dismissed the relation of discipleship as the proper relation with one's educator. In his own case, the exemplars he acknowledged were Wagner and Schopenhauer. Richard Rorty follows him in this respect, in referring to an education by exemplars, but Foucault does not. Nor does Foucault, to my knowledge, use the expression self-creation as such. He seems to prefer the expression 'self-constitution' instead. Rorty's account of self-creation is interesting in that he imposes a relation with education on it not shared either by Nietzsche or Foucault. It begins in *Philosophy and the Mirror of Nature* (1980) where he declares himself in sympathy not with Nietzsche's but with Gadamer's very different "romantic notion of man as self-creative" (p. 358). Gadamer defines education-self-creation as *bildung* or 'edification' (pp. 359–360). Much later Rorty ties self-creation with the pragmatic experimentalism of James and Dewey instead (Saatkamp, 1995). Meanwhile, he engages extensively with the term in *Contingency, Irony and Solidarity* (1989), where Nietzsche is his point of reference. In *Philosophy and the Mirror of Nature*, under Gadamer's influence, edification is described as something that is acquired socially, through conversational engagement, so that, in effect, he views education like MacIntyre and Habermas, as requiring a public—a liberal public like Habermas's. Things change very drastically, however, in *Contingency, Irony and Solidarity* where he describes self-creation-education as the cultivation of private irony. In the book, he acknowledges Nietzsche as one who "saw self-knowledge as self-creation. The process of coming to know oneself, confronting one's contingency, tracking one's causes home," a process he describes as "identical with the process of inventing a new language—that is, of thinking up new metaphors" (p. 27). Self-creation-education- ethics becomes a matter of self re-description, of re-describing oneself in terms of an ironist vocabulary to which the notion of contingency is central.

But Rorty also makes limitations and qualifications on this self re-description, or self-creation, as he sees it; it is one's private self *only* that one recreates through ironic, or poetic re-description. One's public self, where one is a citizen, is re-described differently; through the democratic processes of conversation, dialogue, and pragmatic negotiation. Here, his point of reference, as he says himself, is not Nietzsche but Dewey (and other "fellow citizens" besides, like Marx, Mill, Habermas, and Rawls (Rorty, 1989, p. xiv). Private self-description or self-creation, he says, and this *is* Nietzsche, is a matter of coping with one's aloneness, of making one's own meaning in a contingent universe. This is where reading authors like Nietzsche, Kierkegaard, Baudelaire, Proust, Heidegger and Nabokov, Rorty says, can help; they are the exemplars, the educators, those who illustrate "what private perfection—a self-created, autonomous, human life—can be like" (p. xiv). Any other use of them, in his view, any political use of them, would be mistaken and dangerous. They have no use in the public sphere where the discourse is one of solidarity not self-creation. Rorty emphasises, in fact, that solidarity and self-creation cannot come together in a common project, and should therefore be confined to the separate realms of the private and the public. Unsurprisingly, therefore, he is unsympathetic, to put it mildly, with Foucault's ironic re-descriptions, or unmasking, of the power structures of modern liberal-democratic state and of its institutions and of their implements of subjectivation, though the ironist's ethics also contemplates a radical re-evaluation of the conventional truths which one is raised with in the home and the school and on which one builds one's identity in childhood and youth.[5] Foucault's ethics, however, takes form in the public sphere through his self re-description as an activist and a specific intellectual who practices *parrhesia*, which is the practice not of irony but of truth, and where the inspiration is Socrates more than Nietzsche.[6]

Of course, the difference between Rorty and Foucault, as Rorty (1989) himself says, is one of attitude towards liberal institutions, to which Rorty is sympathetic and to which Foucault, influenced by Nietzsche, is hostile. Rorty contends that the current liberal-democratic order is the only route to social and political progress currently available in today's world, and its societies the only ones that permit the ironist or self-creating poet to flourish. He claims that liberalism contains everything that is politically important in Nietzsche and that what is not so contained can be safely discarded. David Owen (1995), however, rightly claims that Rorty's "liberal perspectivism" is more accurately contrasted with the agonistic politics of Nietzsche's perspectivism than likened to it. Foucault's self-constitution as a specific intellectual in the public sphere, on the other hand, in its endorsement of an agonistic and particularistic politics, is of Nietzschean inspiration. The practice of *parrhesia* was, in this respect, *one side of his ethics*, of his work on himself. Unsurprisingly, apart from their political differences, Rorty and Foucault speak very different moral languages too; while Rorty's is that of solidarity which he translates into a morality of we-intentions, and which appeals to moral psychology, namely to our imaginative ability to see others, strangers included, as "one of us," (1989, pp. 193–194) Foucault's morality, as we shall see, speaks a language of governance instead, and the operation of fields of force that employs and operates with a very different kind of ethics of care for the self. I return to Foucault's ethics of care and his morality later, meanwhile Rorty makes a point about self-creation and its relation with education that is critically important and true; namely, that there is no self-creation without enculturation, without the induction first into a conventional morality, into a self to refuse. The language of self-creation, of freedom, he says, is always in some sense parasitic on the language of conventional truth, such as it may be. Self-creation, he argues (1980)), is not possible *ex nihilo*, so that a conventional morality cannot be dispensed with though it may be repudiated, even radically so, in the name of self-creation. So that education, understood as self-creation, is always also parasitic on enculturation.

Self-creation and Immoralism

To what extent are Foucault's ethics influenced by Nietzsche's immoralism? That he was influenced by Nietzsche's ethics in general is beyond doubt and self-declared. Nietzsche's immoralism was also self-declared. Indeed, he used the term 'immoralist' for himself in a variety of contexts. The same is not true of Foucault. Nietzsche described himself "'as the first immoralist'; identifies Zarathustra with the achievement of immoralism – 'the self-overcoming of morality, out of truthfulness'; and claims the word immoralist as 'a symbol and badge of honour for myself'" (Berkowitz, 1995, p.280n). He described himself an immoralist in a letter to Carl Fuchs where he also referred to immoralism as "the highest form till now, of 'intellectual integrity'" (Berkowitz, 1995, p.280n). Elsewhere, Nietzsche described its achievement as "'the *self-sublimation of morality* [Italics in original text]'" (Berkowitz, 1995, p. 280n). In *The Gay Science*, in a section named 'Our ultimate gratitude to art,' he writes about the playfulness of the immoralist, which he compares with the playfulness of the fool and the artist. He writes about "the *freedom above things* that our ideal demands of us." He continues to maintain that "It would mean *a relapse* for us with our irritable honesty to get involved entirely in morality," and he goes on to refer to people who become too engrossed in morality as "virtuous monsters or scarecrows." "We should be *able* also to stand *above* morality," he continues, "and not only to stand with the anxious stiffness of a man who is afraid of slipping and falling any moment, but also to float above it and play" (Nietzsche, 1974, p. 164). Nietzsche is clear about the kind of morality these negative statements refer to; one that "trains the individual to be a function of the herd and to ascribe value to himself only as function," as an instrument. Because there will be different herds and communities, he says, there will be many different moralities—"Morality is herd instinct in the individual" (Nietzsche, 1974, p. 175). The immoralist, on the other hand, is the individualist, one who "feels responsible only for one's will and actions, and [one] finds one's pride in oneself" (Nietzsche, 1974, p. 164). Nietzsche (1974) senses a turning of the tide in his favour. In the past, such individuality was regarded as

> not a pleasure but a punishment; one was sentenced 'to individuality.' [It was seen as] something painful and as real misery [and associated] with every fear and misery, [and the expression of] 'free will' was very closely associated with bad conscience; and the more 'unfree' one's actions were and the more the herd instinct rather than any personal sense found expression in an action, the more moral one felt. (p. 175)

It is important to understand at this point that Nietzsche's immoralism and his ethics of self-creation was not an attack on morality as such. His immoralism should not be read as the abandonment of all morality. As Leiter (2002) points out Nietzsche: (a) explicitly embraced the idea of a 'higher morality' in his writing, a morality which would inform the lives of 'higher men,' and (b) he "aims to offer a re-evaluation of existing values in a manner that appears, itself, to involve appeal to broadly 'moral' standards of some sort" (p. 74). Leiter (2002) quotes Nietzsche's Preface in *Daybreak*: "'In this book faith in morality [*Moral*] is withdrawn—but why? *Out of morality* [*Moralität*]! Or what else should we call that which informs it—and us? . . . [There] is no doubt that a 'thou shalt' [*du sollest*] speaks to us too'" (p. 74). So, it is not that we can live without moral imperatives but that the imperatives should be our own and original, not the imperatives of the herd but the imperatives, it turns out, of self-mastery. What confuses matters, as Leiter points out, is that he uses "the same German word—typically *Moral*, sometimes *Moralität*—for both what he attacks and what he praises" (Ibid.). Leiter also rules out the view that Nietzsche was simply attacking a specific morality, the Judeo-Christian or European (though no doubt he was too). What he was attacking more generally was the kind of morality, the morality of the 'last man,' that runs contrary to the affirmation of life, which is, to the contrary, the concern of the 'higher man,' the overman. In the famous part where Zarathustra shows us the last man, he describes him as one who invented happiness, neighbourly warmth and comfort, equality, certainty, and reconciliation, as 'his' great values. The last man 'blinks' before the truly life-enhancing values of love, creativity, longing, and adventure that are, on the other hand, the values of the overman.[7]

When we speak of benevolence, Nietzsche (1974) says, we need to distinguish

> between the impulse to appropriate and the impulse to submit, and ask whether it is the stronger or the weaker that feels benevolent. Joy and desire, [he continues] appear together in the stronger that wants to transform something into a function; joy and the wish to be desired appear together in the weaker that wants to become a function. (p. 176)

Pity is the form benevolence will take with the first, the overman, where the will to power is strong—women are typical of the second. What we learn from artists, he says, is how we can "make things beautiful, attractive, and desirable for us when they are not" (1974, p. 240). Only for the artist "this subtle power usually comes to an end where art ends and life begins; but we want to be the poets of our life—first of all in the smallest, most everyday matters" (ibid, p. 240). Poets believe that life is not something to be contemplated but to be made, to be created, to be fashioned; they need to be distinguished from spectators and actors; those who merely observe life and those, "the so-called practical human beings

…who learn their roles and translate everything into flesh and actuality, into the everyday" (1974, p. 242) To be a poet is to give oneself style "to 'give style' to one's character—a great and rare art!" (p. 232). It is to survey all the strengths and weaknesses of one's nature "and then fit them into an artistic plan until every one of them appears as art and reason and even weaknesses delight

the eye" (Ibid). It requires long practice and daily work on oneself; adding, re-
moving, concealing, reinterpreting and making sublime, refining, shaping until,
"when the work is finished, it becomes evident how the constraint of a single
taste governed and formed everything large and small" (p. 232). What matters,
in fact, is not so much whether this 'taste' is good or bad but that it is single,
unified and original. Weak characters are dissolute, they lack this unity of the
overman, they also lack power over themselves. They can never be poets because they "*hate* the constraint of style," of the single, unified, and original. Ultimately, Nietzsche (1974) continues, one thing is needful

> that a human being should *attain* [Italics in original text] satisfaction with himself,
> whether it be by means of this or that poetry and art; only then, [he claims] is a human
> being at all tolerable to behold. Whoever is dissatisfied with himself is continually ready
> for revenge, and we others will be his victims, if only by having to endure his ugly sight.
> For the sight of what is ugly makes one bad and gloomy. (p. 233)

Undoubtedly, there is an element of narcissism in the motivation of the
poet described in this way, as a matter of attaining satisfaction with oneself, and
in the ethics of self-creation as such. But Nietzsche's narcissism is not a kind of
self-absorption; it takes the form of an interest in style, and style is public.
Nietzsche knew better than anyone the danger that self-absorption can become
a morbid narcissism antithetical to life. The italicization of the word *attain* in the
earlier quotation links the achievement of poetic self-creation with education. If
we are interested in Nietzsche's ethics of self-creation what brings us under the
influence of educators is their poetry, their style demonstrated in their art of
living. Regarding them as exemplars of style prevents us from being unduly
captured by the content of their life and work and enables us to turn away from
them, and even against them (as Nietzsche did with both Schopenhauer and
Wagner, and, in Nehamas's (1998) view, though in a perverse kind of way, Socrates); to reject them eventually in order to find one's own way, establish one's
own originality. "One repays a teacher badly," says Zarathustra, "if one remains
nothing but a pupil" (1969, p. 103). As we saw earlier, the job of education, for
Foucault, is like Nietzsche's "to refuse what we are," in order to promote "new
forms of subjectivity". In an interview with Catherine Porter he also contended,
along these lines taken by Nietzsche, that "the key to the personal poetic attitude of a philosopher is not to be sought in his ideas, as if it could be deduced
from them, but rather in his philosophy-as-life, in his philosophical life, his
ethos" (Rabinow 1984, p. 374), his 'manner of being' a philosopher (ibid, p. 377).
But, the central quest for education, for Nietzsche is not to promote new forms
of subjectivity but to discover "How one becomes what one is," as he puts it in

the subtitle of *Ecce Homo*; to discover one's authentic self. A process that requires *amor fati*, a notion Foucault has no room for:

> the fact that a man wishes nothing to be different, either in front of him or behind him, or for all eternity. Not only must the necessary be borne, and on no account concealed . . . but it must also be loved love it," that one is perfectly satisfied with the life one has lived. (Nietzsche, 2004, p. 54)

This difference between them may be why Foucault seems unhappy with describing education as self-creation (though essentially this is how he regards it, though not in the strong form described by Nietzsche) and opts for the term 'self-constitution' instead.

Foucault's ethics contains none of the trappings of Nietzsche's immoralism though he subscribes to the same quest for uncompromising intellectual integrity and truthfulness, and shares the philosophical source of Nietzsche's immoralism, namely his perspectivism; his scepticism about the claim to objective truth about anything, not just morality. Jonathan Glover (2001) shows how the perspectivist logic leads to an ethics of self-creation. If the world has no intrinsic meaning, it goes, we are faced with either of two options; to live with its meaninglessness or to create our own meaning and impose it on the world, or on that part of the world which is touched by our lives. Whichever we choose, the collapse of objective meaning leaves us free to create our own lives and ourselves. And Foucault is with Nietzsche on this conclusion (2001). Nietzsche's unwillingness to impose any model of self-creation on anyone, Glover points out, also arises from his rejection of the idea of a core self that imposes a general pattern on human behaviour and experience. Foucault also shares this rejection; he similarly denies the notion of a core self and rejects the imposition of any model of self-creation on anyone. Foucault, as we shall see, also gave ethics an aesthetic dimension and connected it with giving oneself a style. Nietzsche's understanding of self-creation, however, as Glover points out, was masculinist. Nietzsche, he says, did not believe self-creation possible for women because he identified it with qualities that, by his own account, are typically male; with self-discipline, with a strong, self-controlled, will; with an attitude of hardness towards oneself, with egoism, and with the overcoming of 'bad conscience'. In Part 1 of Zarathustra, Glover (2001) points out, he identified the 'higher' self-creating

> man with the figure of the warrior; with the *hard* 'philosophers of the future, [with] philosophers whose hardness would be the hardness of the hammer; hard toward themselves and others—knowing how to wield the knife— in *Beyond Good and Evil* knowing how to be cruel. (p. 13)

At the same time, he concedes that "Nietzsche's idea of self-creation has a degree of truth" in it, in that while there are certain aspects of one's identity that one does not choose, "there is also the identity people create for themselves, typically elaborating on, or branching out from, this 'given' identity" (Ibid, p. 145). He also concedes the value of this 'self-creation' that "gives part of the sense people have of their lives being worthwhile" (ibid), and argues that one might subscribe to the idea of self-creation without necessarily following Nietzsche; that the "chilling Nietzschean conclusions do not follow from his premises about the value of self-creation and the absence of an external moral law" (ibid, p. 17).

Glover (2001), in fact, suggests a re-definition of self-creation that acknowledges that it can be "at best only partial"; that one's 'given' identity is always in the way, (p. 402) and that "to value self-creation is not necessarily to think that it is the only object of life, which has to override everything else" (p. 17). One's self-creation need not absorb one's life to the point where it is *unrestrained* and becomes the ruthless egoism admired by Nietzsche. It could fit with an ethic of care for other people. "My caring about the sort of person I am motivates the project of self-creation. Why should not my caring about other people," he asks "set limits to it?" (p. 17). This seems to have been the late Foucault's view also. His last work, in fact, was devoted to the exploration of an ethics of care for self, a morality within which the ethical project of self-creation could be contained in a way that it was not for Nietzsche. It could not be otherwise for Foucault since, as I said earlier, he understood the self as being a social construct. He says by way of explanation of his interest in ethics,

> I would say that if now I am interested, in fact, in the way in which the subject constitutes himself in an active fashion, by the practices of self, these practices are nevertheless not something that the individual invents by himself. They are patterns that he finds in his culture and which are proposed, suggested and imposed on him by his culture, his society and his social group. (Bernauer & Rasmussen, 1994, p. 11)

In short, like Rorty and Glover, Foucault declares the inevitability of enculturation; its continued, lurking influence on one's life. How he redefines self-creation within this ethics of care for self will be the subject of the next section. Meanwhile, though Foucault's understanding of self-creation is less radical and weaker than Nietzsche's it is more radical and stronger than Glover's. He wants self-creation to be something more, much more, than "elaborating on" or "branching from" one's given identity. Like Nietzsche he wants it to be a *refusal*, an overcoming, of one's given identity, of the way one has been made subject through "the simultaneous individualization and totalization of modern power structures." Like Nietzsche also, he regards this self-overcoming as violent and painful; a "limit experience," involving the "task of 'tearing' the subject from itself" (Foucault, 1991, p. 31) At the same time, the "new forms of subjectivity" that he wants us to seek out, to constitute in the name of education, implies a far less obsessive undertaking, a more fluid, uncertain, and open-ended approach to ethics, than one defined by Nietzsche's single-minded project of self-creation as that of becoming what one is.

Self-Creation and the Ethics of Care

In effect, Foucault's ethics is complex and multi-dimensional. Some reference was made earlier to one dimension—his self-understanding and self-constitution in the public sphere as a citizen-intellectual where he adopts the ethics of a *parrhesiast*. There are, in fact, two others besides. One the poetic, private, aestheticist side that Rorty refers to in the context of the self-creation of his ironist, that has to do with the way one copes with one's "aloneness in the world," as Rorty (1989) puts it, and that coincides, as we saw earlier, with his perception of his philosophical life. This is where Rorty consigns philosophical activity too. The other the public-private side where one interacts, interrelates, with others not as a citizen but as a fellow human being, a person, as we are wont to refer to it, with whom one could share a whole spectrum of relations from the most intimate to the casual. This interpersonal informal dimension of our relationship with others as fellow human beings is the moral. It is generally informally regulated by moral imperatives whether autonomous or heteronymous, while our relationship with others as citizens is formally regulated by laws, statutes, constitutions, and so on. We are used to referring to the latter as political, but moral relationships are also political, as Foucault would insist, in the sense that they involve relations of power. They are not, however, for Foucault (unlike Nietzsche), like the ethics of citizenship, essentially agonistic, nor do they involve an ethics of aesthetic self-creation, but that of care, of self-care but also care of others. The ethics of self-care, like the Kantian ethics of autonomy, which Foucault locates in the realm of morality is one of self-regulation understood in his case as an ethics of self-mastery rather than submission to natural law. For it, he goes not to Nietzsche, nor to the making of modernity, but to Antiquity for his inspiration.

The Ancient Greeks, Foucault tells us, connected ethics with "deportment and the way to behave" (Bernuer & Rasmussen, 1994, p.6). They, thereby, affirmed its public and aesthetic dimensions. What comes into play in the Greek understanding of ethics as the practice of freedom is "the subject's mode of being and a certain manner of acting visible to others" (Bernuer & Rasmussen,

1994, p.6). One's ethos for the ancient Greeks, "was seen by his dress, by his bearing, by his gait, by the poise with which he reacts to events, etc." This public demonstration of oneself was the "the concrete expression" of one's ethics as an ethics of freedom. Foucault gives this ethics the aesthetic dimension related to his philosophical life referred to earlier ". . . for me intellectual work is related to what you would call aestheticism, meaning transforming yourself" (Bernauer & Rasmussen, 1994, p. 6). It is not, he elaborates elsewhere about his work, about transforming the world, still less about the academic status of what I am doing . . . My problem is my own transformation by one's own knowledge," which is "something rather closer to the aesthetic experience. Why should a painter work," he asks by way of illustrating his meaning, "if he is not transformed by his own painting?" (Dreyfus & Rabinow, 1983, p. 14)

There is in this aesthetic aspect of ethics, as he understood it, both an affinity with this Ancient Greek notion of giving oneself a style, related to one's public comportment and appearance, and with Nietzsche's understanding of giving oneself a style related to the work of self-creation which he also, as we saw, illustrated through the same metaphor of the artist. Foucault refers to yet a third source; the ethics of modernity as described by Baudelaire, namely as "*dandysme*": "the asceticism of the dandy who makes of his body, his behaviour, his feeling and passions, his very existence, a work of art ... the man who tries to invent himself" (Foucault, 1997, p. 312) This is the aesthetic side of education understood as self-creation.

However, once one takes ethics out of the ascetic-aesthetic realm and becomes concerned instead with the realm of the interpersonal, especially that of morality, one ceases to speak the language of self-creation or self-constitution and reverts to the language of self-mastery and governance instead. Beginning with self-master; ancient morality "supposes that one establishes over one's self a certain relation of domination, of mastery, which was called *arche* – power, authority" (Bernauer & Rasmussen, 1994, p. 6). The notion of self-mastery, in fact though, like self-creation, falls within the realm of freedom (from mastery by others or by another), and within that of control and governance. Indeed, it exists in tension between the two. To the contrary, like autonomy, self-government implies obedience to rules that one makes for oneself. Foucault summarizes the relationship between care for the self and morality. He says,

> the care for self is of course knowledge of self—that is the Socratic-Platonic aspect—but it is also the knowledge of a certain number of rules of conduct or of principles which are at the same time truths and regulations. To care for self is to fit oneself out with these truths. This is where ethics is linked to the game of truth, (Bernauer & Rasmussen, 1994, p. 5)

(i.e., the game of politics and morality). But there is also the other side: "I don't think," he says, "there can be a morality without a number of practices of self." (Kritzman, 1990, p. 260) In other words, every morality has its own ethical practices. This is how, to return to O'Leary (2002), ethics is "a sub-set of the category of 'morality'" (p. 11). This applies both to conventional moralities (i.e., where the work one does on oneself is constrained within "systematic, constricting codal structures"), and to morality understood simply as a focus around which reflection develops, where "the practices of self take on the form of an art of self relatively independent of moral legislation" (ibid, p. 260). Thus it was understood in Antiquity, but Christianity reinforced the principle of law and codal structure, even if practices of asceticism continued to give importance to the practices of the self. With "Christianity, with the religion of the text … we pass from a morality that was essentially the search for a personal ethics to a morality as obedience to a system of rules" (ibid, p. 49)

The first, approved of by Foucault, requires a higher ethical sensibility than one based on obedience to impersonal rules (Connolly as cited in Moss 1998). In the ancient world, as a way of living one's liberty it was related negatively to non-slavery, positively to being just to another but also to oneself and one's appetites. In both respects, as in Aristotelian ethics, it was a matter of self-control, of governing one's excessive behaviour, rather than a matter of content, of areas of total prohibition. One was expected to exercise one's moderation in the governance both of oneself and of others. In this way, self-care was identified with the practice of governing oneself against excessive self-indulgence. In the moral realm where what is at stake is care for others, it responds to an ethical sensibility that recognises such care as a necessary extension of one's care for oneself. It recognises that the governance of our relations with others is not separate from our own self-governance. Indeed, it is intrinsic to it. Although essentially a path one seeks to oneself in which one seeks to escape all dependencies and enslavements, an ethics of self-care, Foucault contends, does not mean escaping one's social and political responsibilities, indeed the contrary is the case. Though it implies a *certain* narcissism marked by a sense of one's delight in oneself "as a thing one both possesses and has before one's eyes," (1990, p. 65) it requires "an intensification of social relations," (p. 53) and a weakening of the self that Nietzsche himself suggested in his later work, where the accent in ethics as a conflict of forces is placed more on the aim of self-protection than on that of self-assertion, and is never guided by the will to dominate. This is how Foucault describes it:

> The care of the self is ethical in itself; but it implies complex relationships with others insofar as this ethos of freedom is also a way of caring for others . . . the problem of relationships with others is present throughout the development of the care of the self.

His interlocutor in the interview I am quoting from Rabinow (1997, p. 287) suggests that maybe what he meant was that "The care of self always aims for the well-being of others; it aims to manage the space of power that exists in all relationships, but to manage it in a non-authoritarian manner" (Rabinow 1997, p. 287). Foucault does not disagree, and goes on to describe "the particular position of the philosopher" as "the man who cares about the care of others," rather than one, as with Rorty, who cares about one's aloneness. But not, he adds quickly, one who puts the care of others before the care for oneself. To the contrary, "the care of the self," he insists, 'is ethically prior in that the relationship with oneself is ontologically prior" (Rabinow, 1997, p. 287)

What I take him to mean by 'ontologically prior' is that the question of one's self-care, as care of one's own proper self, is always more immediate and pressing for one than that of one's care for the other in the sense that, in the final analysis, it is always oneself and one's own behaviour that is in question and over which one has the most immediate control, even where what is at issue is one's relation to another or to others. Foucault, however, is not, I would suggest, suggesting any sequential ordering of one's concerns with proper care for oneself preceding one's care for the other, any more than he suggests that self-refusal needs to precede self-affirmation. To the contrary, he is very clear in my earlier quote that one's care for the other is intrinsic to one's care for oneself, not something that follows it, just as one's self-refusal occurs together with, in the very process of one's self-affirmation not prior to it. We are always, as Levinas says, in the process of caring for the other because the face of the other is always present for us and invites our response-responsibility. Foucault understands this response-responsibility as an ethics of self-mastery that comprehends a proper governance of one's relation with the other in the practice of one's freedom (i.e., a use of one's power with respect to the other that is always respectful of his or her freedom). An ethics that avoids dominating him or her, or them, in any way, and that is, therefore, moral because it requires rules, even though they are self-imposed. The amoralist, on the other hand, is one who is unwilling or unable to respond morally to the presence of others in our lives; one who is unwilling to see them as an intrinsic feature of one's own ethical project which is always, in any case, as Glover (2001) suggests, social, and who is, therefore, not disinclined to dominate.

Notes

1   See Wain, K (2004) *The Learning Society in a Postmodern World*, Peter Lang (New York).
2   See Foucault's late essay 'What is Enlightenment' (1997, p. 305).

3   MacIntyre (1981, p. 11) defines emotivism as "the doctrine that all evaluative judgements and more specifically all moral judgements are *nothing but* [italics in original text] expressions of preference, expressions of attitude or feeling, insofar as they are moral or evaluative in character."

4   For a discussion of both publics and the differences between them see Wain, K (2004) quoted in (1).

5   See 'Education without Dogma' (1990) Dialogue, No. 2, 44-47.

6   Foucault takes up the notion of *parrhesia* most extensively in a series of lectures he gave at the University of California at Berkeley in the Fall term of 1983 which were later published as a book edited by Joseph Pearson (2001) entitled *Fearless Speech*, Semiotext(e). In it *parrhesia* is defined precisely in this way, as "fearless speech"; "the parrhesiastes," Foucault says, "primarily chooses a specific relationship to himself: he prefers himself as a truth-teller rather than as a living being who is false to himself." (p.17)

7   See Prologue 5 of the book.

Bibliography

Berkowitz, P. (1995). *Nietzsche: the ethics of an immoralist.* Cambridge: Harvard University Press.

Bernauer, J., & Rasmussen, D. (Eds.). (1994). *The final Foucault.* Cambridge: The MIT Press.

Dreyfus, H. L., & Rabinow, P. (1983). *Michel Foucault, beyond structuralism and hermeneutics.* Wheatsheaf, UK: Harvester

Foucault, M. (1990). *The care of the self.* London: Penguin Books.

————. (1991a). *Discipline and punish: the birth of the prison.* London: Penguin Books.

————. (1991b). *Remarks on Marx.* New York: Semiotext(e).

————. (1997). 'The Ethics of Concern for Self as a Practice of Freedom'. In Rabinow, Paul (ed.) *Michel Foucault the essential works 1, ethics,* London: Allen Lane, The Penguin Press.

————. (2001). Fearless Speech. Los Angeles: Semiotext(e).

Glover, J. (2001). *Humanism.* New Haven, Ct: Yale University Press.

Habermas, J. (1994). *The past as future (Interviews with Michael Haller).* Oxford: Polity Press.

Kritzman, L. D. (Ed.). (1990). *Michel Foucault: Politics, philosophy, culture.* London and New York Routledge.

Leiter, B. (2002). *Nietzsche on morality.* London and New York: Routledge.

MacIntyre, A. (1981) *After virtue.* London: Duckworth.

————. (1987). 'The idea of an educated public'. In G. Haydon (Ed.), *Education and values* (pp. 15–36). London: London Institute of Education.

Moss, J. (Ed.). (1998). *The later Foucault.* London: Sage Publications.

Nehamas, A. (1998). *The art of living.* Berkeley: University of California Press.

Nietzsche, F. (1969). *Thus spoke Zarathustra.* Harmondsworth, UK: The Penguin Press.

————. (1974). *The gay science.* New York: Vintage Books.

————. (2004). *Ecce Homo.* Mineola and New York: Dover Publications.

O'Leary, T. (2002). *Foucault and the art of ethics.* London: Continuum.

Owen. D. (1995) Nietzsche, Politics and Modernity. London: Sage Publications.

Rabinow. P. (1984). *The Foucault reader.* London: Penguin Books.

————. (1997) (ed.) *Michel Foucault ethics: the essential works 1*. London: Allen Lane, The Penguin Press.

Rorty, R. (1980). *Philosophy and the mirror of nature*. Oxford, UK: Basil Blackwell.

————. (1989). *Contingency, irony, and solidarity*. Cambridge: Cambridge University Press.

————. (1990). 'Education without dogma'. *Dialogue*, No. 2. 44–47.

Saatkamp, H. J. (Ed.). (1995). *Rorty and pragmatism*. Nashville: Vanderbilt University Press.

Wain.K. (2004). *The learning society in a postmodern world*. New York: Peter Lang.

ಬ Chapter 12 ಆ

Educational Research: 'Games of Truth' and the Ethics of Subjectivity

Michael A. Peters

Of ourselves we are not "knowers" ... (Nietzsche, 1956)

Introduction: Foucault and Educational Research[1]

Foucault's influence on educational research is undeniable and rapidly growing, both in terms of a thinker described under the broader label of "poststructuralist" (Peters & Wain, 2002) and as a unique philosopher who transcended his own time (Peters, 2000a). In particular, his genealogies of the human subject, his histories of subjectivities, and his analysis of how power relations and discourses shape processes of ethical self-constitution have proved to be powerful approaches to providing critical histories of childhood, students and schools as well as helping researchers to problematize educational concepts, categories and institutions. Foucault's impact on educational research is still in the process of development and assessment (see Peters, 2003a; Peters & Burbules, 2004) but it is clear that his influence, nearly twenty years after his death, is extensive and his approach provides researchers in education with a *critical* perspective based on an original theory of power that owes nothing to liberal or Marxist thought. Foucault also provides a set of historical methodologies (archaeology and genealogy), and a refinement of tools of analysis that enable social and spatial epistemologies of discursive and institutional regimes.

Yet, given these developments I do not think that the use and development of Foucault's work is well enough established in educational research to begin to talk about clear differences or orientations in English-speaking countries in the way that we might distinguish among various national or distinctive readings of Foucault in sociology, history or political studies. We can, I think, talk of the French Foucaultians, for example, comprised of Foucault's students, including Jacques Donzelot and François Ewald or we might talk of the Anglo-Australasian governmentality group based around the journal *Economy and Society* established by Nikolas Rose and including Barry Hindess, Vikki Bell, Mitchell Dean, Ian Hunter, Pat O'Malley, and Barbara Cruikshank, among others.[2] We might also mention specifically Foucaultian historians, even although these do not constitute a group, such as Hayden White and Mark Poster, or Foucaultian sociologists such as Barry Smart, Alan Hunt, and Clare O'Farrell. It would be important to mention in this regard the US, French, or Australian feminists (whose complexity defies easy classification, but see, for example, Lois McNay).

Even so, it is important to note that a group of American scholars organised a number of pre-conference sessions at American Educational Research Association (AERA) meetings and established in the mid 1990s a Foucault SIG (Special Interest Group) "Dedicated to the historical and philosophical studies of education that engage the writings of Michel Foucault."[3] In the educational literature, at least the English-speaking world we can begin to track some of the lines of Foucaultian research in education.

In Britain during the mid 1980s Valerie Walkerdine's (1984, 1988) critical psychology approach to child development exerted a strong influence in British educational circles. Thereafter, the use of Foucault has been dominated by the ethno-sociological orientation of Stephen Ball (1990, 1994), although David Hoskin's (1979) work also has exerted an important influence, as has Norman Fairclough's (1995, 2000), whose discourse analysis based on Foucault has been applied to understandings of educational policy. More recently, a special issue of the *Journal of Education Policy* has been dedicated to poststructuralism and educational research in which Foucault figures prominently (Peters & Humes, 2003). In North America a more epistemological and feminist appropriation of his work can be seen in the writings of Tom Popkewitz (Popkewitz & Brennan, 1997), Bernadette Baker (2001), St Pierre & Pillow (2000), and Maureen Ford (1995). While in New Zealand the philosophical appropriation of Foucault's work by Jim Marshall (1995a, 1995b, 1996a, 1998) exercised a strong critical and philosophical direction not only over his students in his own home country, but also internationally.

New Zealanders have worked on Foucault in diverse ways: Mark Olssen's (1999, 2003) materialist interpretation of Foucault seeks to view him in close proximity to Gramsci; Tina (A.C.) Besley (2002, 2003) has put Foucault to work in understanding the significance of power relations in school counselling and, more broadly, in the construction of the self and youth cultures; Sue Middleton (1998), as a feminist, has not uncritically appropriated his work on sexuality, while I have sought to understand Foucault within the wider context of "poststructuralism," focusing on themes of governance, subjectivity and ethics in relation to education policy (Peters, 1988, 1996, 2000a, 2001a, 2001b, 2003c).

I have described Foucault's many faces of educational research in terms of eight overlapping directions, which are not exhaustive of the educational research utilising Foucault but appear among the most significant currents (Peters, 2003d).

Figure 1: The Many-Sided Foucault in Anglo-American Educational Research

Foucault as naturalised Kantian: J. D. Marshall

Foucault as critical ethno-sociologist: Stephen Ball

Foucault as Nietzschean genealogist: Tina Besley

Foucault as historian of systems of thought: Bernadette Baker

Foucault as historical materialist (and democrat): Mark Olssen

Foucault as social epistemologist: Tom Popkewitz & Marie Brennan

Foucault as crypto-feminist: Sue Middleton

Foucault as poststructuralist: Michael A. Peters

These eight directions in Foucauldian educational research are distinguished in terms of book contributions rather than papers. This is, of course, only what I take to be the major or most interesting directions and I confess that the selection is biased in terms of my country of origin and own theoretical position. There are many more scholars writing on education in the English-speaking world—for example, those who have contributed to Foucault SIGs at AERA over the years and those contributing to various education and Foucault conferences and journals.[4]

Foucault studies in education provide tools for analysis that have inspired historical, sociological and philosophical approaches that cover a bewildering array of topics: genealogies of pupils, students, teachers, and counsellors; the social constructions of children, adolescence, and youth; social epistemologies of the school in its changing institutional form, and studies of the emergence of the disciplines; philosophical studies of educational concepts that grew up with European humanism, especially in its Enlightenment and specifically Kantian formations focusing on the key concepts: Man, freedom, autonomy, punishment, government and authority. In all cases the Foucauldian archive provides an approach to problematizing concepts and practices that seemed resistant to further analysis *before* Foucault—in other words, that seemed institutionalised, ossified and destined to endless repetition in academic understandings and interpretations. *After* Foucault, it is as though we must revisit most of the important questions to do with power, knowledge, subjectivity and freedom in education.

My interests in Foucault have had two main directions: social and educational policy, on the one hand; and a more strictly philosophical approach to the subject or the self, on the other. In relation to the first direction I have focused on Foucault's understanding of space and its significance in understanding educational postmodernity (Peters, 1996, 2003b), applications of the notion of governmentality to the neoliberal paradigm of educational policy (Peters, 2001a), to managerialism and self-governance in education (Peters et al., 2000), and to entrepreneurial culture and the entrepreneurial self (Peters, 2001b). I have also sought to indicate how Foucault, as part of the wider poststructuralist movement, might be of use to educational researchers (Peters, 1999; Peters & Humes, 2003; Peters & Burbules, 2004). In relation to the second direction, I have attempted to locate Foucault in the wider philosophical context of the philosophy of the subject (Peters, 2000a), especially in respect of "writing the self" (Peters, 2000b) and in relation to Wittgenstein (Peters & Marshall, 1999). It is this connection between Foucault's genealogies of the subject and governmentality that provides the most fertile land to be tilled: truth-telling as an educational practice of the self (Peters, 2003b), on the one hand, and what I call the "new prudentialism in education" focusing on a notion of "actuarial rationality" in the constitution of the entrepreneurial self, on the other (Peters, 2003c).

This chapter begins by examining Foucault's approach to truth telling (*parrhesia*) in relation to the changing practice of educational research. It applies Foucault's notion of 'games of truth' to educational research using it to investigate the politics of knowledge and the ethics of the researcher's identity.

Foucault, Games of Truth and Educational Research

In the early eighties, Denis Huisman (1993) asked François Ewald to reedit the entry on Foucault for a new edition of the *Dictionnaire des philosophes*. As the translator, Robert Hurley remarks in a footnote to the text 'Foucault' "The text submitted to Huisman was written almost entirely by Foucault himself, and signed pseudoanonymously 'Maurice Florence'" (Foucault, 1998, p. 458). Foucault begins that text with the following words: "To the extent that Foucault fits into the philosophical tradition, it is the *critical* tradition of Kant, and his project could be called *A Critical History of Thought* (p. 459). Later he defines a critical history of thought as:

> an analysis of the conditions under which certain relations of subject to object are
> formed or modified, insofar as those relations constitute a possible knowledge [*savoir*]

...In short, it is a matter of determining its mode of 'subjectivation' . . . and objectivation . . . What are the processes of subjectivation and objectivation that make it possible for the subject qua subject to become an object of knowledge [connaissance], as a
subject? (Foucault, 1998, pp. 450–60).

He describes himself as undertaking the constitution of the subject both as an
object of knowledge within certain scientific discourses or truth games we call
the 'human sciences' (both empirical and normative) and as an object for himself, that is the history of subjectivity insofar as it involves 'the way the subject
experiences himself in a game of truth where it relates to himself' (p. 461), such
as in the history of sexuality. It is the kind of self-description that Foucault gives
elsewhere. As we remarked in the Introduction to this book in a text written a
year before his death, Foucault (2001a) stated that his real quarry was *not* an investigation of power but rather the history of the ways in which human beings
are constituted as subjects.

The history of the human subject for Foucault was intimately tied to the
development of the human sciences in relation to knowledge and truth. In his
early work Foucault treated truth as a product of the *regimentation* of statements
within discourses that had progressed or were in the process of progressing to
the stage of a scientific discipline. In this conception, the subject, historicized in
relation to social practices, is effectively denied its freedom or effective agency.
This early conception of Foucault's is to be contrasted with his later notion of
the subject where freedom and truth-telling is seen to be an essential aspect of
its constitution as in the concept of "governmentality" and in his studies of the
history of sexuality. For the early Foucault: "'Truth' is to be understood as a
system of ordered procedures for the production, regulation, distribution, circu-
lation and operation of statements" (Foucault, 1980, p. 133).

Foucault makes a shift from "regimes of truth" to "games of truth" that
reflects a change in his thinking concerning the agency of the subject and also
his notion of truth. Foucault says in an interview with Gauthier (1988):

I have tried to discover how the human subject entered into games of truth, whether
they be games of truths which take on the form of science or which refer to a scientific
model, or games of truth like those that can be found in institutions or practices of
control (p. 3).

He, then, elaborates the concept of 'game' in the following way:

when I say 'game' I mean an ensemble of rules for the production of truth...It is an ensemble of procedures which lead to a certain result, which can be considered in function of its principles and its rules of procedure as valid or not, as winner or loser (ibid.,
p. 15).

In a little known paper delivered to a Japanese audience in 1978, Foucault takes up the concept of game in relation to analytic philosophy (and probably Wittgenstein's influential notion of "language-games," although his name is not mentioned) to criticise its employment without an accompanying notion of power. Arnold Davidson (1997) mentions a lecture "*La Philosophie analytique de la politique*" in which Foucault (1978) makes an explicit reference to Anglo-American analytic philosophy:

> For Anglo-Saxon analytic philosophy it is a question of making a critical analysis of thought on the basis of the way in which one says things. I think one could imagine, in the same way, a philosophy that would have as its task to analyse what happens every day in relations of power. A philosophy, accordingly, that would bear rather on relations of power than on language games, a philosophy that would bear on all these relations that traverse the social body rather than on the effects of language that traverse and underlie thought (cited in Davidson, 1997, p. 3).

Language in Foucault's conception "never deceives or reveals" rather as Foucault states: "Language, it is played. The importance, therefore, of the notion of game." Further on, he makes the comparison: "Relations of power, also, they are played; it is these games of power that one must study in terms of tactics and strategy, in terms of order and of chance, in terms of stakes and objective" (cited in Davidson, 1997, p. 4). As he tried to indicate, discourse considered as speaking, as the employment of words, could be studied as strategies within genuine historical contexts, focusing upon, for example, the history of judicial practices or "even the discourse of truth, as rhetorical procedures, as ways of conquering, of producing events, of producing decisions, of producing battles, of producing victories. In order to 'rhetoricize' philosophy" (cited in Davidson, 1997, p. 5).

"Games of truth" then, signifies a changed sense of agency on the part of Foucault, who, investigating practices of self, becomes interested in questions of the ethical self-constitution of the subject and self-mastery, especially in his analysis of classical texts. Thus,

> Unlike Habermas who postulates an ideal speech situation wherein games of truth would have the best chance of success, Foucault is a realist…Instead of an absolutely free discourse community, the best one can attain is a community in which one commands the requisite rules of procedure, as well as the "ethics, the ethos, the practice of self, which would allow these games of power to be played with a minimum of domination (Gauthier, 1988, p. 12).

Paul Veyne (1997) commented after Foucault's death that in his very first lecture at the Collège de France,

Foucault contrasted an 'analytic philosophy of truth in general' with his own preference 'for critical thought that would take the form of an ontology of ourselves, of an ontology of the present'; he went so far, that day, as to relate his own work to 'the form of reflection that extends from Hegel to the Frankfurt School via Nietzsche and Max Weber' (p. 226).

Veyne warns us not to take that circumstantial analogy too far and he puts us on a course that connects Foucault strongly to Nietzsche and Heidegger, correctly in my view.

Foucault's preference for a form of critical thought related to 'truth games' rather than an analytic philosophy of truth, he discovers in our classical Greek heritage: the two—the analytic and the critical—emerged side by side. It is clear that Foucault, at least toward the end of his life, neither denied the classical ideal of truth as correspondence to an independently existing world nor the 'analytics of truth'. Foucault's innovation was to historicize 'truth,' first, materially in discourse as 'regimes of truth' and, second, in practices as 'games of truth.'

In a brilliant series of lectures entitled *Discourse and Truth: The Problematization of Parrhesia*, given at Berkeley during the months of October-November in 1983 and later published in English as *Fearless Speech* (2001b), Foucault outlines the meanings and the evolution of the classical Greek word '*parrhesia*' and its cognates, as they enter into and exemplify the changing practices of truth-telling in Greek society. In particular, Foucault investigates the use of *parrhesia* in specific types of human relationships and the procedures and techniques employed in such relationships. Central to his analysis is the importance of education and its relations to 'care of the self,' public life and the crisis of democratic institutions (see Peters, 2003a).

With Foucault we can distinguish at least two major models for understanding educational research. First, along with the early Foucault we might hypothesise that educational research is a set of practices that are strongly influenced by more general epistemic cultural formations and codes which shape the conditions of possibility for educational knowledge and determine the "rules of formation" for discursive rationalities that operate beneath the level of the researcher's subjective awareness. These rules Foucault calls the *historical a priori* that operate as a "positive unconscious" and constitute a whole epistemological field, or *episteme*. The rules of discursive formation are not the invention of the researcher but rather the *historical a priori* of a dynamic research community. We can expand this epistemological insight to talk of different and competing kinds of educational research and their different epistemological foundations (see e.g., Pring, 2000), although a Foucaultian account, even an archaeological one, would need to be a critical history of emerging systems of research practices within which researchers found themselves socially embedded. On this 'structuralist' or archaeological model of education as one of the "sciences of man" both the researcher and the researched are located within the modern episteme based on the discourses of 'Man.' Both researcher and researched are constituted beings, effects of discourse and regimes of truth.

In his later work, Foucault shifts from 'regimes of truth' to 'games of truth' and the emphasis according falls on how the human subject constitutes itself by strategically entering into such games and playing them to best advantage. Forms of educational research historically embedded within its various institutional contexts (research associations, conferences, journals, training regimes) thus constitute 'games of truth' where researchers constitute themselves and constitute the researched. The genealogical model makes room for human agency in the processes of subject constitution attending to local and "subjugated knowledges" that both positivistic sciences and Marxism marginalize. In this context genealogies are "anti-sciences" because they contest "the [coercive] effects of the centralising powers which are linked to the institution and functioning of an organised scientific discourse" (Foucault, 1980, p. 84). As Best (1994) remarks: "Genealogy therefore seeks to vindicate local, disordered, and fragmentary forms of discourse and struggle and to battle the operations of power within modern scientific discourses that attempt to assimilate or disqualify local knowledges" (p. 36).

In terms of the subjectivity of the educational researcher we can perhaps best highlight the Foucaultian notion of 'practices of the self' by briefly examining qualitative research and the way in which the now traditional concept of "participant observer" already tacitly begins the process of 'unbracketing' the subjectivity of the researcher—that is, challenging the objectivist ideology associated with the bracketing one's own beliefs, assumptions, tastes and preferences—in order to acknowledge how deeply they enter into knowledge constructions. Foucault also provides us with the means to begin to question the relation between researcher as author and text, between *doing* research and *reporting* on it. There are diverse modes of reporting none of which has sole purchase on the truth. Qualitative educational research, which is based on the researcher's 'understanding' rather than on the constructed dialogue that takes place among participants—albeit with different roles and responsibilities—can no longer be sustained. In the late Foucault we find a greater emphasis on the self-awareness of the researcher, on the identity of the researcher and on the ethics of self-constitution, which brings into focus anew and challenges the researcher/subject relation and its discursive and methodological representations.

Notes

1 This essay draws on Peters (2003a, 2003c).
2 Ian Hunter's (1998) book on reschooling is particularly worthy of mention in relation to this group.
3 Useful websites with proposals are available, at least for the AERA 2001 session. See the roundtables "Foucault and Education: How do we know what we know?" (chaired by Katharina Heyning with participation by Andrea Allard, Colin Green, Ruth Gustafson, Michael Ferrari & Rosa Lynn Pinkius, Stephen Thorpe, Cathy Toll, Kevin Vinson, Huey-li Li) and "Tinkering with Foucault's Tool-kit Down Under" (chaired by Stephen Ball, with participation by Elizabeth McKinley, Mary Hill, Nesta Devine, Michael Peters, James Marshall, Sue Middleton).
4 See, e.g., Broadhead & Howard (2001), Covaleskie (1993), McDonough (1993), and Mayo (1997).

Bibliography

Baker, B. (2001). *In perpetual motion: Theories of power, educational history, and the child.* New York: Peter Lang.

Ball, S. J. (1990). (Ed.) *Foucault and education.* London: Routledge.

————. (1994). *Education reform: A critical and post-structural approach.* Buckingham: Open University Press.

————. (2002). *Counseling youth: Foucault, power and the ethics of subjectivity.* Westport, CT: Praeger.

————. (2003, August). Truth-telling (Parrhesia)—A risky business in education. Paper presented at the 21st World Congress of Philosophy, Istanbul, Turkey.

Best, S. (1994). Foucault, postmodernism and social theory. In D. R. Dickens & A. Fontana (Eds.), *Postmodernism and Social Inquiry* (pp. 25–52). London: UCL Press.

Broadhead, L. A. & Howard, S. (2001). The Art of Punishing: The research assessment exercise and the ritualisation of power in higher education." *Educational Policy Analysis,* 6 (8), [retrieved on July 6th, 2006 from] *http://epaa.asu.edu/epaa/v6n8.html*

Covaleskie, J.F. (1993). Power goes to school: Teachers, students, and discipline. *Philosophy of Education Yearbook,* [retrieved on July 6, 2006 from] *http://www.ed.uiuc.edu/EPS/PES-Yearbook/93_docs/COVALESK.HTM*

Davidson, A. (1997) (Ed.) *Foucault and His Interlocutors.* Chicago, University of Chicago Press.

Fairclough, N. (1995) *Critical Discourse Analysis,* London: Longman.

————. (2000) *New Labour, New Language?* London: Routledge.

Ford, M. (1995). 'Willed' to choose: Educational reform and Busno-power (Response to Marshall). *Philosophy of Education Yearbook* [retrieved on July 6, 2006 from] *http://www.ed.uiuc.edu/EPS/PES-Yearbook/95_docs/ford.html*

Foucault, M. (1978) La philosophie analytique de la politique. In D. Defert & F. Ewart with J. Lagrange (Eds.), *Dits et écrits, 1954–1988,* Vol. 4. (pp. 540–541). Paris: Gallimard.

————. (1980). *Power/knowledge: Selected interviews and other writings 1972–1977.* London: Harvester.

————. (1998) *Michael Foucault: Aesthetics, Method, and Epistemology: Essential Works of Foucault, 1954–1984 Volume 2,* James Faubion, (Ed.; Paul Rainbow Series Ed.; Robert Hurley and Others, Trs).

————. (2001a) The Subject and Power. *Michel Foucault: Power.* In P. Rabinow (Ed.), *The Essential Works of Michel Foucault 1954–1984, Vol 3* (pp. 326–348). London: Allen Lane and The Penguin Press. (Original work published in 1983)

————. (2001b) *Fearless Speech.* LA, Semiotext(e).

Gauthier, J. D. (1988). The ethic of the care of the self as a practice of freedom. In J. Bernauer & D. Rasmussen (Eds.), *The Final Foucault* (pp. 1–20). Cambridge, MA: MIT Press.

Hoskin, K. (1979). The examination, disciplinary power and rational schooling. *History of Education* *8*(2), 135–146.

Hunter, I. (1998) *Rethinking the School: Subjectivity, Bureaucracy, Criticism.* Sydney: Allen & Unwin.

Huisman, D. (1993) *Dictionnaire des philosophes,* 2 vol. Paris: PUF.

Marshall, J.D. (1995a). Foucault and neo-liberalism: Biopower and Busno-Power" *Philosophy of Education Yearbook* [retrieved on July 6th, 2006 from] *http://www.ed.uiuc.edu/EPS/PES-Yearbook/95_docs/marshall.html*

————. (1995b). Skills, information and quality for the autonomous chooser. In M. Olssen & K. Morris Matthews (Eds.), *Education, democracy and reforms* (pp. 63–76). Auckland: NZARE.

————. (1996a). *Michel Foucault: Personal autonomy and education.* London: Kluwer Academic.

————. (1996b). Education in the mode of information: Some philosophical considerations. *Philosophy   of   Education   Yearbook* [retrieved   on   July   6th,   2006   from] *http://www.ed.uiuc.edu/EPS/PES-Yearbook/96_docs/marshall.html*

Mayo, C. (1997). Foucauldian cautions on the subject and the educative implications of contingent identity. *Philosophy of Education Yearbook* [retrieved on July 6th 2006, from] *http://www.ed.uiuc.edu/EPS/PES-Yearbook/97_docs/mayo.html*

McDonough, K. (1993). Overcoming ambivalence about Foucault's relevance for education (Response to Covaleskie). *Philosophy of Education Yearbook* [retrieved on July 6th, 2006 from] *http://www.ed.uiuc.edu/EPS/PES-Yearbook/93_docs/MCDONOUG.HTM*

Middleton, S. (1998). *Disciplining sexuality: Foucault, life histories, and education.* New York, London: Teachers College.

Nietzsche, F. (1956). *The Birth of tragedy* and *the genealogy of morals.* (F. Golffing, Transl.). New York: Anchor Books.

Olssen, M. (1999). *Michel Foucault: Materialism and education.* Westport, CT and London: Bergin & Garvey.

————. (2003). Invoking democracy: Foucault's conception (with insights from Hobbes). *Policy Futures in Education,* 1(3), [retrieved on July 6th, 2006 from] *http://www.triangle.co.uk/ PFIE.*

Peters, M. A. (1996). *Poststructuralism, politics and education.* Westport, CT and London: Bergin & Garvey.

————. (Ed.). (1999). *After the disciplines? The emergence of cultural studies,* Westport, CT.and London: Bergin & Garvey.

————. (2000a). Michel Foucault 1926–1984. In J. Palmer & D. Cooper (Eds.), *100 Key Thinkers on Education* (pp. 170-174). London, Routledge.

————. (2000b). Writing the self: Wittgenstein, confession and pedagogy. *Journal of Philosophy of Education*, 34(2), 353–368.

————. (2001a). Foucault and governmentality: Understanding the neoliberal paradigm of education policy. *The School Field* XII (5–6), 61–72.

————. (2001b). Education, enterprise culture and the entrepreneurial self: A Foucauldian perspective. *Journal of Educational Enquiry*, 2 (1), [Retrieved on 27th August, 2006 from] (*http://www.education.unisa.edu.au/JEE/*).

————. (2003a). Truth-telling as an educational practice of the self: Foucault, *parrhesia* and the ethics of subjectivity. *Oxford Review of Education*, 29(2), 207–223.

————. (2003b). Heidegger and Foucault on space and bodies: Geographies of resistance in critical pedagogic practices. In R. Edwards & R. Usher (Eds.), *Spatiality, Curriculum and Learning* (pp. 184-196). International Perspectives on Curriculum Series. Buckingham: Open University Press.

————. (2003c, August). The new prudentialism in education: Actuarial rationality and the entrepreneurial self. Paper presented at the Roundtable on Education and Risk at the World Congress of Philosophy, Istanbul.

————. (2003d). Why Foucault? New directions in Anglo-American educational research. Keynote address presented at the "After Foucault: perspectives of the Analysis of Discourse and Power in Education", 29-31 October, The University of Dortmund.

Peters, M. A., Fitzsimons, P., & Marshall, J. D. (2000). Managerialism and education policy in a global context: Neoliberalism, Foucault and the doctrine of self-management. In N. Burbules & C. Torres (Eds.), *Globalization and education: Critical perspectives* (pp. 109–132). New York and London: Routledge.

Peters, M. A. & Wain, K. (2002). Postmodernism/Poststructuralism. In N. Blake, P. Smeyers, R. Smith & P. Standish (Eds.), *The Blackwell guide to the philosophy of education* (pp. 57-72). Oxford: Blackwell.

Peters, M. A., & Humes, W. (Eds.). (2003). Poststructuralism and educational research. Special issue of *Journal of Educational Policy*.

Peters, M. A., & Burbules, N. (2004). *Poststructuralism and educational research*. Lanham & Oxford, UK: Rowman & Littlefield.

Popkewitz, T., & Brennan, M. (Eds.). (1997). *Foucault's challenge: Discourse, knowledge and power in education*. New York: Teachers College Press.

Pring, R. (2000). *Philosophy of educational research*. London and NewYork: Continuum.

St.Pierre, E. A. & Pillow W. S. (Eds.). (2000*). Working the ruins: Feminist poststructural theory and methods in education*. New York: Routledge.

Veyne, P. (1997). The final Foucault and his ethics (C. Porter & A. I. Davidson, Transl.) In A. I. Davidson (Ed.), *Foucault and his interlocutors* (pp. 225-42). Chicago: University of Chicago Press.

Walkerdine, V. (1984). Developmental psychology and child centered pedagogy. In J. Henriques et al., *Changing the Subject* (pp. 157–174). London: Methuen:.

————. (1988). *The mastery of reason: Cognitive development and the production of rationality*. London: Routledge.

❧ Chapter 13 ☙

Critically Framing Education Policy: Foucault, Discourse and Governmentality

Robert Doherty

Policy analysis is a diverse and interdisciplinary field involving many researchers and specialists, in varying institutional setting, working under such banners as policy advocacy, policy research, policy development. One sector of the field of policy analysis, 'critical policy analysis,' has emerged around a focus and commitment to unmask or decode the ideological dimensions, values and assumptions of public policy. A feature of education policy in late modernity is its relentless predisposition to fix the boundaries and horizons of national projects of education at all levels. Such policy production now takes place in an atmosphere infused by the economic, political, social and cultural affects of globalisation. As a consequence, education policy is now cast in moulds that reflect this 'new complexity' in the policymaking climate, a complexity comprised of the interrelation between the supranational, the nation state and the regional.

In approaching policy analysis in the context of the new complexity, this chapter assumes a political dimension to the phenomena of education policy. Education policy is taken to be an expression of political rationality, and as a constituent of the scaffolding that establishes and maintains certain hegemonic projects. This section considers two ideas; 'governmentality' and 'discourse,' and their related theorisation, provided by the thought and analytical approaches of the French philosopher and historian Michel Foucault. Discourse and governmentality offer us the possibility of marking out a distinctive and penetrating analytical approach with which to undertake the task of critically reading education policy. The main focus of this chapter will be on governmentality, but it seems inopportune in considering approaches to critical policy analysis not to highlight the usefulness of Foucault's treatment of discourse.

Discourse

Discourse, from a mainstream social science perspective, could perhaps be thought of as a body of ideas, concepts and beliefs that have become established as knowledge, or as an accepted way of looking at the world. Such discourses form a set of lenses that have a profound influence on our understanding and action in the social world. Texts could be thought of as establishing, embodying, symbolising or expressing such discourses. A variety of approaches to the study of texts, across different disciplines, would understand and identify their techniques in terms of being discourse analysis. However, there is no commonly agreed definition of the idea of discourse or of the nature and scope of discourse analysis, this is an area marked by ongoing and complex theoretical debates. One common assumption underlying various approaches to discourse analysis is an intellectual commitment to understanding discourse as 'constructing' the social world, rejecting a realist perspective on language as a neutral medium that allows the describing and categorising of that world. Foucault's work has been a major inspiration in the growth of interest and engagement with the idea of discourse across the humanities and social sciences. The centrality of discourse in the work of Foucault is illustrated by its dominance in the intellectual manifesto he sets out in his inaugural lecture upon taking up his chair at the elite College de France:

> Here is the hypothesis which I would like to put forward tonight in order to fix the terrain – or perhaps the very provisional theatre – of the work I am doing: that in every society the production of discourse is at once controlled, selected, organized and redistributed by a certain number of procedures whose role is to ward off its powers and dangers, to gain mastery over its chance events, to evade its ponderous, formidable materiality. (Foucault, 1984, p.109)

The 'statement' is a central constituent of Foucault's analytics of discourse, statements or speech acts, or elemental parts of texts, are not of interest in terms of a detailed textual analysis, but in discerning the rules by which certain statements, or truth claims, as opposed to others, can emerge, operate, and come to comprise a discursive system: "…the term discourse can be defined as the group of statements that belong to a single system of formation; thus I shall be able to speak of clinical discourse, economic discourse, the discourse of natural history, psychiatric discourse" (Foucault, 1969, p. 121).

Central to Foucault's understanding is a commitment to a materialist conception of language; this goes beyond attention to signs and meaning in language to embrace its affects in the social world. Olssen (2004) points to Foucault's formulation of discourse as functioning as an alternative conception to what we would understand as ideology. This formulation of ideology operates, not in a Marxist sense of false consciousness, but as a more or less coherent system of ideas shared by a particular group within the social order. Such an ideology attempts to establish and maintain the normalisation, the naturalization, of the values, assumptions and prescriptions for action shared by its adherents and sponsors. Discourses are not simply texts, they are a form of power. For Foucault, power relations cannot be established, maintained, extended, resisted or mobilised into action, or given material form, without the mediation of discourse. Statements may be patterned into discursive formations according to sets of rules, but such formations have a tangible, concrete affect in structuring practices, relations of power and subjectivity, hence the materiality of language. This relation of power, ideology, language and discourse marks out the territory of interest and engagement for critical policy analysis. Discourses are the resources, the very fibre, from which policy texts are produced. Dominant, complimentary, persuasive, legitimating, contrasting and discordant discourses form the fabric of policy texts. The breadth of this fabric extends to include, policy documents, statements, legislation, speeches, events, training materials, websites, and the whole plethora of locations that embody authoritative statements of values, prescriptions, futures, priorities and obligations.

Policy texts, and their context of production in the incubator of the state apparatus or institutional context, form a primary locus for the forensic analysis of their form, ideological ambitions, components and identity. The work of uncovering the ideological influences and ambitions of texts, unmasking the social relations of power and domination that they submerge, is a central preoccupation for critical policy analysis. Foucault's development of discourse provides a powerful critical orientation and line of analysis and has been a major inspiration to those who have extended and developed discourse theory (Fairlough, 1989,1995, 2003; Luke, 1995). Commonly, the discourses embedded in policy texts operate to constitute, position, make productive, regulate, moralise and govern the citizen. Such texts are also indelibly marked by hidden conceptions of government, the task of governing, and its associated technologies. Foucault understood the activity of governing as only becoming possible through the development, harnessing, incorporation and active employment of discourse.

Governmentality

The idea of governmentality, as patented by Foucault (1991), offers a second horizon in relation to education policy scholarship. A number of researchers have noted the fragmentary and uncollected nature of Foucault's writing on governmentality, a line of enquiry that emerged in the latter period of his work. His investigation into this question of government informed a series of lectures delivered at the *College de France* in 1978. Foucault's approach to the concept of government was not problematized within the conventional terms of the state, constitutional theory or political philosophy, but in a broad sense of the 'conduct of conduct,' embracing all procedures, inventions, calculations, tactics and institutions implicated in this 'specific' and 'complex form of power.' In this sense, the practice of government leads to consideration of the multitude of techniques, schemes, structures and ideas deliberately mobilised in attempting to direct or influence the conduct of others. For Foucault, the family, the workplace, the profession, the population, are just some of the many sites within which the operation of government is to be found. In relation to the state, Foucault is concerned with unearthing the evolving rationalities of government, illustrated by his identification of the movement away from Machiavelli's problematic of reinforcing the power of the prince, to a new rationality for the state in relation to itself and its own flourishing.

> But government is not just a power needing to be tamed or an authority needing to be legitimised. It is an activity and an art which concerns all and which touches each. And it is an art which presupposes thought. The sense and object of governmental acts do not fall from the sky or emerge ready formed from social practice. They are things that have to be—and which have been— invented. (Burchell et al. 1991, p. x)

Governmentality is a prism that illuminates a particular stratum of enquiry, a perspective that examines, with a historical gaze, governing, as a deliberate, purposeful, technicised activity, directed at the subject, the society, or some consciously categorized subdivision of the social body. This activity resides and operates in a conflictual milieu, complicated by the contingent, the unexpected, and continually unbalanced by the outworking of discursive struggles. Governmentality is a perspective that resists systemisation or a neat explanatory theoretical ordering of government or politics, but tends to complexity, silhouetting a multi-dimensional matrix of intersecting problems, ambitions, protagonists, struggles, technical apparatuses, and discursive structures. For Foucault, the central labour around which such a matrix forms, under a liberal mentality of governing, is directed toward the constitution of the self, the configuration of the subject under the action of government.

An examination of political power from the vantage point of a history of governmentality focuses on such strategies, techniques, methods and technologies that have been deliberately employed or incorporated by the state in maximising its resources (crucially, its population). Foucault's attention is drawn to the task of giving an account of 'government reason,' its evolving nature, historical increments, periods of ascendancy, its changes and discontinuities. This analysis is particularly sensitive to patterns of state intervention into the lives of citizens. For Foucault, the state in modernity is characterised by an increasing governmentalization of the social order as the state intervenes on behalf of what it perceives as its own interest. The arrival of liberalism marks the advent of a distinctly modern form of government. Liberalism is identified by Foucault as the propagator of a unique form of the art of government, emerging out of the breakdown of the restrictions of feudalism and the dawn of a market capitalist society.

Critical to this is the 'freedom' of the citizen of the liberal state as they internalise norms and directions to regulate their own behaviour. Liberty, therefore, becomes a resource for government. This is a novel understanding of the operation of freedom in the theorisation of how the state can be governed. This theory of governing evolves in reaction to a realisation of the limits of the state to know, to see, to govern through pervasive observation, measurement and the regulation of every detail of life. The liberal state assumes a certain type of citizen, a responsiblised, socialised citizen, who within, and because of, their arc of freedom, serves the well being of the state. Governmentality is as much about what subjects do to themselves as what is done to them. As Peters (2001) puts it, " . . . government in this sense only becomes possible at the point at which policing and administration stops; at the point where government and self-government coincide and coalesce" (p. 1).

The Liberal Tradition

Liberalism has become that dominant political tradition of the modern age, it has both battled and evolved in relation to its challengers, Marxist socialism, and conservatism. Liberalism defines the problem space of 'governing' in a distinctive way, the state under the liberal insignia, is charged with the maintenance of conditions in which two vital sectors; the market and civil society, can operate and thrive. Critically, Foucault locates the emergence of 'society' with the advent of liberalism and its establishment as the culture of government. A key constituent of the intellectual architecture of the liberal art of governing is the identification of the state as the potential cause and agent of harmful government. In governing this sphere of the social, the liberal state is at pains to govern within what it understands as the logic of civil society's own internal systems of regulation and order. The social sphere, together with the market, the free space of economic activity, requires a sensitive governance so as not to unbalance their intrinsic mechanisms for order, success and maintenance. Burchell (1996) describes early, or classic, liberalism in terms of 'naturalism':

> It is in relation to this dynamic, historico-natural, both economic and non-economic domain that government as the exercise of nationally unified political sovereignty comes to define its tasks. Liberal governmental reason does not so much set out what in a particular case government policy should be, as define the essential problem space of government, and define it in such a way as to make a definite art of government

both thinkable and practicable. Early liberalism determines the questions of how to govern in relation to an object-domain which is a kind of quasi-nature with its own specific self-regulating principles and dynamic. This natural space is both what must be governed and what government must produce or, at least, maintain in the optimum condition of what naturally it is. Civil society becomes at the same time both object and end of government. (p. 24)

The late 19th century witnessed the emergence of social liberalism, or the 'new liberalism' in response to what perhaps could be described as the failures of classical liberalism to deliver in the realm of the social. It was the fate of the 'masses' under the demands of industrial capitalism that began to undermine the classical formulation of liberalism. It became apparent that the possession of 'liberty' did not compensate for poverty, economic hardship and social disintegration. Older liberal practices of philanthropy and regulation had failed as a response to the plight of the 'pauperised urban poor.' This new strain of state reason was marked by a more 'positive' view of freedom. In defence of this notion of freedom, under threat for a range of social evils, there followed a renegotiation of the liberal art of government. This 'welfare' liberalism, characterised by a more interventionist state, lasted into the early years of the 20th century and echoed beyond. The re-emergence, in the 1980s, of powerful strains of classical liberal thought into governmental reason marks the latest resurgence of liberal thought in the guiding rationality for governing. This emerging and remerging tradition of liberalism is characterised in one respect through the agenda, and importantly, the non-agenda of the state. This backdrop, of changing political rationality, can form a context for the consideration of public policy as an expression of governmentality.

Education Policy

Policy is commonly defined as a statement of government intentions. It is purposeful, directed toward a problem, need or aspiration, specifying principles and actions designed to bring about desired goals. The process of policymaking can be modelled in a number of ways, privileging, for example, process, reason or expert knowledge. This paper would endorse a view of policy making as essentially conflictual. Olssen et al. (2004) and his colleagues define policy in terms of "…any course of action (or inaction) relating to the selection of goals, the definition of values or the allocation of resources," (p. 71) policy is, therefore, bonded to the exercise of political power. This assures contestation, conflict, differing interests and competing views, reflecting asymmetries in power, representation and voice, in a political milieu fractured by divisions of class, race and gender. There is an inextricable link between policy, and policymaking, and politics as the art of government. Public policymaking, in essence, is the machinery of the modern state, the very tissue of state physiology. Engaging in the study of public policy, both in relation to the policymaking process or specific policies, assumes some understanding of the state. The task of policy analysis is made possible by approaching the question of the nature and function of the state through recourse to a range of theoretical problemizations and the recognition of policy as an expression of political rationality.

In the shaping of conduct, power is exercised through the active construction of representations of the economic and social systems and through the issuing of complementary sets of instructions, requirements and guidance on how subjects should behave and respond. The educational state is both incorporated into such representations and is simultaneously persuaded to understand its identity in relation to such narratives. Approaching the analysis of a field like education policy from a 'governmentality' stance can open up a critical space, a space that centres on "…that dimension of our history composed by the intervention, contestation, operationalization and transformation of more or less rationalised schemes, programmes, techniques and devices which seek to shape conduct so as to achieve certain ends" (Rose, 1999, p. 20).

I want to suggest a *two directional critique* offered by an analysis of governmentality as applied to public policy. If we consider the application of a governmentality reading to education policy, individual policies and related sectors of policy can be analysed in a backward direction in search of specific ambitions, deliberate objectives. Policy can be examined in a forward direction, in search of the technical forms, organisational arrangements, practices and forms of knowledge that are mobilised in making political reason operational and material. From this viewpoint, policy is read as an intervention, as the initiation and legitimation of a set of practices, as the planting and nurturing of certain screens of subjectivity, and as a retrospective display of 'state reason.' Policy is exposed, within a governmentality framework, as a direct, naked expression of state rationality, it becomes the theatre par excellence from which to view the living, breathing, evolving drama of government's understanding of governing. Policy, on a self-consciously governmentality reading, provides a window onto the troubled and ambitious soul of 'state reason.'

> Very broadly, we might say that governments attempt to represent the short-term interest of the temporarily dominant coalition of forces within a social formation; these coalitions are represented in political parties, and party policy reflects, on the one hand, the shifts of interest and the influence between the groups making up the coalition and, on the other, its conceptions of what is required to secure majority electoral support. In

one sense, then, the government acts to mediate the State and its subjects to each other.
(Dale, 1989, p. 53)

In thinking of 'government' and the state, it is useful to position the executive in relation to the dispersed structures, bureaucracies, institutions and apparatus of the state infrastructure. The executive may in one sense be at the helm
of this great vessel, but the state machine is a matrix of institutions and social
actors with its own political economy, contestations, rivalries, contradictions
and nodes of operation. The gravity around such nodes creates differing intellectual and policy climates through which the executive must prevail in its project of governance. In this context, it is perhaps instructive to ask an important
question in relation to governmentality and public policy. Where, we may reflect, does governmentality reside? Where, or within whom, is reason of state,
rationalities of the art of government, embodied?

Principally, we can assert that the knowledge that makes an art of modern
government possible is widely distributed in a political and administrative elite.
In the liberal state there is a legacy of knowledge and technical apparatuses that
make, to use Burchill's phrase, 'a definite art of government both thinkable and
practicable.' Nonetheless, primarily we must look to the executive of the current
political project as the most unambiguous embodiment of state reason. Key
components of this mentality of government will include an articulation of what
the prosperous, secure, influential state looks like, together with a set of ideas
and convictions as to how government must be enacted, operationalised in pursuit of this purpose. It is perhaps possible in attempting to answer this question
more fully, to point to hierarchies of actors and networks within and around the
organisational structure of the state. This ferment of intellectual and ideological
activity is both a resource for the executive, a provider of technical and intellectual innovations in pursuit of its aims, and a privileged lobbyer and influencer of
its project.

At this level, what perhaps we could think of as the *meso* level of state reason, policy scholarship has developed a range of approaches to conceptualising
those spaces where governmental rationality resides. There would appear to be
common conceptual ground between the focus of an analytics of governmentality and such conceptions as policy context, policy climate, policy culture, theories of agenda setting and control, think tanks, networks of influence, advocacy
coalitions and epistemic communities. In applying one dimension of our two
directional analysis, we can look back, in relation to a policy event, at its antece-
dents, looking to unearth the deliberate, purposeful, intentionality behind this
expression of political rationality. The trajectory of intention can be traced back
through the *meso* level to the principal level of ideological framing. This sector,
composed of a political and administrative elite together with the multifarious

networks of experts, professionals, researchers, advisors that infuse and surround the apparatus of government, is the main depository of governmental reason. It is here, at this altitude, new mutations and selections of governmental reason, and its technical means of effect, develop and evolve.

The other dimension of our analysis looks to discover the technical character of policy, the disciplines, practices, techniques, conventions, and forms of knowledge arranged and mobilised to give concrete form to political thought. A governmentality reading considers critically the resulting outcomes, implications, distributions, subversions, miscalculations, and alterations of such operationalised political thought.

Policy, at differing levels of creation, transmission and implementation, can be approached through an analysis of governmentality. Dimensions of government thought emerge into view under the application of this two directional critique. At the level of policy initiation, 'invention' or creation there is a searching for a 'rationality' that defines a policy trajectory, and shifts into a search for a *techne*[1] of implementation. At the *meso* level of policy production, we see a replication of the dynamic of the level above. This is a level of refinement, operationalization, a level of rendering practical, of discourse annunciation, text production, a surface of emergence and transmission. At the micro level of implementation, of arrangements, of techniques, all kinds of practices (administrative, bureaucratic, monitoring, auditing, training, performance managing) are enacted. Discourses, rationales and forms of knowledge support these socially mediated arrangements. Again the two directional critique can be applied. Remembering Foucault's conception that power is flexible, exercised, rather than possessed, productive as well as repressive, a governmentality reading has an insatiable concern for the resistance, subversion, penetration, failures and conflicts of operationalised policy.

Neoliberalism

The politics of the later part of the 20th century have been marked by the latest incarnation of liberal thought, the emergence of neoliberalism. Peters (2001), drawing on the work of British neo-Foucauldians, offers a very concise anatomy of neoliberal governmentality. He maps among its essential characteristics such elements as: retaining the liberal commitment to a perpetual critique of the state; the movement from naturalism toward an understanding of the market as an artefact shaped by cultural evolution and a focusing on the legal, regulatory framework of the economic sphere; the extension of economic rationality as a basis for the political; a revival of the rational, self-interest, utility maximising subject of classical economics; the unlashing of the techniques and rationality of business, the commercial, the private, into the public services and operations of the state.

Liberal democracies now subsist in a more or less neoliberal terrain, a dispensation that continually seeks to extend its reach. We live in an age in which a hegemonic neoliberalism is "...the closest thing to a global metanarrative we experience at the start of the twenty-first century" (Peters 2001, p. viii). We are all neoliberals now, or a least we live and move in a world whose geography is being refashioned by the evolving project of an imperious neoliberalism. The market state, whose arc of concern, or more precisely, its role, as allocated by this hegemonic discourse, and its mediations and compromises of electoral calculation, has become the recognisable face of contemporary governmental reason. The liberal democratic state, enclosed within the boundaries allocated by the global emissaries of neoliberalism, develops an art of government constrained by the limited options for self-interest that unfold within the operational possibilities of its allotted field of movement. This 'positioned state' is a contextual marker for the propagation of certain forms of state reason. Such a contour map of state prerogative allocates zones to the private, the public and new combinations and couplings of public, private, and third sector.

Late capitalism has an inherent reluctance to concede to the state anything other that a restricted field of movement, function or sector of control. At the same time, it seeks to co-opt, cajole and lobby the state to place its resources behind and around supporting those zones within which it has been declared trespasser or alien. The state is engineered as regulator, decontaminator, caretaker, insurer, actuary, keeper and curator of the markets infrastructure. It is within such an ideologically demarcated construction yard that the levers of state are assembled, connected and allocated a control function. The machinery of state is configured and designed to press, tension and be conspicuously demobilised within designated fields of action. This is the mechanical incubator that supports the growth of new strains of state rationality, evolving schemas for the activity of government that have as their object the: 'conduct of conduct.'

The global policy climate of developed, and developing nations is now impregnated by the tenets, assumptions, ambitions and operational technologies of a neoliberal ethos of government. When Tony Blair,[2] in the most high profile speech of the political calendar, addresses the governed as *'consumer and citizen,'* then the student of governmentality cannot be anything other than jolted by the implications of this powerful collocation. This observation, on the policy climate, has particular application to the construction of education policy, as it has moved into to a more central position in the strategic thinking of nation states.

This movement can be accounted for by a number of factors, notwithstanding, the primarily reason for its prominence can be attributed to the pressure exerted by the policy juggernaut of neoliberal economics.

A governmentality analysis would seem to offer policy studies a potent and interrogative framework from which to examine educational change and reform. A reading of education policy from a governmentality stance centres the use of freedom as a resource of the state, the constitution and regulation of the self, the development of subjectivities, and the active formation of the citizen. It also draws our attention to the reformation of the citizen, the modernisation of the citizen of former projects, the reengineering of the citizen to harmonise with current projects of state reason.

Notes

1   Greek term for the art, craft, or skill involved in deliberately producing something.

2   The leaders speech to the annual party conference; a discursive event invested with cultural significance and authority. Labour Party Conference, Winter Gardens, Blackpool, Tuesday 1st October 2002.

Bibliography

Burchell, G., Gordon, C., & Miller, P. (Eds.) (1991). *The Foucault effect*. Chicago: The University of Chicago Press.

————. (1996). Liberal government and techniques of the self. In A. Barry, T. Osborne, T & N. Rose (Eds.), *Foucault and political reason* (pp. 19–36). London: Routledge.

Dale, R. (1989). *The state and education policy*. Milton Keynes [England] Open University Press.

Fairclough, N. (1989). *Language and power*. Harlow [England] Longman.

————. (1995). *Critical discourse analysis*. London: Longman.

————. (2003). *Analysing discourse: Textual analysis for social research*. London: Longman.

Foucault, M. (1969). *The archaeology of knowledge*. London: Routledge.

————. (1984). The order of discourse. In M. Shapiro (Ed.), *Language and politics* (pp. 108–138). Oxford: Blackwell.

————. (1991). Governmentality. In G. Burchell, C. Gordon & P. Miller (Eds.), *The Foucault effect* (pp. 87–104). Chicago: The University of Chicago Press.

Luke, A. (1995). Text and discourse in education: An introduction to critical discourse analysis. In M. W. Apple (Ed.), *Review of research in education*, Vol. 21 (pp.194–210). Washington; American Educational Research Association.

Olssen, M., Codd, J., & O'Neill, A. (2004). *Education policy: Globalization, citizenship and democracy*. London: Sage.

Peters, M. A. (2001a). Foucault and governmentality: Understanding the neoliberal paradigm of education policy, *The School Field*, *XII*(5/6), 61–72.

———. (2001b). *Poststructuralism, Marxism and Neoliberalism*. Maryland: Rowman and Littlefield.

Rose, N. (1999). *Powers of freedom: Reframing political thought*. Cambridge: University of Cambridge Press.

ഌ Chapter 14 ‍ଔ

Invoking Democracy: Foucault's Conception (With Insights from Hobbes)

Mark Olssen

William Connolly (1998) has suggested that:

> Foucault does not articulate a vision of democracy. His early objections against political ideals such as prisons militates against it; and his later cautious affirmation of a positive political imagination never takes this form. But numerous comments in the context of his participation in public protests and demonstrations are suggestive on this score. It seems to me that a series of correspondences can be delineated between the ethical sensibility cultivated by Foucault and an ethos of democracy they invoke. (p. 120)

It is in this spirit of the ethos of democracy invoked by Foucault that my article takes root. Like Connolly, I will supplement Foucault with ideas and thoughts that extend beyond him, until I create a picture coherent enough to satisfy. I will of course differentiate Foucault's thought from the extensions and supplementations I provide. To the extent that Foucault advanced no overarching theory of democracy, the questions become, which of his ideas and formulations are relevant for a theory of democracy; how might he have problematised existing conceptions and formulations; and what lines of argument might he suggest for future explorations. My approach is premised on the fact that while Foucault showed little interest in, and indeed some distaste for, normative political theorising, I have no such inhibitions.[1] My tactic is to piece together the fragments of a theory of democracy, to show how Foucault approached democracy as a set of historically contingent practices, and to reveal the latent normative conceptions and suggestions within his texts. My argument, and conclusion, will be that Foucault *suggests* a theory of democracy and suggests a series of conceptions of democracy that takes us beyond our current models and practices.[2] I endeavour to outline what such a conception might look like. The basis for such an argument stems from Foucault's later writings on ethics and self-creation, liberty, autonomy and rights. More specifically, I will consider the following areas of his thought.

- a relational and dialogical conception of ethics with implications for agency, liberty, autonomy and interdependence;
- a conception of liberty as nondomination or as involving an equalization of power relations;

- a pragmatic political principle that would necessarily oppose government policies that conflict with or inhibit the cultivation of the self;
- a critique of philosophical and political monism and a argument for political pluralism;
- a historico-political discourse on rights;
- insights derived from his writings on power and resistance;
- an advocacy of *parrhesia* or speaking the truth to power.

Liberty, Ethics and Domination

Foucault's conceptions of liberty and ethics can be seen to presuppose a democratic context. Although historically democracy has been associated, as Weber argued, with an expanding hierarchical bureaucracy and as a form of technical expertise as ends in themselves, Foucault would see these tendencies as contingent historical episodes and challenges to be surmounted rather than as the necessary consequences of the expansion of the democratic process.

Foucault's conceptions of liberty, ethics and more broadly in relation to his writings on the cultivation and constitution of the self presuppose several normative themes related to democracy. In his later two volumes of *The History of Sexuality*, and in a variety of articles and interviews, Foucault develops a conception of the self which while avoiding liberal humanist conception of the autonomous chooser, incorporates a sense of agency and freedom. In this new-found concern with an active subject, there is on the surface a shift in relation to Foucault's interest away from knowledge as a coercive practice of subjection to being a practice of the self-formation of the subject. Yet, this positing of a more active, volitional subject does not involve a radical break with his earlier work, nor is it inconsistent with it. As Foucault states in his essay 'The Concern for Truth' (1989: p. 296) whereas in *Madness and Civilization* it was a matter of knowing how one 'governed' 'the mad'; in his later two works, it is a matter of how one 'governs' 'oneself'. In addition, in another essay he says:

> If now I am interested…in the way in which the subject constitutes himself in an active fashion, by the practices of the self, these practices are nevertheless not something that the individual invents by himself. They are patterns that he finds in his culture and which are proposed, suggested and imposed on him by his culture, his society and his social group. (Foucault, 1991, p. 11)

Cultivating the self is the basis of ethical work. Ethical work, says Foucault, is the work one performs in the attempt to transform oneself into an ethical subject of one's own behaviour, the means by which we change ourselves in order to become ethical subjects. Such a history of ethics is a history of aesthetics. In his interview *On the Genealogy of Ethics*, Foucault (1984b) explains that there is,

> another side to the moral prescriptions, which most of the time is not isolated as such but is, I think, very important: the kind of relationship you ought to have with yourself, *rapport à soi*, which I call ethics, and which determines how the individual is supposed to constitute himself as a moral subject of his own actions. (p. 352)

Ethics, as such, is part of morality, but rather focus exclusively on codes of moral behaviour, it concentrates on the self's relationship to the self, for the way we relate to ourselves contributes to the way that we construct ourselves and form our identities, as well as the way we lead our lives and govern our conduct.

Foucault's understanding of ethics and liberty invoke a particular form of community. Hence, Foucault's conception of ethics is not the narrow individualist conception of western modernity. Rather it refers to what Kant termed *Sitten*—customs or practices. Hence, ethics for Foucault is not intended in the Kantian sense, as Ian Hacking (1986) puts it, as "something utterly internal, the private duty of reason" (p. 239), but more in the sense of Ancient Greece where ethics was concerned with the good life. As Foucault (1991) states it:

> The Greeks...considered this freedom as a problem and the freedom of the individual as an ethical problem. But ethical in the sense that Greeks could understand. *Ethos* was the deportment and the way to behave. It was the subject's mode of being and a certain manner of acting visible to others. One's *ethos* was seen by his dress, by his bearing, by his gait, by the poise with which he reacts to events, etc. For them that is the complete expression of liberty. (p. 6)

Foucault's understanding of the care of the self involves a politically active subject acting in a community of subjects, involving practices of the self that require governance as well as the problems of practical politics. Foucault speaks for instance of liberty as implying complex relations to others and self. Ethical action is not for Foucault an individual affair but presupposes a certain political and social structure with respect to liberty. For liberty or civic freedom to exist, there must be a certain level of liberation conceived as the absence of domination. Thus, the subject's activity is intrinsically mediated through power, which coexists with freedom in that relationships of power are changeable relations that can modify themselves. But where states of domination result in relations of power being fixed "in such a way that they are perpetually asymmetrical [then the] margin of liberty is extremely limited" (Foucault, 1991, p. 12). Foucault

(1991) gives the example of the traditional conjugal relation in the eighteenth and nineteenth centuries:

> We cannot say that there was only male power; the woman herself could do a lot of things: be unfaithful to him, extract money from him, refuse him sexually. She was, however, subject to a state of domination, in the measure where all that was finally no more than a certain number of tricks which never brought about a reversal of the situation. (p. 12)

Invoking democracy, the normative inference is the counterfactual: resistance should oppose domination wherever it finds it. Such an inference suggests that domination is an imbalance of power, it is one of many structurings of power, and what resistance aims at is an 'equalisation'; and rather than a concentration, it suggests a dispersment. The emphasis on 'minimising domination' appears again in his remarks on Habermas. Criticising Habermas for advocating a form of 'utopian' thinking, whereby communicative action operates in a powerless vacuum, Foucault (ibid.) says:

> I don't believe there can be a society without relations of power . . . The problem is not of trying to dissolve them in the utopia of perfectly transparent communication, but to give oneself the rules of law, the techniques of management, but also the ethics, the *ethos*, the practice of self, which would allow these games of power to be played with a minimum of domination. (p. 18)

In this sense,

> liberty is itself political. And then it has a political model, in the measure where being free means not being a slave to one's self and to one's appetites, which presupposes that one establish over one's self a certain relation of domination, of mastery, which was called *arche* – power, authority. (p. 6)

When one practices liberty one is engaged in moral conduct, which is to say that liberty must be practiced ethically. As Foucault (1991) puts it: "Liberty is the ontological condition of ethics. But ethics is the deliberate form assumed by liberty" (p. 4). This means that the 'care for the self' involves liberty and ethics, which presumes a certain form of social structure: a certain degree of liberation.

In this sense, ethical action also takes place in a community, in that care for the self involves care for others. In Foucault's words:

> The care for the self always aims at the good for others . . . This implies also a relation with others to the extent that care for self renders one competent to occupy a place in the city, in the community or in interindividual relationships...I think the assumption

of all this morality was that one who cared for himself correctly found himself, by that very fact, in a measure to behave correctly in relationship to others and for others. A city in which everyone would be correctly concerned for self would be a city that would be doing well, and it would find therein the ethical principle of its stability. (1991, p. 7)

Such a community is both *borderless* and *complexly differentiated*. These are the two essential conditions of what I have called elsewhere (Olssen, 2002) a 'thin community.' In such a conception difference and unity are balanced. Thin communities are linked to other communities and to the global order. Foucault's rejection of Hegelianism and forms of monist communitarinism establish difference as an important political principle, which ensures and safeguards pluralism, globalism, democracy and inclusion. In such a conception, democracy is the protection of difference. For Foucault, the principle of difference underpins his approach to the political as well as his global conception of citizenship. It is the theory of difference that establishes relationality and diversity as fundamental social and political attributes. It is also his conception of difference that establishes the particular character of Foucault's communitarianism as 'thin,' and which regulates the legitimate sphere of state and group actions vis-à-vis individual and group discretion.

Democratic tactics comprise a multifaceted range of mechanisms and processes. Its advantage for a Foucauldian politics is not simply that it enables the participation and approval of concerns by the entire collectivity and of all the major groups within it, but more importantly, it permits continued debate, modification, rejection, or revision of agreed decisions while enabling a maximum of freedom and autonomy, an ongoing possibility of negotiation and dialogue, and the most effective opposition possible to abuses of power. Government is important for Foucault, as Mitchell Dean (1999a) says, "according to whether it allows rather than inhibits the 'self-directed use and development of capacities'" (p. 184). There is an obvious sense in which democracy is the form of government best suited to these ends.

In his "unfashionable interpretation of Michel Foucault"[3], James Johnson (1997) maintains that Foucault's commitment to concepts and principles such as those cited in the quotations above suggest a normative analysis of power contra the fashionable postmodern interpretations of his work. Johnson further supports his case by tracing similar references to canonical works such as *Discipline and Punish* as well as in Foucault's articles and interviews. In *Discipline and Punish*, Foucault (1977, p. 222) speaks of institutions such as prisons and schools as having the role of "introducing insuperable asymmetries and excluding reciprocities". Here Foucault talks of the disciplines as being "essentially nonegalitarian and asymmetrical" (p. 222). Johnson accepts the view contra the postmodern interpretations of Foucault, "that disciplinary power is *normatively objectionable* [for Foucault] precisely *because* it imposes unequal, asymmetrical, nonreciprocal relations and *because*, in doing so, it obliterates the sorts of extant communicative relation that, potentially at least, could produce social relations characterized by equality, symmetry and reciprocity" (1997, p. 572). Hence, says Johnson, power relations for Foucault are "objectionable because they subvert relations of communication, relations of the sort that – if more fully specified – might sustain the vision of political agency that is implicit in his commitment to resistance or dialogical ethics" (572).

As against totalizing approaches, such as Marxism, Hegelianism, and liberalism, the normative emphasis of Foucault's position is that all power relations must be characterized by *openness* (i.e., not be "set", "congealed", "nonegarlitarian", "asymmetrical" or "nonreciprocal"). As a consequence, such principles give a normative basis to a conception of democratic justice, while at the same time recognizing that justice will require different things at different times and places. Although principles, of varying degrees of importance and weight, will relate to all aspects of conflicts in local situations, such principles will always underdetermine any actual ethical dilemma, and hence never fully resolve issues internal to such conflicts. While power relations must remain dialogically open, and be normatively skewed toward power equalization[4], they must also be context-sensitive to the specific contingencies of historical circumstance.

Rights as a Historico-Political Discourse

I want now to look at three practices of democracy, or better tactics or strategies that can be called *democratic*: rights; contestation; and deliberation. A genealogy of democracy would trace the historical descent and emergence of the multiple processes, strategies, mechanisms, and tactics that societies instantiate as discourses of protection against war and conquest. That is, it would trace the shifting historically contingent conceptions of what constituted democracy in different societies at different times. Rather than government 'by the people' in any direct or unmediated sense of 'pure' democracy,[5] as in Greek society, or in eigtheenth century Europe and North America, or as in the later 'representative' traditions, Foucault would see practices of democracy more broadly as representing "historico-political" discourses, comprising an assortment of tactics, strategies and mechanisms.

What are such tactics, strategies and mechanisms aimed at? In Foucault's view the discourse of rights is a 'historico-political discourse' aimed at the protection of lives. As he puts it (2003):

The jurists of the seventeenth century and especially the eighteenth century were, you see, already asking this question about the right of life and death. The jurists ask: when we enter into a contract, what are individuals doing at the level of the social contract, when they come together to constitute a sovereign, to delegate absolute power over them to a sovereign? They do so because they are forced to by some threat or by need. They therefore do so in order to protect their lives. (p. 241)

Thus, viewing the development of rights in relation to "mechanisms, techniques and technologies of power" (p. 241) they assumed prominence because, "in the seventeeth and eigtheenth centuries we saw the emergence of techniques of power that were essentially centered on the body" (Ibid). In this, rights were a device,

> devices that were used to ensure spatial distribution of individual bodies (their separation, their alignment, their serialization, and their surveillance) and the organization around those individuals of a whole field of visibility. They were also techniques that would be used to take control over bodies. (p. 241)

Rights are part of the 'individualizing-totalising' disciplinary technology. They were juridical technologies charged with protecting the *pluribus* while promoting the *unum*. Although rights constituted individualising technologies of power, a new form emerged at the end of the eighteenth century, which also applied to rights in that it enabled individuals to be monitored, counted, compared, processed, treated equitably.

> This technology of power does not exclude the former, does not exclude disciplinary technology, but it does dovetail into it, integrate it, modify it to some extent, and above all, use it by sort of infiltrating it, embedding itself in existing disciplinary technologies...So after a first seizure of power over the body in an individualizing mode, we have a second seizure of power that is not individualizing, but, if you like, massifying, that is directed not at man-as-body, but man-as-species...What I would call a "biopolitics" of the human race (p. 242)

Hobbes is, in this sense, the father of rights, for he saw the issue was security. As Foucault (2003) notes:

> Leviathan's strategic opposite number is, I think, the political use that was being made in political struggles of a certain historical knowledge pertaining to wars, invasions, pillage, dispossessions, confiscations, robbery, exaction, and the effects of all that, the effects of all these acts of war, all these feats of battle, and the real struggles that go on in the laws and institutions that apparently regulate power . . . Leviathan's invisible adversary is the Conquest. (p. 98)

It was a fear of the Conquest that led Hobbes to stress the role of the State:

> Hobbes may well seem to shock, but he is in fact being reassuring: he always speaks the
> discourse of contracts and sovereignty, or in other words, the discourse of the State.
> After all, philosophy and right, or philosophico-juridical discourse, would rather give
> the State too much power than not enough, and while they do criticize Hobbes for giv-
> ing the State too much power, they are secretly grateful to him for having warded off a
> certain insidious and barbarous enemy. (pp. 98–99)

Rights crystallize whatever given imbalance of power and wealth exists in a society. In the seventeenth century, natural rights theories were developed by conservative thinkers in the defense of property and competition and other
bourgeois values. A system of rights constituted part of a historico-political *settlement*. A settlement can be represented, in Rawl's (1996) sense, as a *modus
vivendi*, which is to say, a treaty, or alliance of diverse interests, which may at
times constitute an overlapping consensus. In situations of war the settlement
collapses and rights mean nothing. In this sense, the concept of settlement, although not explicitly used by Foucault, is useful in that it attests to the historical
character of rights as they are embodied in broader discursive arrangements at a
particular time.[6] Rights are a *war-preventing* strategy. They constitute a system of
universal regulation of what is due whom and what is owed.

   In this sense, what is to be made of Hart's (1955) claim that rights are natural? And, if there are no natural rights, is the discourse of rights redundant?
What Hart failed to see is that moral rights may be built on a historically constituted settlement, and they will reflect the injustices and iniquities built into that
settlement. In this sense, the existence of moral rights does not mean there
must exist a natural right of liberty amongst men.[7] For Foucault, rights systems
take effect as a settlement against war. They are a technology, a fixing the relation of the individual to the society; they differentiate; they are one of the 'divid-
ing practices.' Foucault (2003) cites and endorses the views of Boulainvilliers
who argues that the idea of a natural right is "no more than a useless abstraction" (p. 156). In Boulainvilliers' view you can study history for as long as you
like but you will never discover any natural rights. Behind the existing divisions
between groups or strata in society are wars and struggles. Freedom, specifically,
is not natural, for freedom is only conceivable if there are no relationships of
domination between the individuals concerned. Freedom for Boulainvilliers is
essentially the freedom to trample on the freedom of others. In this sense, freedom is the direct opposite of equality. Whatever the relation between the two, it
is something that is decided and enjoyed according to "difference, domination,
and war, thanks to a whole system of relations of force" (ibid, p. 157). In these

relations, any laws of nature, if indeed they do exist, are weaker than the "none-galitarian law of history":

> It is therefore natural that the egalitarian law of nature should have given way—on a permanent basis —to the nonegalitarian law of history. It was because it was primal that natural right was not, as the jurists claim, foundational; it was foreclosed by the greater vigor of history. The law of history is always stronger than the law of nature. This is what Boulainvilliers is arguing when he says that history finally created a natural law that made freedom and equality antithetical, and that this natural law is stronger than the law inscribed in what is known as natural right. The fact that history is stronger than nature explains, ultimately why history has completely concealed nature. When history begins, nature can no longer speak, because in the war between history and nature, history always has the upper hand. There is a relationship of force between nature and history, and it is definitely in history's favor. So natural right does not exist, or exists only insofar as it has been defeated: it is always history's great loser, it is 'the other.' (2003, p. 157–8)

A further point Boulainvilliers suggests is that "war is both the starting point for an analysis of society and the deciding factor in social organisation" (Foucault, 2003, p. 158). What is meant here is that wars and struggles determine the particular form of the relation of force between freedom and equality in the settlements or agreements that separate wars and contain struggles. The nature of military institutions, or the problem of "who has the weapons" is crucial to the maintenance of order between wars. The "problem of who has the weapons" is bound up, says Foucault (2003) "with certain technical problems, and it is in this sense that it can provide the starting point for a general analysis of society" (p. 159). He continues:

> History now looks essentially like a calculation of forces . . . Once the strong become weak and the weak become strong, there will be new oppositions, new divisions, and a new distribution of forces: the weak will form alliances among themselves, and the strong will try to form alliances with some and against others….For his part Boulain-villiers makes the relationship of war part of every social relationship, subdivides it into a thousand different channels, and reveals war to be a sort of permanent state that exists between groups, fronts and tactical units as they in some sense civilize one another, come into conflict with one another, or on the contrary, form alliances. There is no more multiple and stable great masses, but there is a multiple war. In one sense, it is a war of every man against every man, but it is obviously not a war of every man against every man in the abstract and – I think—unreal sense in which Hobbes spoke of the war of every man when he tried to demonstrate that it is not the war of every man against every man that is at work in the social body. With Boulainvilliers, in constract, we have a generalised war that permeates the entire social body and the entire history of

the social body; it is obviously not the sort of war in which individuals fight individuals, but one in which groups fight groups. (p. 161)

The upshot of this conception is that war is a "disruption of right" (ibid, p. 163). Here, says Foucault:

> War turns the very disruption of right into a grid of intelligibility, and makes it possible to determine the force relationship that always underpins a certain relationship of right. Boulainvilliers can thus integrate events such as wars, invasions, and change—which were once seen as simply naked acts of violence—into a whole layer of contents and prophecies that covered society in its entirety…A history that takes as its starting point the fact of war itself and makes its analysis in terms of war can relate all these things— war, religion, politics, manners, and characters—and can therefore act as a principle that allows us to understand history. (p. 163)

Citing and summarising Foucault in his account of Boulainvilliers here brings to the fore the functions of democratic practices and tactics—not simply rights, but also the others—contestation, deliberation, the rule of law, parliamentary elections, forms of representation—as part of the settlement against war and chaos.[8] In this sense, rights may recognise, preserve and legitimate the existing unequal relation of forces in society, as they did in the seventeenth century, in consolidating bourgeois relations of property and class.[9] Or they may, in other periods, conceivably extend from the political to the economic domains, seeking to challenge unequal relations and forces. In this sense, rights to life, to a certain minimum level of sustenance and property, to walk the streets in day or night, to speak, to contest, can be endorsed, exchanged, surrendered, or exempted. What is clear, however, is that for Foucault, democracy is the alternative to war, for democracy is nothing but the tactics adopted to resolve conflict, ensure more or less peaceful transitions of power, and to permit each individual their legitimate arena or space, whereby rights—both passive and active—can be exercised and maintained. In this sense, by invoking the normative in Foucault, we can see that democracy is the containment and management of war. Democracy is politics, and "politics," as Foucault (2003) says, inverting Clausewitz's famous aphorism, "is the continuation of war by other means" (p. 15).

Hobbes, rather than Locke, is the preferred starting point for a social conception of rights, for the juridical tradition that passes through Hobbes is more compatible with the priority of the social over nature and, in this sense, of the "triumph of the will" (Rials, 1994, p. 168). For Locke, the law restores natural right and is subservient to it, which is the basis, ultimately, for Locke, of giving citizens the right to rebel. For Hobbes, the situation is more complex. Although, in *Leviathan* (1885, 65–66) there is a "right of nature" (*jus naturale*) which resides in "the liberty each man hath to use his own power, as he will himself, for the preservation of his own nature, that is to say his own life," a state wherein "every man has a right to everything." hence a state where "there is no security" (p. 66), it would be a mistake to confuse this abstract and unqualified "right of nature" with the modern notion of subjective rights based upon the idea of an individual power. As Rials (1994) notes:

> Hobbes does not think that the "right of nature" dissolves, despite his ambiguous phrasing, into the "natural rights" of individuals. Right is constituted only once the individual "powers" or "forces" come together to constitute a societal machine, the "artificial man" (Leviathan) whose strength is the sum of all prior individual forces that have made him sovereign. This is the difference between Hobbes and the teachers of the modern natural-right school. If there are no natural rights while the social contract is in the making, there surely are none once it is made. In the contract, the "right of nature" gives way entirely to the "civil right," which is the fruit of law's exaltation. With Hobbes one already has voluntarist positivism. (p. 168)

Contestation and Deliberation

Foucault's writing on rights, as summarised above, from his lecture of the 11th February 1976 at the *Collège de France* show his serious consideration in relation to the themes of war, peace, and security. Such considerations also give substance to his political work on behalf of prisoners and other marginalised groups. In June 1984, *Libération* carried his brief article *Confronting Governments: Human Rights*, where he states:

> There exists an international citizenship that has its rights and its duties and that obliges one to speak out against every abuse of power, whoever its author, whoever its victims. After all, we are all members of the community of the governed, and thereby obliged to show mutual solidarity. (2001, p. 474)

The conception of rights here invoked seems to be one beyond both sovereignty and discipline; one which Foucault (1980) hinted at towards the close of the second lecture on power (January 14th, 1976) where he said:

> If one wants to look for a non-disciplinary form of power, or rather, to struggle against disciplines and disciplinary power, it is not towards the ancient right of sovereignty that we should turn, but towards the possibility of a new form of right, one which must indeed be anti-disciplinarian, but at the same time liberated from the principle of sovereignty. (p. 108)

A conception of right not subject to normalisation, and not legitimating the interests of the monarch might then exist in contestation as is entailed in Foucault's discussions of resistance to power. Such resistance occurs wherever domination occurs. It is present also in relation to his later discussions concerning *parrhesia,* which has a range of meanings and uses, the main one of which functions in relation to democratic institutions, and means essentially speaking the truth to power. Foucault (2001a) points to an ancient tradition revolving around free speech, as embodied in *parrhesia,* which he defines as "frankness in speaking the truth" (p. 11).[10] Ordinarily translated into English as 'free speech,' *parrhesiazomai* or *parrhesiazesthai* is to use *parrhesia,* and the *parrhesastes* is the one who uses *parrhesia* (i.e., the one who speaks the truth). But someone is said to use *parrhesia* "only if there is a risk or danger for him in telling the truth . . . the *parrhesiastes* is someone who takes a risk" (2001a, p. 16). In addition:

> The function of *parrhesia*...has the function of criticism...*Parrhesia* is a form of criticism, either towards another or towards oneself, but always in a situation where the speaker or confessor is in a position of inferiority with respect to the interlocutor. The *parrhesiastes* is always less powerful than the one with whom he speaks. (ibid)

Finally, "in *parrhesia,* telling the truth is regarded as a duty" (ibid). Foucault (2001a) draws the various elements together. Thus,

> *Parrhesia* is a kind of verbal activity where the speaker has a specific relation to truth through frankness, a certain relationship to his own life through danger, a certain type of relationship to himself or other people through criticism...and a specific relation to moral law through freedom and duty. More precisely, *parrhesia* is verbal activity in which a speaker expresses his personal relationship to truth, and risks his life because he recognizes truth telling as a duty to improve or help other people (as well as himself). In *parrhesia,* the speaker uses his freedom and chooses frankness instead of persuasion, truth instead of falsehood or silence, the risk of death instead of life and security, criticism instead of flattery, and moral duty instead of self-interest and moral apathy. That, then, quite generally, is the positive meaning of the word *parrhesia* in most of the Greek texts...from the Fifth Century B.C. to the Fifth Century A.D. (pp. 19–20)

In relation to Greek uses, *parrhesia* was potentially seen as dangerous to democracy. As Foucault explains:

> The problem, very roughly put was the following. Democracy is founded on *politeia,* a constitution, where the *demos,* the people, exercise power, and where everyone is equal in front of the law. Such a constitution, however, is condemned to give equal place to all forms of *parrhesia,* even the worst. Because *parrhesia* is given even to the worst citizens, the overwhelming influence of bad, immoral, or ignorant speakers may lead the

citizenry into tyranny, or may otherwise endanger the city. Hence *parrhesia* may be dangerous to democracy itself. (Ibid, p. 77)

Thus, Foucault cites the third book of Plato's Republic [Book VIII, 557a–b], where Socrates tells Adeimantus that: "When the poor win the result is democracy. They kill some of the opposite party, banish others, and grant the rest an equal share in civil rights and government, officials being usually appointed by lot" (pp. 83–84).

Socrates goes on to enquire as to what people are like in a democracy: First of all, they are free. Liberty and free speech [*parrhesia*] are rife everywhere; anyone is allowed to do what he likes…That being so, every man will arrange his own manner of life to suit his pleasure.

Plato's concern here, says Foucault (2001a) is that in a democracy there is:

> no common *logos*, no possible unity, for the city. Following the Platonic principle that there is an analogous relation between the way a human being behaves and the way the city is ruled, between the hierarchical organization of the faculties of the human being and the constitution makeup of the polis, you can see very well that if everyone in the city behaves just as he wishes, with each person following his own opinion, his own will or desires, then there are in the city as many constitutions, as many small autonomous cities, as there are citizens doing whatever they please. And you can see that Plato also considers *parrhesia* not only as the freedom to say whatever one wishes, but as linked with the freedom to *do* whatever one wants. It is a kind of anarchy involving the freedom to choose one's own style of life without limit. (p. 84)

Plato's treatment occludes difference, or fails to allow for difference within unity. *Parrhesia* is not condemned because all citizens are given rights to influence the city, or to have a say. For Plato, it is because of this very quality that it is opposed. Yet, within the context of security and war, this democratic right (*parrhesia*) becomes the condition on which peace is maintained. *Parrhesia* contributes to the democratic settlement against war that constantly threatens to erupt, or become uncontainable. Such insights are potentially continuous with the republican tradition in political theory, where rights of contestation are prior to consent, and where public decisions are legitimate so long as they are capable of withstanding group and individual contestation under procedures agreed by all. In this sense, contestation is a hedge against arbitrariness in decision making. Essentially, contestation introduces the fundamental idea of democracy as 'self-rule.'

If *parrhesia* could contribute to an ideal of democracy within the law, according to the constitutional rules that limit its scope, in talking about moving beyond sovereignty and discipline, Foucault seems to acknowledge a more fundamental right to *resistance* when power becomes damned up, resulting in domination. Thus, in his interview 'Truth and Power,' he (1980a) speaks of *strategies of resistance* taking effect when surveillance and oppression become "unbearable" (p. 122). In this sense, it would constitute a right, not because it relates back to nature, but in that it becomes the condition on which war and chaos are avoided and survival assured. While such strategies don't guarantee the avoidance of war, they become its best hope, and its minimum condition. Let us say, without such a right, war, which is really the suspension of all rights, all security, becomes almost certain. Resistance—short of war—becomes a condition of pluralist democracy, which is itself a strategy for the avoidance of war.

Strategies of contestation are linked to deliberation, which requires the fostering of institutions in which political action, with all its limitations, can be pursued. Deliberative democracy acknowledges that viewpoints and preferences will conflict, and allows for uncoerced or open context as essential to the arrival at an agreed outcome. Such strategies for Foucault are essentially group based where the views of individuals are transformed in the process. Deliberative democracy thus counts to insure against open conflict.

In the Foucauldian sense, deliberation recognises and tolerates differences to a much greater sense than in Habermas's understanding. Habermas's post-Kantian conception of a transcendent communicative consensus, embodied through the ideal speech situation is replaced by a much looser context of shared agreements, more of the character of Rawls' (1996) *modus vivendi* than a consensus reached based on epistemological grounds of the force of the better argument alone. As a *modus vivendi* is simply a loose treaty, or agreement, it is based sometimes on nothing more than a shared interest in survival. The aim of deliberation is not epistemic consensus, pace Habermas, but rather, a new concordance, or settlement, based on a workable balance between different views, a pragmatic consensus of sorts, based on epistemic factors, conceptions of justice, as well as a range of pragmatic factors, such as the priorities for peace and stability at a particular moment in time.

Extending Foucault and Democracy Post 9/11

If a settlement is an historically contingent accord or agreement which constitutes a system of rules whose function is the containment of conflict and prevention of open hostilities, in the Hobbesian sense, it is motivated by the quest for security. In his essays in *Society Must Be Defended* Foucault clearly accepts such a view, but whether he would accept Hobbes' skepticism in international relations is more doubtful. The standard view of international relations accords with the Westphalian model of free independent states, organised and run on the basis of autonomy and non-interference. Such a view represents an extrapolation from Hobbes views about individuals in the state of nature to ethical skepticism concerning relations between states in the international arena. For Hobbes there were no *effective* moral principles in the state of nature.[11] The fact that one individual cannot trust another individual to abide by a moral rule or norm, makes it pointless acting in such a way oneself—which is why life in the state of nature is 'solitary, nasty, brutish and short.' In the international system of states, ethical skepticism means that there are no moral restrictions on a state's interpretation of its own interests. Hence, as moral rules would be inappropriate, the system is seen as 'anarchic.'

Kant rejected such a conception, as did Grotius and Pufendorf before him. Rather than support an anarchic conception of international relations based on individual state interests, they supported an ethical view of the role of the state acting in accord with an objective moral rule.[12] Initial plausibility of such a view can be seen in the existence of human rights accords, international charters, and initiatives towards international peace, which would seem to suggest that some conception of international morality does exist, and does influence states in their actions towards each other. Before the Peace of Westphalia, Grotius had defined international relations as a moral community of states.[13] Pufendorf also developed a conception of the 'morality of states,' interpreting international relations from within a natural law tradition.[14]

Globalisation, terrorism and weapons of mass destruction make such a model, based on an 'ethical' conception of the global order, more of a necessity than a plausible option in the twenty first century. The rise of international terrorism and weapons of mass destruction, as well as phenomenon like climate change, SARS, AIDS and Bird-Flu alters the 'equation,' for they make individual and collective survival an important ethical concern. The possibilities of nuclear terrorism, together with the democratisation of knowledge and of access to nuclear knowledge and technology, make the challenges facing humanity even more formidable. In this situation, survival constitutes a new imperative, a 'final settlement,' to justify a global law of morality amongst nations. Acting according to principles becomes compelling if by so doing acts of terrorism are *minimised*, and the possibilities for survival are *enhanced*. Similarly, the possibility of acts of terror or of violence, or unintended developments like climate change, AIDS or Bird-Flu, increases the need for a discourse of safety and security. We may not agree with Hobbes on very much, but the priority of *security* over *freedom*, was indeed a profound insight. Globalisation and terrorism raise the issue of 'survival' both for individuals and nations.

Such a thesis would argue that given these new realities of acts of terror and weapons of mass destruction, the *self-interest* of states, like the *self-interest* of individuals, is a poor basis for action and ethics. Indeed, actions calculated in terms of short-term interests may not be realised as in the long-term interests of either. The interests of survival are normative in that they impose requirements of action in the interests of all. The self-interests of humanity cannot be calculated on the basis of the interests of each, however, but must involve a collective consideration. This necessitates a conception of democracy, as Beitz (1979) puts it, which expresses a "moral point of view":

> The moral point of view requires us to regard the world from the perspective of one person among many rather than from that of a particular self with particular interests, and to choose courses of action, policies, rules, and institutions on grounds that would be acceptable to any agent who was impartial among the competing interests involved...From the moral point of view...one views one's interests as one set of interests among many and weighs the entire range of interests according to some impartial scheme. (p. 58)

This principle of democracy is *non-foundational* but *universal*. It is not based upon any fixed conception of human nature, or of a premise, as with Habermas, of universal rationality, but rather purely on a principle of a *mutual interest in universal survival. In an age of terrorism democracy is the condition upon which survival can best be assured.* Such a conception is universal to the extent that it is *willed*. The inspiration is Nietzschean rather than Kantian. It is also, I think, Foucauldian, in the sense that it constitutes *a universalism of democracy as a contingent discourse of open protection and facilitation in a world of dangers.*[15]

Although survival may justify democracy, as an end or goal it is too thin to be fully adequate, of course, for mere survival cannot possibly satisfy a complete account of life's ends and aims. And it may not be universally agreed to, if we mean by universal 'agreed to by all,' for there are no doubt some, including 'suicide bombers,' for whom it holds no sway at all. Ultimately, that is the choice of course, and certainly it focuses the concentration. For if democracy is the *precondition* of survival, then it requires a democratic mandate to be effective, even so.

Beyond this, it is possible to build a much richer conception of democracy on this basis. If survival is a final justification, and focuses our attention as to why democracy is important, survival with dignity resonates of a more traditional concern with *ends*. This of course is the classic conception of democracy as a doctrine based on the ultimate worth and dignity of the human being, as espoused in the republican tradition. Thus, it is not the narrow 'realist' theory of democracy that has been articulated and advocated by postwar American political science, commonly associated with the writings of Joseph Schumpeter (1976) *Capitalism, Socialism and Democracy*, which refers to a narrow system of representative government and a means of changing governments through a system of elections. Rather, if safety, dignity, and survival are to be possible, it must be deepened, once again, to refer to a substantive ends which is something more than mere utility, but encompasses the well-being and safety 'of each and all.' Such a conception must once again entail a certain idea of participation, equality, inclusion, social justice, and freedom as well. Democracy must in this light be seen as a comprehensive discourse of (1) safety and security, (2) freedom and autonomy, (3) inclusion, (4) fairness and justice, (5) equality of resources and capabilities. In an age of terrorism, where a global *Leviathan* is feared, a *comprehensive discourse of democracy becomes the best answer to the Hobbesian problem of order.*

While some political theorists might sense a resonance here with Rousseau's general will, this would be mistaken. The model suggested here is, in the sense of Foucault, not a totalising one, which presupposes unity between individual and collective, but a *detotalising* one that is based on the notion of general well-being, while recognising the diversity and differences between cultures and people. In terms of social ontology such a conception could possibly be reconciled with Martha Nussbaum's (1995) "thick, vague conception" (p. 456) of the good. Nussbaum advances "a soft version of Aristotelian essentialism" (p. 450) which incorporates a "determinate account of the human being, human functioning and human flourishing" (p. 450). While in formal terms it recognises that all individuals and cultures have certain developmental and lifestyle needs, this "internal essentialism" [is] "an historically grounded empirical essentialism" (p. 451). As such, it is purely formal, for within this broad end, and subject to the limits necessary for its realisation and continuance, it permits and recognises a multitude of identities and projects and ways of life.

Of course, in that Nussbaum claims to be influenced by Aristotle, there is a clear difference with Foucault, who was more influenced by Nietzsche. Thus, Foucault would reject the essentialist teleological conception of the subject as 'realising' their *ends* or *destiny*, in preference for a more constructivist Nietzschean emphasis on 'self constitution.' But beyond this, it can be claimed that self-constitution presupposes certain 'capabilities' in the ways Nussbaum claims. Also, the models of social relations, and specifically of the ontological priority of the social to the individual, are similar in both traditions. It should also be noted that Nussbaum has been challenged on her dependence on Aristotle (see Arneson, 2000; Mulgan, 2000). In defense of locating herself in an Aristotelian tradition, she maintains that she is inspired by the basic ontological postulates, but not the detailed arguments, of Aristotle, and she admits that her identification as 'Aristotelian' has a great deal to do with her own biography and early philosophical commitments and training (see Nussbaum, 2000).

Nussbaum's conception of the good is concerned "with the overall shape and content of the human form of life" (p. 456). Such a conception, she says, is "vague, and this is deliberately so...for it admits of much multiple specification in accordance with varied local and personal conceptions. The idea is that it is better to be vaguely right than precisely wrong" (p. 456). Such a conception is not metaphysical in that it does not claim to derive from a source exterior to human beings in history. Rather, it is as "universal as possible" and aims at "mapping out the general shape of the human form of life, those features that constitute life as human wherever it is" (p. 457). Nussbaum calls this her "thick, vague conception...of the human form of life" (p. 457). Hence, her list of factors constitutes a formal list without substantive content, allowing for difference or variation within each category. Amongst the factors are (1) mortality: all human beings face death; (2) various invariant features of the human body, such as "nutritional, and other related requirements" regarding hunger, thirst, the need for food and drink and shelter; (3) cognitive: "all human beings have sense perception...the ability to think"; (4) early development, (5) practical reason, (6) sexual desire, (7) affiliation with other human beings, and (8) relatedness to other species and to nature (pp. 457–460).

As purely formal factors or generic species characteristics, which can admit to cultural and historical variation, Foucault, in my view, could be rendered consistent with the general tenor of Nussbaum's list, although he may wish to enter qualifications or caveats on specific features (sexual desire?). Foucault himself says that universal forms may well exist. In *What is Enlightenment*, Foucault (1984) suggests there may possibly be universalizing tendencies at the root of western civilization, which include such things as "the acquisition of capabilities and the struggle for freedom," as "permanent elements" (pp. 47–48). Again, more directly, in the preface to the *History of Sexuality, Volume II*, Foucault (1984a) says that he is not denying the possibility of universal structures:

> Singular forms of experience may very well harbor universal structures; they may well not be independent from the concrete determinations of social existence . . . this thought has a historicity which is proper to it. That it should have this historicity does not mean that it is deprived of all universal form, but instead that the putting into play of these universal forms is itself historical. (p. 335)

Like Nussbaum, the factors he recognises as invariant do not derive from any "extrahistorical metaphysical conception" (Nussbaum, 1995, p. 460). Also, Foucault's conception is very much in keeping with Nussbaum's "thick, vague conception" in that it is concerned to identify "components that are fundamental to any human life" (p. 461). Of course, the recognised features of human life should be seen as largely in relation to *form* rather than *substance*, for Foucault would be skeptical that the *essential substantial* properties of a human being can be distinguished from the *accidental* properties, in that the human being is historically constituted in the process of history.[16]

Richard Bernstein (1994) notes Habermas's criticism that when critique is totalised it is caught in a contradiction as it has no standard. Thus, as Habermas (1987) put it, genealogy "is overtaken by a fate similar to that which Foucault had seen in the human sciences" (pp. 275–276). Yet, Bernstein seeks to defend Foucault's position by relating critique to the exigencies of the environment, not in terms of truth, but in terms of the ever-present dangers in which people in history face. What is dangerous is that "everything becomes a target for normalisation."[17] What is dangerous is that war and violence destroy the possibilities of *any* form of human order of life. What is at issue is survival itself. In this sense, Foucault's "archaeological-genealogical analyses of problematiques are intended to specify the changing constellation of dangers" (Bernstein, 1994, p. 227). For as Foucault (1984b) said, "everything is dangerous", and "if everything is dangerous, then we always have something to do" (p. 343).

Notes

1   I am not suggesting that Foucault could not have justified his own position, but simply indicating that my own interest is in deriving normative inferences from his analysis. Foucault's reasons for rejecting normative theory, while interesting, are beyond the scope of this paper.

2   In claiming that Foucault "suggests" a theory of democracy, I seek only to selectively link certain social and ontological fragments in Foucault's thinking to assess their implications for a normative conception of democracy. My claims are of a distinctly limited and exploratory nature in relation to both Foucault scholarship, as well as democratic theory. I am quite aware that I am selectively picking out certain themes and emphases in Foucault to assemble my own conception, and that the conception offered is somewhat speculative and far from complete. It is also acknowledged that Foucault's on his own provides only limited value in respect to generating normative principles of democracy and that insights from writers like Heidegger, Neitzsche and Spinoza are needed to flesh the picture out and make it coherent. Such an enlarged perspective is beyond the scope of this enquiry however.

3   This is the subtitle to his 1997 article in *Political Theory*.

4   Such an emphasis on equalization, or equilibrium of powers has potentially interesting affinities to Montesquieu's theory in *The Spirit of the Laws*. The jurist Charles Eisenmann (1933) maintains that the representation of Montesquieu's thesis as a "separation of powers" thesis is a myth, and that Montesquieu was really advancing a thesis concerning the equilibrium of powers, where the concern was with 'balance' or 'combination' rather than separation. Although interesting as a future area of equiry, it is not possible to explore such affinities in this paper

5   Term used by Tom Paine, 1989, p. 170.

6   The concept of 'settlement' in that it suggests a contingent assemblage of elements at a particular time is consistent with historicist theories like Foucault's. It would constitute a form of 'discursive apparatus'. In that Foucault did not himself use this concept, I appreciate that I am 'extending' Foucault's frame of reference somewhat.

7   For Hart says, "if there are any moral rights, it follows that there is at least one natural right, the equal right of all men to be free" (1955, p. 175). For Hart, natural rights are clearly non-conventional and pre-political.

8   Although he doesn't necessarily concur with everything writers like Hobbes or Boulainvilliers says, it is the function of rights as a historical;ly specific strrategy against war and chaos that Foucault extracts from their writings as a central theme.

9   Foucault's point here seems to be that the disacourse of rights can serve to both protect individuals and crystallize power and wealth simultaneously. In this sense, rights can have multiple functions.

10   Writers like Nancy Fraser (1989) and Jurgen Habermas (1987) accuse Foucault of "crypto-normativism" by which they partly mean that he invokes liberal arguments while critiquing liberalism. The concept of *parrhesia* might count in this sense being indistinguishable from the right to free speech. But Foucault would easily respond to such a charge for while he clearly agrees with many liberal ideals and values, he would maintain that the ontological and epistemological basis of liberalism is incapable of supporting them. Part of his quest can be seen as the search for a different type of philosophical support for such ideals.

11   Hobbes did maintain there were natural principles and proposes nineteen laws of nature (see Hobbes, *Leviathan*, Chaps. 14 and 15). The trouble in international relations, as in the state of nature, is the difficulty in being sure that others would act on them.

12   For contemporary work in this tradition, see the English School of Martin Wright (1992) and Hedley Bull (1977).

13   Grotius's was a 'pre-liberal' conception, and notably, he argued against the principle of 'non-interference,' arguing that it is sometimes justifiable (see Beitz, 1979, p. 71)

14   Although he argued against Hobbes, as Beitz (1979, p. 60) notes, he produces similar conclusions about the weakness of moral rules in international relations.

15   My view is that survival is a better basis to justify democracy than the idea of a founding or original 'social contract.' Survival is an end that comprises two aspects: self preservation (individually and collectively) and well being. It is not grounded in human nature but constitutes a choice which must be enacted. The inspiration here is more Spinozian than Foucauldian, although I would claim that they are not inconsistent with Foucault's approach.

16   Such a reconciliation between Foucault and Nussbaum would require far greater effort than is possible here. There is some point to the argument that Nussbaum's focus on survival and well-being would only be fruitful if re-opackaged in a more constructivist frame of reference influenced by Nietzsche and Spinoza.

17   Bernstein is citing Hiley, (1988, p. 103).

Bibliography

Arneson, R.J. (2000). Perfectionism and politics. *Ethics, 111*(1), 37–63.

Beitz, C. (1979). *Political theory and international relations*. Princeton, NJ: Princeton University Press.

Bernstein, R. J. (1994). Foucault: Critique as a philosophical ethos. In M. Kelly (Ed.), *Critique and power: Recasting the Foucault/ Habermas debate* (pp 211–242). Cambridge, Mass.: MIT Press.

Bull, H. (1977). *The anarchical society*. New York: Columbia University Press.

Connolly, W. (1998). Beyond good and evil: The ethical sensibility of Michel Foucault. In J. Moss (Ed.), *The later Foucault: Politics and philosophy* (pp. 108–128). London: Sage Publications.

Dean, M. (1999). *Governmentality: Power and rule in modern society*. London: Sage.

Eisenmann, C. (1933) *L'Esprit des Lois et la séparation des Pouvoirs*. Paris: Mélanges Carré de Malberg, pp. 163–192.

Foucault, M. (1977) *Discipline and Punish*. (trans. A. Sheridan) New York: Pantheon.

———. (1980). Two Lectures. In C. Gordon (Ed.), *Power/ knowledge: Selected interviews and other Writings, 1972–1977* (K. Soper, Transl.) (pp. 78–108). Brighton: Harvestor Press.

———. (1980a). Truth and power. In C. Gordon (Ed.), *Power/ knowledge: Selected interviews and other Writings, 1972–1977* (K. Soper, Transl.) (pp. 109–133). Brighton: Harvestor Press.

———. (1984). What is enlightenment? (C. Porter, Transl.). In P. Rabinow (Ed.), *The Foucault reader* (pp. 31–50). New York: Pantheon.

———. (1984a). Politics and ethics: An interview (C. Porter, Transl.). In P. Rabinow (Ed.), *The Foucault reader* (pp. 373–380). New York: Pantheon.

———. (1984b). On the genealogy of ethics: An interview of work in progress. In P. Rabinow (Ed.), *The Foucault reader* (pp. 340–372). New York: Pantheon.

———. (1989). The concern for truth. In S. Lotringer (Ed.), *Foucault live: Interviews, 1966–84* (pp. 293–308). New York: Semiotext(e).

———. (1991). The ethic of care for the self as a practice of freedom: An interview. J. Bernauer & D. Rassmussen (Ed.), *The Final Foucault* (J. D. Gauthier, Transl.) [pp. 1–20]. Cambridge, Mass.: The MIT Press.

———. (2001). Confronting governments: Human rights. In J. D. Faubion (Ed.), *Michel Foucault: Power (the essential works 3)* (R. Hurley, Transl.) (pp. 474–476). Allen Lane: The Penguin Press.

———. (2001a). *Fearless speech*. J. Pearson (Ed.), Los Angeles: Semiotext(e).

———. (2003). *Society must be defended: Lectures at the College de France, 1975–76.* (D. Macey, Transl). Allen Lane: The Penguin Press.

Fraser, N. (1989) *Unruly Practices: Power, Discourse and Gender in Contemporary Social Theory*. Cambridge: Polity Press.

Habermas, J. (1987). *The philosophical discourse of modernity* (F. Lawrence, Transl). Cambridge: MIT Press.

Hacking, I. (1986) Self-Improvement. In David Couzens Hoy, *Foucault: A Critical Reader* (pp. 235–240). Oxford: Basil Blackwell.

Hart, H.L.A. (1955). Are there any natural rights? *The Philosophical Review, 64* (2), 175–191.

Hiley, D. (1988). *Philosophy in question: Essays on a Pyrrohonian theme*. Chicago: Chicago University Press.

Hobbes, T. (1885). *Leviathan*. London: George Routledge and Sons.

Johnson, J. (1997) Communication, criticism, and the postmodern consensus: An unfashionable interpretation of Michel Foucault. *Political Theory*, 25 (4): 559–583.

Mulgan, R. (2000). Was Aristotle an 'Aristotelian Social Democrat.' *Ethics*, 111(1), 79–101.

Nussbaum, M. (1995). Human functioning and social justice: In defence of Aristotelian essentialism. In D. Tallack (Ed.), *Critical theory: A reader* (pp. 449–472). New York: Harvestor/Wheatsheaf,.

———. (2000). Aristotle, politics, and human capabilities: A response to Antony, Arneson, Charlesworth, and Mulgan. *Ethics 111*(1), 102–140.

Olssen, M. (2002). Michel Foucault as 'thin' communitarian: Difference, community, democracy. *Cultural Studies-Critical Methodologies, 2*(4), 483–513.

———. (2003). Structuralism, post-structuralism, neo-liberalism: Assessing Foucault's legacy. *Journal of Education Policy, 18*(2), 189–202.

Paine, T. (1989). *Thomas Paine: Political writings*. Cambridge: Cambridge University Press.

Rawls, J. (1996) *Political Liberalism*, New York: Columbia University Press.

Rials, S. (1994). Rights and modern law. In M. Lilla (Ed.), *New French thought: Political philosophy* (pp. 164–177). Princeton, New Jersey: Princeton University Press.

Schumpeter, J. (1976). *Capitalism, socialism, democracy. London*: Allen and Unwin.

Wright, M. (1992). *International theory: The three traditions*. New York: Holmes and Meier.

Tina (A.C.) Besley is Professor in the Department of Educational Psychology and Counseling at California State University, San Bernardino. Tina's areas of scholarship include: youth issues, notions of self and identity; school counseling; education policy; education philosophy; and the work of Michel Foucault and poststructuralism. She is on the editorial boards of five academic journals and is general editor of three book series. Tina has presented seminars and lectures internationally and has published in many reputable journals. Her book, *Counseling Youth: Foucault, Power, and the Ethics of Subjectivity* (Praeger, 2002) is now in a paperback edition (Sense Publishers, 2006). She co-authored with Michael Peters, *Building Knowledge Cultures: Education and Development in the Age of Knowledge Capitalism* (Rowman & Littlefield, 2006).

Thomas Coelen is Deputy Professor of Social Pedagogy at the University of Rostock, Faculty of Philosophy, and head of an evaluation institute in Hamburg, Germany. His main research fields are school-related social work, community education, research methodology, and social theory. He wrote a book on the role of education in Foucault's work: *Pädagogik als 'Geständniswissenschaft'?* (Lang, 1996), his dissertation is on youth work and school: *Kommunale Jugendbildung* (Lang, 2002), and his habilitation is a collection of essays on formal and non-formal education: *Ganztagsbildung* (Bielefeld, 2005).

Robert A. Doherty is a Lecturer in the Department of Educational Studies University of Glasgow, Scotland and is currently undertaking a PhD that focuses on governmentality and Third Way politics in the UK entitled *New Labour: Education, Social Exclusion and Governmentality*. He has written and contributed to a range of publications that reflect his research interests in Education Policy, Poverty and Social Exclusion, Teacher Education, Technology Education and Social Capital Theory. His publications include: "Towards a Governmentality Analysis of Education Policy" in *Gouvernementalität und Erziehungswissenschaft: Wissen - Macht - Transformation.* S. Weber and S. Maurer. Wiesbaden, (VS Verlag. 2006); "Social Exclusion: License Through Ambiguity" *Journal of Educational Enquiry*, 2003 and "Technology Education" in *Scottish Education.* in T. Bryce and W. Humes. (Edinburgh University Press, 2003 with J. Dakers).

Fabian Kessl is Senior Lecturer for Educational Science (Social Work) at the University of Bielefeld, Germany. He is member of the Co-Ordinating Office of Social Work & Society - Online Journal for Social Work & Social Policy. His research interests are in social work theory, governmentality studies, political theory and transformation of the welfare state. His recent books were on a governmentality of social work and a handbook on spatiality: *Der Gebrauch der eigenen Kräfte: eine Gouvernementalität Sozialer Arbeit* (Juventa, 2005) and *Territorialisierung des Sozialen: Regieren sozialer* Nahräume (Barbara Budrich, 2006).

James D. Marshall is research Professor at the University of North Carolina at Chapel Hill, USA and Professor Emeritus at the University of Auckland, New Zealand where he was head of department, then foundation Dean of the Faculty of Education. He has strong interests in critiquing performativity in education and in Wittgenstein and continental philosophy, including the works of, Nietzsche, Bergson, Sartre, Beauvoir, Camus and Foucault. He has published many articles and several books including: *Philosophy and Education: Accepting Wittgenstein's Challenge* (edited with Paul Smeyers, Kluwer, 1995; *Michel Foucault: Personal Autonomy and* Education (Kluwer, 1996); *Discipline and Punishment in New Zealand education* (with Dominique Marshall, Dunmore, 1997); *Individualism and Community: Education and social policy in the postmodern condition* (with Michael Peters, Falmer, 1996); *Wittgenstein: Philosophy, postmodernism and pedagogy* (with Michael Peters, Bergin & Garvey, 1999).

Jan Masschelein is Professor of Philosophy of Education at the Catholic University of Leuven, Belgium. His primary areas of scholarship are educational theory, political philosophy, critical theory, studies of governmentality and social philosophy. Currently his research concentrates on the 'public' character of education and on 'mapping' and 'walking' as critical research practices. He is the author of many articles and contributions in these fields and of three books: *Pädagogisches Handeln und Kommunikatives Handeln* (Deutscher Studien Verlag, 1991), *Alterität, Pluralität, Gerechtigkeit. Randgänge der Pädagogik* (Leuven University Press, 1996 - co-authored with M. Wimmer) and *Globale Immunität. Eine kleine Kartographie des Europaischen Bildungsraums* (Diaphanes, 2005 - co-authored with M.Simons).

Susanne Maurer is Professor of Education and Social Pedagogy at the University of Marburg, Germany. Her primary areas of scholarship are the history (and historiography) of social work and social movements, feminist critique and practices, biography, popular culture and agency. She is the author of many articles and recently co-edited three books: *Handbuch Sozialraum* (VS Verlag für Sozialwissenschaften 2005, with Fabian Kessl, Christian Reutlinger and Oliver Frey); *Soziale Arbeit zwischen Aufbau und Abbau* (VS Verlag für Sozialwissenschaften 2006, with Birgit Bütow and Karl August Chassé); *Gouvernementalität und Erziehungswissenschaft* (VS Verlag für Sozialwissenschaft 2006, co-edited with Susanne Maria Weber).

Mark Olssen is Professor of Political Theory and Education Policy in the Department of Political, International and Policy Studies, University of Surrey. His scholarly interests are centred around Foucault, political philosophy and education policy. He has published articles in many reputable journals. His books include *Michel Foucault: Materialism and Education* (Paradigm Press, 2006); *Education Policy: Globalisation, Citizenship, Democracy*, (with John Codd and Anne-Marie O'Neill) (Sage, 2004) in 2004 an edited volume *Culture and Learning: Access and Opportunity in the Classroom* (Sage, 2004) ; co-editor with Michael Peters and Colin Lankshear, *Critical Theory and the Human Condition: Founders and Praxis* (Peter Lang, New York, 2003) and of *Futures of Critical Theory: Dreams of Difference,* (Rowman and Littlefield, 2003).

Michael A. Peters is Professor of Education at the University of Illinois at Urbana-Champaign. He holds a post as Visiting Professor at the University of Glasgow where he previously held a post as Research Professor. He is executive editor of *Educational Philosophy and Theory* (Blackwells) and co-editor of two international online-only journals, *Policy Futures in Education* and *E-Learning* (Triangle Journals). He has research interests in educational theory and policy, and in contemporary philosophy. He has published over thirty books and edited collections in these fields, including most recently: *Education, Globalisation and the State in the Age of Terrorism* (2004); *Poststructuralism and Educational Research* (with Nick Burbules) (2004); *Critical Theory and the Human Condition* (2003); *Futures of Critical Theory* (2003) (Eds.); *Poststructuralism, Marxism and Neoliberalism: Between Theory and Politics* (2001).

Ludwig A. Pongratz is Professor of General Pedagogy and Adult Education at the Darmstadt Technical University, Germany. His publications and research concentrate primarily on the history of pedagogic theory and the methodology of pedagogy, critical theory and educational philosophy, school pedagogy and adult education. His research includes empirical studies alongside his historical and conceptual works. He is the author of many articles and ten books and edited collections in these fields, including most recently: *Bildungsphilosophie und Bildungsforschung* (with Wolfgang Nieke and Michael Wimmer) (2006); *Untiefen im Mainstream. Zur Kritik konstruktivistisch-systemtheoretischer Pädagogik* (2005); *Nach Foucault – Diskurs- und machtanalytische Perspektiven der Pädagogik* (with Wolfgang Nieke, Michael Wimmer and Jan Masschelein) (2004); *Zeitgeistsurfer. Beiträge zur Kritik der Erwachsenenbildung* (2003); *Kritik der Pädagogik – Pädagogik als Kritik* (with Wolfgang Nieke and Jan Masschelein, 2003).

Maarten Simons is post-doctoral researcher at the Centre for Educational Policy and Innovation, Catholic University of Leuven, Belgium. His research interests are educational policy and political philosophy with special attention for governmentality and schooling, autonomy and higher education and performativity in education. He is co-authored with J. Masschelein of *Globale Immunität: Eine kleine Kartographie des Europaischen Bildungsraums* (Diaphanes, 2005).

Susanne Maria Weber is a professor in the department of social studies at Fulda University of Applied Sciences, Germany. As an educational scientist, she focuses her research on questions of power, knowledge and transformation. From a discourse analytical perspective she works on complex transformation, institutional networking, transversal thinking and practices. Her dissertation was titled "Organisationsentwicklung und Frauenförderung. Eine empirische Untersuchung in drei Organisationstypen der privaten Wirtschaft. (Ulrike Helmer Verlag, 1998). Her habilitation was titled "Rituale der Transformation. Großgruppenverfahren als pädagogisches Wissen am Markt." (VS Verlag für Sozialwissenschaft 2005). She published *Gouvernementalität und Erziehungswissenschaft* (VS Verlag für Sozialwissenschaft, 2006, co-edited with Susanne Maurer).

James Wong holds a PhD in philosophy from the University of Toronto and is currently teaching at Wilfrid Laurier University in Canada, where he has a cross-departmental appointment with the Department of Communication Studies and Department of Philosophy. His research focuses on Foucault, social kinds, and social philosophy. His Foucault-inspired PhD dissertation from the University of Toronto is titled *On the Very Idea of the Normal Child.* Representative publications include 'Sapere Aude: critical ontology and the case of child development in *Canadian Journal of Political Science* (2004), 'Nancy Fraser and the Politics of Identity' (co-written with Andrew Latus) in *Philosophia* (2003), and 'What's in a Name? An examination of social identities' in *Journal for the Theory of Social Behavior* (2002).

❧ Index ❧

Studies in the Postmodern Theory of Education

General Editors
Joe L. Kincheloe & Shirley R. Steinberg

Counterpoints publishes the most compelling and imaginative books being written in education today. Grounded on the theoretical advances in criticalism, feminism, and postmodernism in the last two decades of the twentieth century, Counterpoints engages the meaning of these innovations in various forms of educational expression. Committed to the proposition that theoretical literature should be accessible to a variety of audiences, the series insists that its authors avoid esoteric and jargonistic languages that transform educational scholarship into an elite discourse for the initiated. Scholarly work matters only to the degree it affects consciousness and practice at multiple sites. Counterpoints' editorial policy is based on these principles and the ability of scholars to break new ground, to open new conversations, to go where educators have never gone before.

For additional information about this series or for the submission of manuscripts, please contact:

> Joe L. Kincheloe & Shirley R. Steinberg
> c/o Peter Lang Publishing, Inc.
> 29 Broadway, 18th floor
> New York, New York 10006

To order other books in this series, please contact our Customer Service Department:

> (800) 770-LANG (within the U.S.)
> (212) 647-7706 (outside the U.S.)
> (212) 647-7707 FAX

Or browse online by series:
> www.peterlang.com